FROM
FINANCIAL CRISIS
TO
GLOBAL RECOVERY

FROM FINANCIAL CRISIS TO GLOBAL RECOVERY

Padma Desai

COLUMBIA UNIVERSITY PRESS

NEW YORK

Columbia University Press
Publishers Since 1893
New York   Chichester, West Sussex
Copyright © 2011 Columbia University Press
All rights reserved

Library of Congress Cataloging-in-Publication Data
Desai, Padma.
From financial crisis to global recovery / Padma Desai.
p. cm.
Includes bibliographical references and index.
ISBN 978-0-231-15786-5 (cloth : alk. paper)—ISBN 978-0-231-52774-3 (ebook)
1. Global Financial Crisis, 2008–2009.   2. Financial crises—United States.
3. Recessions—United States.   4. United States—Economic conditions—2009–
5. United States—Economic policy—2009–   I. Title.
HB37172008.D47 2011
330.973—dc22
2011002617

Columbia University Press books are printed on permanent and durable acid-free
paper.
This book is printed on paper with recycled content.
Printed in the United States of America
c 10 9 8 7 6 5 4 3 2 1
References to Internet Web sites (URLs) were accurate at the time of writing. Neither
the author nor Columbia University Press is responsible for URLs that may have
expired or changed since the manuscript was prepared.

For
Martin Wolf
The economics journalist of the day

CONTENTS

PREFACE

The financial crisis has prompted a vigorous outpouring of books from economists, journalists, and financial commentators who have analyzed it from a variety of perspectives. From beginning to end, they tell a complete story of why the American economy spiraled into a devastating financial mess, how the financial crisis evolved into a global phenomenon, and how policymakers sought to put out one fire before turning to the next one. The economists stay away from a personalized narrative, stick with the economic features, explain them engagingly, and occasionally suggest an alternative policy framework that provides a more promising outcome. The journalists create entertaining narratives around the decision making and the personalities involved in the process without providing an analytical model of the origin of the crisis and the policy handling. The financial commentators do set out a rigorous analytical underpinning of the turmoil's origin and its evolution, but without explaining brain twisters such as over-the-counter derivatives and credit default swaps, which are beyond the grasp of most economics students. Even the difference between quantitative monetary softening by the Federal Reserve and discretionary easing via a change in the federal funds rate needs to be spelled out for beginners.

This book is different. I have written it for my undergraduate students who plan to major in economics or financial economics. I have also used some of the material for my lecture course on emerging market economies, which attracts graduate students from the political science department and from the Columbia Schools of Education, Journalism, and International Affairs. Given their diversity of interests and background, I have chosen to develop a story in each chapter, with an anecdote or two and with newspaper citations. Each chapter has charts and the occasional picture or cartoon so that my argument makes a concrete appeal to the reader. Each chapter begins with an introduction that summarizes its content. Most important, I provide an analytical framework in each chapter in order for the reader to go beyond the story, the facts, and the pictures and think rigorously.

In chapter 1, I trace the origin of the crisis to a combination of the easy monetary policy of the Federal Reserve that began in 2001 and a weak regulatory environment, which drove Americans into out-of-bounds home acquisition based on mortgage financing. These mortgages, which were acquired by major Wall Street banks and other financial institutions, turned subprime when the housing boom collapsed as interest rates began moving up from mid-2004. In order for the reader to fully grasp the magnitude and coverage of the government's bailout effort, the chapter also unfolds the rescue programs that were launched by the policy makers in late 2008.

Of particular relevance here, and discussed in chapter 2, is the decisive implementation of the stress tests of major U.S. banks by the Federal Reserve that in turn was followed by financial funding for the needy banks from the Troubled Asset Relief Program legislated by Congress in late 2008. This early restoration of the financial health of major U.S. banks differed from the delayed adoption by EU regulators of a stress test of European banks in the summer of 2010.

In chapter 3, I discuss U.S. economic recovery in terms of precise indicators, among them real GDP growth, the unemployment rate, and the inflation rate, and argue that given the severity of the recession, employment recovery during the current recession will lag sharply behind GDP recovery, more so than in the recessions of 1981 and 2001. Therefore, the White House economic policy team and the Treasury should not be faulted for running a budget deficit aimed at forestalling sharp declines of real GDP and employment. However, as a prudent Keynesian, I argue that although the budget deficit is necessary in the short run for countering the gaps in consumption and investment spending, deficit reduction will remain the biggest challenge for the government and lawmakers in the medium term. By contrast, the Federal Reserve may end up successfully devising a timely exit strategy of monetary policy tightening if inflationary expectations appear in 2011.

In chapter 4, I rank a number of countries from North America, Europe, Asia, and South America in terms of the impact of the crisis on their GDP growth rate in 2009 and its recovery prospects in 2010. The explanatory variables in the exercise relate to the health of an economy's banking sector, the country's export dependence, and finally its inflation rate combined with a continuing budget deficit, which will restrict policy makers' ability to undertake a stimulus. At the top of the ranking hierarchy are the Asian economies, led by China and India, followed by Brazil and Chile in South America. The United States, Germany, and France are in the middle. Among the major economies, Russia and Japan turn up almost at the bottom in terms of the latest GDP growth rate indicators in 2009 and 2010. This ranking, based on these dual GDP growth rates for a select group of countries, is also adopted for the book's cover.

In chapter 5, I describe the financial activities of security traders and hedge fund managers who employ over-the-counter derivatives and credit default swaps via fast electronic trading and flash orders. The details from the get-go provide the necessary background to my readers for understanding the essential features of the financial overhaul that will emerge from the Dodd-Frank Wall Street Reform and Consumer Protection Act, which President Barack Obama signed on July 21, 2010.

Chapter 6 is on the regulatory proposals and provides a blow-by-blow account of the 18-month-long legislative process in Congress that was marked by energetic debates, back-and-forth trade-offs, and softening, by lawmakers, of some regulatory provisions, evidently for minimizing their negative impact on the functioning of the U.S. financial sector. In my view, the enforcement of adequate reserve requirements by banks against their risky assets and the regulation of over-the-counter derivative trading are critical for striking a balance between maintaining an active banking sector in the United States and warding off the impact of the next crisis. At the same time, the regulatory agencies will have to stay ahead technologically in monitoring the activities of the increasingly complex financial vehicles, including fast electronic trading, that are here to stay. In conclusion, the U.S. regulatory stance appears more selective and less restrictive than the regulations being deliberated by EU lawmakers that I discuss in the chapter.

Chapter 7 on the dollar's role as a reserve currency has a complete story of the dollar's emergence in that role and the requirement for it to remain reasonably stable in order for foreign holders of dollar assets, among them the People's Bank of China, to continue amassing these assets. I also provide the background for the Chinese policy makers' resolute determination against raising the yuan-dollar exchange rate at our bidding while the U.S. economy continues posting a massive budget deficit combined with an easy monetary policy that lowers the greenback's value. "The dollar is your currency, but it has become our problem," Chinese policy makers emphasize.

Chapter 8 discusses the contrasting features between the Great Depression and the current financial crisis, narrating the differences in both origin and policy response. A major policy lesson is invoked by Federal Reserve Chairman Ben Bernanke, who referred to the relevance to the current situation of the Fed's premature policy tightening in 1937 in the middle of a fragile recovery of the U.S. economy. The chapter's details provide the readers with a balanced view of the relative seriousness of the current crisis in terms of the worst features in each episode, consisting of GDP growth decline, the stock market plunge, inflation moving into deflation, and the unemployment rate.

As for the future of American capitalism, I argue in the final chapter that it will retain its innovative spirit and entrepreneurial vigor and that the best that regulators will manage in the future is moderating the impact and volatility of a crisis episode. In my judgment, the overhaul of financial rules is intended to provide regulatory guardrails against excessive risk taking by American banks rather than cutting their size and curbing their competitive prowess against foreign banking rivals. As for the role of the proposed Consumer Financial Protection Bureau in protecting Americans' interest with regard to credit and debit cards, checking accounts, and mortgage lending, I believe that American banks will keep ahead of their customers' choices and decision making.

The analytical framework and the major conclusions relating to the current crisis were written up toward the end of October when the manuscript was completed. Indeed, I faced a continuing challenge in keeping ahead of the evolving details and not being overtaken by them in my focus as an economics analyst. These details related not only to the forecasts and actual outcomes of GDP, unemployment, and inflation from quarter to quarter and the stock market and manufacturing sector ups and downs, but also to the state of the housing sector and the on-again, off-again benefits for the unemployed. These features continued to be energetically invoked in the context of the U.S. budgetary and monetary policy making. The mid-November 2010 congressional election results, in which the

Republicans gained control of the House of Representatives, will undoubtedly reshape these policies amid a contentious legislative environment. Across the Atlantic, the recurring sovereign debt problems in the peripheral eurozone economies and their impact on the future of the euro will continue to engage EU policymakers in the months ahead.

In the following paragraphs, I briefly update the major features of the evolving economic scene in the United States and in the eurozone with a view to suggesting that they do not affect the book's conclusions.

With regard to U.S. GDP growth prospects in the second half of 2010, I had ruled out a double-dip recession in the third quarter. Anticipating the November congressional election outcome, I had also suggested that all the Bush tax cuts should be extended for a year in the interest of a bipartisan consensus on the issue. On December 17, 2010, President Obama signed into law the $858 billion tax cut compromise he had reached with congressional Republicans. It extended the Bush tax cuts by two years. The tax cut would temporarily reduce employees' payroll taxes by 2 percentage points and thereby put extra cash in consumer wallets. The long-term unemployed got an extension of unemployment insurance. Prompted by the proposed tax incentives, businesses would release their cash into new investment and equipment purchases.

On the eve of the bipartisan tax compromise, U.S. GDP had already risen 2.6 percent at a seasonally adjusted annual rate in the third quarter, higher than the 1.7 percent of the second quarter. A vigorous growth in consumer spending had lifted retail sales, industrial production, and factory orders. In the last week of December 2010, companies released reports of higher corporate profits, and the Dow industrial average hit a two-year high.

As before, however, the job market lacked decisive momentum in new hiring. The unemployment rate had remained at a high 9.4 percent of the workforce. The high unemployment rate weighed on homeowners' ability to hold on to their properties. At the same time, sales of new homes remained at historically low levels in November 2010, lower by more than 20 percent compared with their level a year earlier. Finally, the fragile balance sheets of state and local governments posed a continuing problem with regard to their economic health and financial maneuverability.

Amid these massive uncertainties in the housing and labor markets and the tortuous bipartisan fiscal wrangling over the Bush tax cuts following the results of the mid-November congressional elections, the Federal Reserve, as before, displayed a consistent policy stance. On December 14,

2010, the Federal Open Market Committee (FOMC) kept the short-term interest rate on hold at near-zero and stayed with its decision (announced on November 3) of purchasing long-term Treasury bonds worth $600 billion by mid-2012. The core consumer price index was up a scant 0.8 percent in November from a year earlier. Including energy and food, it was up 1.1 percent. Inflation, in the Fed's judgment, was not of imminent concern, and December would provide a forward momentum to the economic recovery going into 2011. But the unemployment rate would remain high, close to 9 percent toward 2011-end, even if real GDP grew at 4 percent. It was necessary to undertake a significant quantitative easing of monetary policy and bring down long-term interest rates so that businesses would undertake investment spending as consumer outlays kept apace.

Perhaps the improved growth prospects following the December tax deal would drive investors away from long-term Treasury bonds and their yields would rise. Will the positive feedback work against the Fed's expectation of declining long-term interest rates? In its December decision making, the FOMC announced that "it will regularly review the pace of its securities purchases . . . and will adjust the program as needed to best foster maximum employment and price stability."

How did the year-end policy making among European leaders in Brussels compare with the positive tax compromise and the steady-as-you-go monetary policy stance of the Federal Reserve in Washington?

In late November 2010, the government of Ireland was provided a bailout funding of up to €90 billion ($119 billion) for financing its budget deficit and supporting Irish banks that held government debt. Sovereign debt restructuring that would have unnerved bond investors was thus avoided. But the Irish bailout raised the possibility of similar rescues for Spain and Portugal. That in turn raised the question: Shouldn't the size of the current €440 billion ($559 billion) EU bailout fund be increased? However, despite calls by leading officials of the European Central Bank (ECB) and the International Monetary Fund (IMF) for a larger and immediate European response to such a crisis, the suggestion was opposed by a core group of senior officials from the fiscally prudent northern countries, among them Germany, Finland, the Netherlands, and Sweden. They resisted suggestions for short-term changes in the EU-wide response system. These officials insisted that the Economic and Monetary Union (EMU) operating in the eurozone reemphasize fiscal austerity in the peripheral economies and quickly pass new budgetary rules that would punish its profligate members.

However, the EU leaders adopted an easier option at the December 16, 2010, summit. They approved an amendment to the EU treaty for creating a new bailout system for debt-ridden countries and for setting up a permanent rescue fund in 2013. The amendment must be ratified by all 27 EU member states. It would seem that a here-and-now resolution of the urgent, short-term bailout issues was postponed to a future date.

Can the recurring bailouts of the peripheral members that issued their respective sovereign bonds for financing their budget deficits be held back if the eurozone authorities were to issue common euro bonds, similar to U.S. Treasury bonds? But a common euro bond would require a fundamental change in the treaty that formed the EMU. A common euro bond must be backed by closer economic and budgetary integration. It might even mean minimum standards on pay and welfare policies and corporate taxation. European leaders are not ready for such a great leap forward. It would seem that at the end of 2010, the common bailout fund of €440 billion ($559 billion) supplemented by the IMF funding of €250 billion ($318 billion) that I discussed in chapter 4 would provide the resources for near-term bailouts. No more than that was the response of the better-off EU members.

This implies that the near-term tool at the EU disposal, short of full-scale bailout for troubled peripheral economies, will be the ECB's program of using its own balance sheet for buying sovereign debt (as discussed in chapter 2). The ECB announced on December 24, 2010, that it would nearly double its capital, from €5.8 billion ($7.66 billion) to €10.8 billion ($14.27 billion) by the end of 2012. It will acquire an additional financial cushion for buying distressed bonds of countries such as Greece, Ireland, Portugal, and Spain. The extra funding will flow to ECB coffers from the profits of the national central banks.

It would seem that the policy debates and decisions in Brussels tend to lag behind the urgent requirements for eurozone stability. Every time a bailout is negotiated, the doomsayers raise the possibility of the euro's demise and the breakup of the eurozone. These concerns reflect the formidable challenges of forming a single economic and political union among a diverse group of countries. The issues facing Washington policy makers, by contrast, appear manageable. Perhaps the December 2010 tax compromise will lay the groundwork for tomorrow's badly needed overhaul of the tax code by Congress. Perhaps the Republican-dominated Congress will also stop short of undertaking a major overhaul of the Dodd-Frank Act that I discuss at length in chapter 6. Again, the quantitative easing launched by the Federal Reserve will work out despite the fact that the interest rate on the 10-year Treasury bond went up following Fed purchases. The discussion of these issues, however, belongs to another project.

From Financial Crisis to Global Recovery follows my earlier book *Financial Crisis, Contagion, and Containment: From Asia to Argentina* published by Princeton University Press in 2003. It dealt with the massive destabilizing impact that several emerging market economies experienced when their policy makers prematurely opened up their financial systems to short-term capital inflows in the 1990s. The present book has a well-rounded story with the analytical focus and major conclusions of each chapter firmly in place. I deliberately stayed away from working up a new idea or a novel explanation of this or that aspect of the crisis. I designed it as a textbook. Despite this ostensibly limited goal, I faced an uphill task in managing its comprehensive coverage and analytical rigor amid continuously unfolding data and policy details. In finally accomplishing it, I have profited enormously from classroom discussions and responses from my students. I am immeasurably grateful to Edmond Horsey, my research assistant, for pushing the manuscript from its provisional shape to a successful completion. He collected the necessary information for each chapter and converted it into charts that are uniformly attractive and readily accessible. He tracked down the cartoon sources and persisted with round-the-clock reminders to the copyright holders till he got the necessary permission for their publication in the book. At my request, he located suitable quotations from the works of Robert Triffin, Adam Smith, and John Maynard Keynes that I hope the readers will savor for their current relevance despite their cumbersome prose. I also thank Maria Konovalova and Yuan Wang for their assistance in collecting some information for chapters 3 and 5. I acknowledge partial financial support from the Harriman Institute of Columbia University.

I invite my readers to undertake an exploration of the causes and consequences of the destabilizing financial turmoil with an American origin and a global reach. It is a continuing story that I hope will end soon with a positive outcome for the millions of people who lost their livelihood from its destructive impact.

December 29, 2010, Padma Desai

FROM
FINANCIAL CRISIS
TO
GLOBAL RECOVERY

1

Financial Crisis Origin

A variety of factors contributed to the U.S. economy's recession, which exhibited catastrophic symptoms of a housing bubble toward the end of 2007. Prompted by low interest rates beginning on January 3, 2001, and overlooked by the regulatory agencies, Americans borrowed excessively for home mortgages. This first phase of extensive mortgage financing for eventual home ownership extended from 2001 to 2004. Then from June 30, 2004, interest rates began moving up and these mortgages became unmanageable and ultimately subprime. Marked by escalating foreclosures, this second phase of their conversion into the subprime category intensified from 2005 to 2007. The crashing valuations of mortgage-based assets held by U.S. financial institutions, among them government-supported Fannie Mae and Freddie Mac, and by the American Insurance Group (AIG), required their bailout by the Treasury and the Federal Reserve in late September 2008.

These subprime mortgages were also repackaged into salable assets by savvy operators who sold them to investors, which included large Wall Street banks. This securitization activity via slicing and dicing of the troubled mortgages intensified in 2007. When brought into the act, Congress passed a $700 billon Troubled Asset Relief Program (TARP) for rescuing the banking system.

A major financial breakdown was avoided.

The housing bubble, financed by excessive mortgage lending that plunged the U.S. financial sector into a severe crisis, required its bailout in late 2008 and early 2009. To understand this unprecedented rescue operation, it is necessary to examine the U.S. economy's recovery from the March 2000 collapse of the dotcom bubble.

I. Easy Monetary Policy and Tax Cuts

Beginning in January 2001, the Federal Reserve followed an easy monetary policy for pulling the economy out of the recession that was induced by the collapse of the dotcom bubble in March 2000. It lowered the federal funds rate—which sets the overnight interbank borrowing cost—from 6 to 1 percent on January 3, 2001, and kept it there until June 30, 2004. At the same time, tax cuts, proposed by President George W. Bush and approved by Congress in 2001 and 2003, provided the fiscal stimulus.

Americans began acquiring low-interest-rate mortgages to buy homes. The housing boom, feeding into vigorous construction activity from 2001, provided the impetus to economic recovery, which gathered momentum in 2003 and 2004. The economy recorded a 2003 third quarter GDP growth of 7.5 percent over the preceding quarter. GDP growth rate in 2004 was an exceptional 3.6 percent.

An external factor, combined with the easy monetary policy from 2001 through June 2004, added to the continuing economic resurgence marked by the housing bubble.

Saving Flow from Outside

The emergence of China as a fast-growing economy, with a real annual GDP growth of 8 to 10 percent starting in 1980, represented a new phenomenon in the history of the modern world. By 2005, China's gross domestic investment at 41.2 percent of its GDP was exceeded by its gross saving rate at 49.5 percent, with the rising profitability of the Chinese corporate sector accounting for 70 percent of these savings.[1] At the same time, a booming export sector contributed to the double-digit annual GDP growth of 10 to 11 percent from 2003 to 2006. The People's Bank of China aggressively pumped Chinese currency into the foreign exchange market in exchange for dollars from exporters, which it invested in U.S. Treasury bonds and other foreign currency holdings.[2]

This generous bounty implied that the U.S. Treasury had to borrow less internally. U.S. mortgage rates, steered by the federal funds rate of 1 percent, remained low, which encouraged Americans to take on massive mortgages for home ownership. These mortgages turned into unsustainable burdens as the Federal Reserve began raising the federal funds rate after June 30, 2004. The rate rose to 5.25 percent by June 29, 2006, where it remained until August 17, 2007.

The process of unconstrained home ownership was aided by the failure of consumer protection arrangements that were encumbered by the presence of several agencies responsible for protecting household interests by ensuring regulatory compliance on the part of brokers, mortgage companies, and banks. This is examined in the next section.

II. Failure of Regulatory Arrangements

In the years leading to the crisis, Wall Street banks, flush with cash, were eager to acquire mortgage-backed securities. They encouraged mortgage companies and brokers by steering potential borrowers into high-risk loans. People borrowed beyond their means because appraisers inflated the values of properties that prospective buyers were interested in. Borrowers were led to believe that they had undertaken a standard fixed-rate mortgage only to learn later that their mortgage was a complicated variable-rate contract. Banks could choose their own regulators and switch to a less scrupulous regulator. Federal regulators occasionally sidestepped tougher state requirements that could have prevented such predatory lending activities. Hardly anyone debated the "regulatory capture" by the federal agencies while risky lending practices proliferated.

Mortgage-securitizing banks were not responsible for abuses in the original mortgages. Large American and European banks securitized these subprime mortgages and sold them to global investors with a view to making a profit.

According to the Center for Public Integrity, the top 25 subprime originators had advanced almost $1 trillion in loans to more than 5 million borrowers between 2005 and 2007, the peak of subprime lending. Many of these borrowers' homes were eventually repossessed.[3]

*"Officer, that couple is just walking
away from their mortgage!"*

(© Tom Cheney / The New Yorker Collection / www.cartoonbank.com.)

Would you pay $103,000 for this Arizona fixer-upper? (Reprinted by permission of *The Wall Street Journal*, copyright © 2009 Dow Jones & Company, Inc. All Rights Reserved Worldwide.)

Among mortgage firms that had recklessly extended loans to home owners was Integrity Funding LLC, which had given a $103,000 home equity loan in early 2007 to Marvene Halterman for a little blue house on West Hopi Street in Avondale, Arizona. It was a 30-year mortgage with an adjustable rate that started at 9.25 percent and was capped at 15.25 percent.[4] Halterman, who had bought the house four decades earlier for $3,500, had a long history of unemployment and other problems. She collected junk, and the yard at the house "was waist high in clothes, tires, laundry baskets and broken furniture. . . . By the time the house went into foreclosure in August [2009], Integrity had sold that loan to Wells Fargo & Co., which had sold it to a U.S. unit of HSBC Holdings PLC, which had packaged it with thousands of other risky mortgages and sold it in pieces to scores of investors."[5] A series of similar out-of-bounds decisions had set the stage for the unfolding of the worst financial crisis to hit the United States since the Great Depression.

Why was mortgage lending not regulated? According to the Center for Public Integrity, the big financial players spent $3.5 billion lobbying Washington from 2000 to 2009 and donated $2.2 billion to political campaigns. Wells Fargo Financial, owned by the bank, contributed almost $18 million to election campaigns and lobbying, equally divided between Republicans and Democrats.[6]

(City of Avondale, AZ; Code Enforcement Division.)

Would the crisis have been averted if mortgage lenders' risk management and underwriting practices were more effectively regulated despite the Fed's low interest rate policy from 2001 to 2006? The next section explores this question.

III. What Caused the Crisis:
Lax Regulations or Easy Monetary Policy?

Alan Greenspan, who was chairman of the Federal Reserve from 1987 to 2006, was grilled by the Financial Crisis Inquiry Commission on April 7, 2010, about the Fed's role in the onset of the crisis. Didn't the Fed's failure to curb subprime lending amid the unfolding of the housing bubble fall into the category of "oops"? Phil Angelides, commission chairman, reiterated: "My view is you could have, you should have, and you didn't."[7] Defending his record, the former chairman said: "I was right 70 percent of the time, but I was wrong 30 percent of the time. What we tried to do was

(© 2010, Barry Blitt. Reprinted by permission.)

the best we could with the data that we had."[8] Referring to the ballooning subprime mortgages, he said: "If the Fed . . . had tried to thwart what everyone perceived as . . . an unmitigated good, then Congress would have clamped down on us." Then again: "If we had said we're running into a bubble [of house prices] and we need to retrench, the Congress would say, 'We haven't a clue what you're talking about.'"[9]

The Fed chairman's policy handling prompted this response from a *New York Times* columnist: "If the captain of the *Titanic* followed the Greenspan model, he could claim he was on course at least 70 percent of the time too."[10]

Current Federal Reserve Chairman Ben Bernanke also defended the Fed's record by distinguishing between regulatory failure and low interest rates as factors contributing to the housing bubble. The easy interest rate regime prevailed from 2001 to 2006—he was a member of the Board of Governors of the Federal Reserve for most of that period. In his remarks at the annual meeting of the American Economic Association in early January 2010, he said: "When historical relationships are taken into account, it is difficult to ascribe the house price bubble either to monetary policy or to the broader macroeconomic environment."[11] Earlier Bernanke had referred to the flow of saving from China that had kept U.S. interest rates low. Wasn't it necessary therefore to moderate the Fed's easy monetary policy?

Alicia H. Munnell, a former research director at the Federal Reserve Bank of Boston, provided an insightful assessment: "The Fed is this powerful and privileged institution, and it has a bully pulpit that it can use even when it doesn't have the direct authority to regulate . . . it's never appropriate for a Federal Reserve official to say, 'It's not our job.' In some ways, Alan Greenspan is saying that."[12] Clearly the Federal Reserve, in charge of the financial regulatory setup, should have been aware of its massive policy shortcomings. Wouldn't the borrowing binge have been moderated or even cut short if it had raised the federal funds rate earlier and adequately? Weren't community banks around the country, which issued mortgages and chose their own regulators for the purpose, under the supervisory umbrella of the Federal Reserve? At the same time, shouldn't the Securities and Exchange Commission have extended its regulatory oversight to the activities of financial institutions that were recklessly packaging these subprime mortgages and selling them to investors, which included large Wall Street banks?

In any case, while the Fed defaulted in its policy-making and regulatory roles, were banks poised to manage the hit from the subprime mortgage holdings in their portfolios? Let's examine that question.

IV. Consequences of Excessive Securitization of Subprime Mortgages by Banks

Bank holdings of securitized mortgages were diversified across regions of the United States. One region may suffer a crash, but the property market would not collapse across the country as a whole. Besides, in the first half of 2007, large western banks had posted a record $425 billion in aggregate profits and had capital reserves that vastly exceeded the minimum required by international banking rules. Global banks alone were estimated to hold core capital (known as tier 1) of $3.4 trillion against their assets.

However, losses on the securitized mortgage assets turned out to be so large in the second half of 2007 that they started eating up bank capital. Between June and late November of 2007, more than $240 billion had been wiped off the market capitalization of the 12 largest Wall Street banks. Banks stopped trusting one another. They refused to lend to one another and hoarded their cash.

As the cash shortage intensified, New York, London, and Zurich bankers sought capital infusions from Asian and Middle Eastern sovereign funds estimated at about $3 trillion. Citigroup Inc. was the first to get an infusion, in late November 2008, of $7.5 billion from the Abu Dhabi Investment Fund, the world's biggest sovereign fund. UBS and Merrill Lynch followed.

The crisis of confidence—the loss of "animal spirits"—affected not only the banking sector, but also the stock market, the Treasury bond market, and, most of all, American households struggling with the burden of mortgage payments and home foreclosures as 2007 wound down. In a parallel to the stock market crash of 1929, the market experienced its worst week in October 3. The interest rates on three-month U.S. Treasury bills veered into the negative range in September 2008, for the first time since 1941. Caught in this erosion of animal spirits, American consumers cut back their spending. Business and consumer confidence needed to be revived.

It was time for the Federal Reserve to act. On January 21, 2008, Martin Luther King Day, Chairman Bernanke convened a videoconference of the Federal Open Market Committee and convinced the committee to opt for a king-sized rate cut of three-quarters of a percentage point to 3.50 percent, with a decisive hint of more to come. "It was the first time the Fed had cut rates in between regularly scheduled meetings since the aftermath of September 11, 2001. Although no one realized it at that time, Mr. Bernanke's new strategy was born that day. Whatever it takes."[13]

As 2008 advanced, the stock market began its volatile and sharp descent from a height of 13,000 (registered by the Dow Jones Industrial Average) in April 2008 to 6,500 in February 2009. At the same time, accelerating home foreclosures and subprime mortgages took a toll on mortgage-based assets of banks, mortgage-lending giants Fannie Mae and Freddie Mac, and AIG, the largest American insurer. The rescue called for a joint effort on the part of the Treasury and the Fed, as we see in the next section.

V. The Joint Treasury–Fed Rescue Deals in 2008

The earliest bailout, jointly brokered by the Treasury and the Fed, related to Bear Stearns.

JPMorgan Chase Takeover of Bear Stearns

In March 2008, JPMorgan Chase & Co. bought the collapsing Bear Stearns in a deal that was brokered jointly by former Treasury Secretary Hank Paulson and Bernanke with a transfer of Bear Stearns's troubled assets of $29 billion to the Treasury. In the aftermath of the staggering bailouts that were to follow toward the end of the year, the Bear Stearns takeover by the Treasury was a minor exercise of ownership transfer.

On September 6, the government took over mortgage-lending giants Fannie Mae and Freddie Mac as they teetered near collapse with a portfolio of home loans worth $5.5 trillion out of a total estimated at $10 trillion.

Fannie Mae and Freddie Mac Takeover by the Treasury

For over half a century, Fannie and Freddie enabled Americans to buy homes as the two agencies purchased loans from mortgage banks and provided them with cash for making more loans. It was not the purpose of Fannie and Freddie to directly extend loans to people. The two agencies had a political and legal mandate, prescribed by the U.S. Department of Housing and Urban Development, to support low-income housing by acquiring loans "with lower credit standards." From 2005, the two agencies increased their share of mortgages for affordable housing for moderate-income borrowers living in "underserved areas." The lower credit standards,

"Oh, yeah? Well, my dad bailed out your dad!" (From *The Wall Street Journal*, permission Cartoon Features Syndicate.)

however, meant that, over time, they acquired loans that borrowers could not afford.

As defaults and foreclosures mounted, the two agencies increasingly held worthless assets on their balance sheets, and they needed cash inflow in order to avoid bankruptcy. In September 2008, the Treasury extended a loan of $200 billion each to the two companies and took charge of running them under a conservatorship until they revived. "A failure [of Fannie and Freddie] would affect the ability of Americans to get home loans, auto loans, and other consumer credit and business finance. [Their] failure

*"Well, this is one way to keep the kids
from moving back home."*

(© Tom Cheney / The New Yorker Collection / www.cartoonbank.com.)

would be harmful to economic growth and job creation," Treasury Secretary
Paulson announced in a Washington press conference.

Having received the funding, Fannie and Freddie continued to mod-
ify the loans on their balance sheets in order to keep people in their
homes.

LOAN MODIFICATION PROGRAMS OF FANNIE AND FREDDIE

One of the loan modification programs involved the agencies buying defaulted loans directly from home owners. They also acquired delinquent
loans from pools of mortgage-backed securities (that they had guaranteed) and kept them in their investment portfolios.

In an innovative wrinkle, instead of modifying the loans of home
owners facing foreclosure, the agencies agreed to allow the home owners

to stay in their homes and rent them at a cost lower than their mortgage payments. Fewer foreclosures would stabilize communities and the housing market as well. But there was a catch. If the agencies continued these programs until home prices stabilized, it was entirely possible that they would use up the funding assigned to them by the Treasury—$200 billion each, all of which was free from congressional oversight.

According to the Treasury, Fannie and Freddie needed a longer financial leash. They could not be burdened with the requirement that they reduce their portfolios of mortgages and mortgage-backed securities, which had reached a total of $1.5 trillion. On December 24, 2009, the Treasury, which owned 79.9 percent of the mortgage giants, favored them with a Christmas Eve offering. It suspended for three years the combined $400 billion *limit* on the bailout allowances with which they operated their programs. In another retreat, the Treasury and the Federal Housing Finance Agency also approved significant cash bonuses for top Fannie and Freddie executives. In addition, the agencies would not be required to sell mortgage-backed securities from their portfolios in order to trim their balance sheets. In any case, the market for these tainted assets was weak. Besides, the Federal Reserve was planning to wind down its program of buying mortgage-backed securities by March 31, 2010. Instead, Freddie and Fannie could buy them from the market and keep mortgage interest rates low.

Was the Treasury too lenient with Fannie and Freddie and, in effect, with delinquent home owners who lacked the cash to afford their homes and needed to be rescued? Nearly 15 million American home owners owed their creditor banks more than their homes—in which they owned no equity— were worth. They would be ready to accept foreclosures rather than continue making payments on their outstanding balances. The loan modification program deliberately did not compel banks to write down these balances, which meant that more banks would need to be rescued via taxpayer bounty. The loan modification arrangement only required delinquent home owners to pay lower interest on their mortgages. A faster rate of foreclosures would have thrown millions out of their homes and destabilized entire communities. Fannie and Freddie, endowed with substantial financial resources, would implement the loan modification agenda cautiously.

Caution notwithstanding, the two siblings had run up losses of $126.9 billion in 2009. Both are outside congressional oversight, but shouldn't the taxpayers who will ultimately bear the costs of bailing them out of the mortgage mess they created receive an honest accounting of their exposure? Shouldn't the toxic twins, both government-sponsored entities, be brought openly onto the federal budget with respect to the subsidies they poured into the housing market?

REFORMING FANNIE AND FREDDIE

Opinions differed. Treasury Secretary Tim Geithner informed Congress in late February 2010 that Fannie and Freddie would be reformed in 2011 so that the mortgage catastrophe did not happen again. Representative Barney Frank (D-MA) declared that he would have them abolished in their current avatar, but he fell short of presenting a plan outline. In early March, Representative Scott Garrett (R-NJ) introduced the Accurate Accounting of Fannie Mae and Freddie Mac Act, which would require that taxpayers receive an accurate accounting of the activities of the two behemoths. As 2010 was an election year, Republicans sought opportunities to take a stab at the government's financing accountability.

Continuing the debate, Spencer Bachus, ranking Republican member of the House Financial Services Committee, went further, asking whether Fannie and Freddie should be phased out within four years, whether private mortgage financing be reinvigorated, and whether the original hybrid model of Fannie and Freddie operating as private companies with government financial backing should be gotten rid off once and for all. In response, Treasury Secretary Geithner acknowledged the limitations of the hybrid arrangement: "We should not re-create that fatal mix of public and private shareholders in the same institution." But a government guarantee to facilitate a stable housing market would, in his view, continue, although that support needed to be priced appropriately so as not to burden the taxpayers excessively. Nevertheless, according to Geithner, an outright privatization of Fannie and Freddie was out of the question.[14]

By mid-June 2010, Fannie and Freddie, which held 95 percent of U.S. housing mortgages in their portfolios, reported a massive slump in their share values. Fannie's shares, which traded at $60 per share in September 2007, had collapsed by 99 percent, to about 55 cents. Freddie's exchanged for 74 cents per share, down 98 percent from $60 in September 2007. The New York Stock Exchange, which requires minimum trading guidelines for shares to trade above $1 a share, delisted both from its trading platform on June 16.

Their banishment from the New York Stock Exchange notwithstanding, Fannie and Freddie continued acquiring foreclosed homes, removing owners who could not afford them, selling these units, and extending

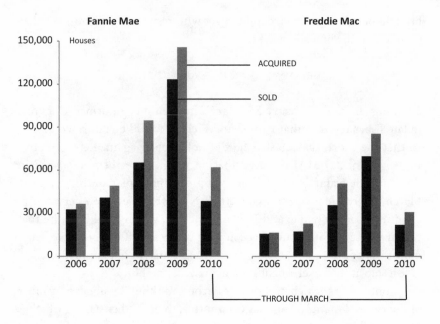

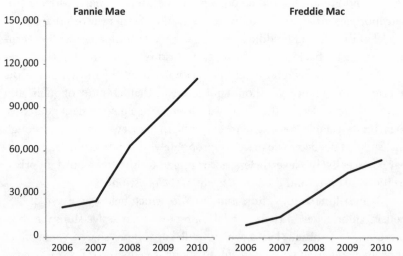

Figure 1.1.
Total Mortgage Holdings of Fannie Mae and Freddie Mac. (Fannie Mae, Freddie Mac.)

mortgage loans to new owners. From 2006 to March 2010, they had acquired foreclosures faster than they could sell them (figure 1.1). During the same period, their ballooning housing inventories had converted them into the country's largest landlords supported by taxpayer bounty. In view of the massive holdings in subprime mortgages on the agencies' balance sheets, their outright privatization would be an unwise public policy choice in the Treasury's judgment. In the meantime, Fannie and Freddie must keep the homes, cover their utility bills and pay their taxes, and hire thousands of contractors to maintain the homes, mow the lawns, and clean the pools. The maintenance cost of these properties was $13 billion in the second quarter of 2010.[15] But the homes could not be disposed of because the housing market was unstable. A private owner would acquire money-losing mortgages at throwaway prices, dispossess the mortgage holders, and resell the properties when the housing market revived. By contrast, Fannie and Freddie had allowed such mortgage holders to continue occupying their homes under modified arrangements. The financial reform legislation that President Barack Obama signed on July 21, 2010, required the Treasury to submit proposals to overhaul Fannie and Freddie no later than January 1, 2011. The public was invited to make suggestions.

Not every troubled company was as lucky as Fannie and Freddie in continuing to get life support from the American taxpayer. On September 15, 2008, Lehman Brothers Holdings Inc., a 150-year-old firm employing 25,000 workers, was forced to initiate the largest bankruptcy proceedings in U.S. history.

Lehman Brothers

Why wasn't Lehman saved? After all, the government had allowed JPMorgan Chase to buy and rescue Bear Stearns. Perhaps Congress did not want to undertake another bailout on the heels of Fannie and Freddie just a week before. Lehman's balance sheet was excessively leveraged without adequate collateral. Lehman's global derivatives with a notional face value of $39 trillion included deals with 8,000 counterparties. The derivatives, split into numerous strands, presented a daunting challenge to its computer platforms and technology staff. Despite Lehman's being smaller than Merrill Lynch and, unlike Merrill Lynch, having no ties with either Main Street or Wall Street and despite prodding by the Treasury, Lehman could not find a partner with deep pockets to team up with. "In retrospect, if you had to choose one firm to throw under the bus to save everyone else, you would choose Lehman."[16]

A year later, former Treasury Secretary Paulson reminisced in his memoir about his decision to let Lehman go under: "Only after Lehman Brothers failed did we get the authorities from Congress to inject capital into financial institutions. . . . Amazingly, U.S. government regulators still lack the power to wind down a nonbank financial institution outside bankruptcy."[17] Without Lehman's collapse, Congress would not have been activated to pass the $700 billion TARP on October 3, 2008, aimed at saving the financial system.

AIG was the final item on the Treasury–Federal Reserve's bailout list.

AIG Rescue

On September 16, 2008, the Federal Reserve rescued AIG with an $85 billion loan, and the U.S. government got a 79.9 percent equity stake in the company in the form of warrants, called equity participation notes. The Fed loan was secured with AIG's insurance business assets, and the government's equity stake could turn out to be profitable with the rebound of the market. "A disorderly failure of AIG could add to already significant levels of financial market fragility," the Fed said in a prepared statement. Indeed, after Congress passed TARP to bolster the financial health of U.S. banks, AIG received $49 billion from the program.

The AIG rescue saved the company—but was it proper? Not according to an audit conducted more than a year later by the special inspector general for TARP, Neil Barofsky. According to his severe admonition, the New York Federal Reserve under the presidency of Geithner had paid 100 cents to the dollar for the complex securities that AIG trading partners (among them, Goldman Sachs Group Inc., Merrill Lynch, and Société Générale) had insured with AIG. These credit market bets in the bank portfolios, amounting to $60 billion, were tied to the collapsing mortgage-linked securities and were worth much less. Of course, the banks desperately tried to get AIG to post adequate collateral to cover the securities, which it could not do. Instead, the government bought these securities from the banks, which then cancelled their insurance contracts with AIG and freed it from the pressure to post matching collateral. AIG was rescued. So were the banks, its partners—with full coverage from U.S. taxpayers.

"We've decided that it would be wise to dissolve the corporation and form a cult."
(From *The Wall Street Journal*, permission Cartoon Features Syndicate.)

On November 19, 2009, Treasury Secretary Geithner defended his decision to rescue AIG when he was New York Fed president. In his view, the government lacked the power to rescue a company such as AIG, which was not legally set up as a bank. "Coming into AIG, we had, basically, duct tape and string." It was, however, critical to keep AIG liquid, whereas Lehman, a nonbank company, could be allowed to disappear. Did this imply double standards?

In the autumn of 2008, the policy-making team was driven more by trial-and-error problem solving than by personal preferences. The escalating turmoil demanded seat-of-the-pants action, often with limited information and little time to think. Of course, hindsight is 20-20—and every decision at each stage of the crisis would end up being evaluated in the great American tradition of Monday-morning quarterbacking. In late May 2010, the Congressional Oversight Panel for TARP held a hearing about the government bailout of AIG. Several questions were raised, but the most crucial was: When will AIG repay the $83.2 billion it owed to the Federal Reserve? The company had sold off some assets, paid down its debts, and had become a smaller entity. Ultimately, AIG would shrink to international general insurance (including property and casualty) and domestic life insurance. It might continue insuring mortgages. Everything else had been closed or sold or put up for sale. Perhaps AIG will repay the Fed's loan in 2011. But would it ever become profitable enough for the Treasury to recover its $49 billion TARP bailout funding?

In late September 2010, AIG's board of directors floated a scheme for consideration by government overseers that would provide an affirmative nod to the question. Under the plan, the Treasury could convert the $49 billion of preferred shares in its possession into common shares. That would initially raise the Treasury's stake in AIG from the current 79.9 percent to greater than 90 percent. The Treasury would then gradually sell off the shares to private investors. That would reduce its ownership stake in the company and perhaps earn it a profit if the shares rose in value. The Treasury exit plan could begin as early as the first half of 2011. If the plan succeeded, the Treasury could argue that the initial investigation undertaken by lawmakers with regard to the government bailout of AIG was off the mark.

An even more damaging after-the-event scrutiny was mounted by congressional watchdogs with regard to Bank of America's purchase of Merrill Lynch.

Bank of America Takes Over Merrill Lynch

In December 2008, Bank of America bought Merrill Lynch for $50 billion. But before the deal could be consummated, Bank of America CEO Kenneth Lewis, worried about the deteriorating toxic assets of Merrill Lynch, called Bernanke and Paulson and told them that he was thinking of pulling out of the deal. Terrified by the prospect of panic in the financial market that this might set off, they loaned Bank of America an additional

$20 billion from TARP funding. Almost 10 months later, Lewis, Bernanke, and Paulson appeared before the House Committee on Oversight and Government Reform on plausible charges of having worked up a secret deal without the knowledge of Merrill Lynch shareholders and then arranging a cover-up. At the end of the day, Merrill had to be saved from a collapse, and Lewis took the heat and defended the deal. "I would say [Bernanke and Paulson] strongly advised and they spoke in strong terms, but I think it was with the best intentions," he said in his testimony on June 11, 2009. Months later at a conference of Japanese investors in Tokyo, he waxed eloquent about his mission: "I began my tenure as CEO of this company with a vision for a global, integrated, multiproduct financial services company. . . . Merrill Lynch will help bring this vision to life." He also invoked a Japanese proverb in support of his mission, saying, "Vision without action is a daydream. . . . Action without vision is a nightmare."

More than a year later, Kenneth Lewis's nightmare was not over. In early February 2010, Andrew Cuomo, New York State Attorney General, filed a civil fraud lawsuit against Bank of America, Ken Lewis, and the bank's Chief Financial Officer Joseph Price, accusing them of "duping shareholders and the federal government in order to complete a merger deal with Merrill Lynch."[18] In other words, the management of Bank of America intentionally concealed massive losses at Merrill in order for the shareholders to approve the deal. In hindsight, Bank of America's takeover of Merrill Lynch did not seem to have hurt U.S. taxpayers. Bank of America has since repaid the TARP bailout fund, and Merrill's investment bank has turned the corner into reporting profit. Andrew Cuomo, who was planning to run for governor of New York State, was evidently catching a moment under the sun to play politics.

In September 2008, the Bank of America takeover of Merrill Lynch was the least costly and controversial item on the firefighting agenda of the Treasury and the Federal Reserve for rescuing the financial system as a whole, which was heading toward a collapse. It was urgent to get Congress into the act. The next section describes what Congress did.

VI. Congress to the Rescue

In the midst of this frenzy of rescues, the stock market had continued to fall sharply, and the yield on U.S. short-term Treasury bonds had sunk to zero as risk-averse investors flooded to these safest of assets. It was time to bring Congress into a big-time rescue plan. On September 18, 2008, Paulson and Bernanke (accompanied by Chris Cox, chairman of the Securities and Exchange Commission) went to Capitol Hill to alert the congressional leadership. "'No economy has ever faced the financial meltdown we're facing without undergoing a major recession,' [Bernanke] told the stunned leadership behind closed doors. Without congressional action, it would be deep and prolonged."[19]

In the original version of the rescue legislation, the $700 billion in funding was intended to be for the Treasury to buy the toxic assets of the banks rather than provide them with cash infusions. But the House voted down the proposed bill. In the view of the legislators, voters were angry and in no mood to bail out a bunch of profligate bankers who sought to be saved via taxpayers' cash. Representative Frank consoled Secretary Paulson: "Sometimes you have to let the kid run away from home. He gets hungry, he comes back."[20] In its revised and final version, TARP, with its $700 billion in funding, included not only subprime mortgage assets but also other financial instruments in the rescue operation.

Frank provided the final word on the rescue package: "You can't go out and shoot the bankers. You can't have an economy without a functioning credit system. People are angry. They're furious. But you have no option but to live with these people."[21]

Great Depression No. 2 was avoided by the lawmakers with a timely but ironic show of generosity in favor of the bankers.

2
Banking Sector Stress Tests
United States Versus the European Union

Toward the end of 2008, the U.S. economic recession continued to worsen. The banking sector was in unprecedented uncertainty. Credit to businesses had dried up, forcing them to lay off workers and postpone investment. Banks had been posting lackluster revenues throughout the year. Investors and depositors fled large banks because they were not sure if these banks would remain solvent.

In response, the Federal Reserve announced a stress test in February 2009 for 19 major banks in order to assess the potential impact of a severe recession on their earnings. The Treasury advanced the banks a cash buffer from the Troubled Asset Relief Program (TARP), which they needed for gaining adequate capital reserves. TARP represented a set of initiatives undertaken by the Treasury for rescuing major U.S. banks and for acquiring a stake in the auto industry. The share of TARP set aside for rescuing banks was designated the Capital Purchase Program.

By the end of 2009, the banks had returned most of the taxpayer-financed TARP bailout funding, although they were still holding back from advancing credit to U.S. businesses and households. At the same time, however, the Federal Deposit Insurance Corporation (FDIC) had to take over a fair number of small banks around the country that were holding subprime mortgage assets, which situation, in turn, emptied that agency's funding resources.

In contrast to the Federal Reserve's decisive implementation of a stress test for major U.S. banks, European Union (EU) policy makers lagged behind, until July 2010, in mounting a test for assessing the health of European banks. These banks carried subprime mortgage securities as well as sovereign bonds of the heavily indebted governments of Greece, Ireland, Portugal, and Spain. Their balance sheets called for a careful screening in terms of decisive criteria of the burden they would need to surmount if the EU economic recession turned out to be worse than expected and if their reserves had to deal with a likely decline in the values of their sovereign debt holdings.

The EU stress test results announced on July 23 cleared the majority of EU banks from a severe impact on their capital adequacy arising from a severe recession and a decline in the valuations of the sovereign bonds in their portfolios. Only seven of the 91 major banks needed to raise additional capital for meeting the emergencies defined in the stress test. The positive results raised doubts among observers about the stringency of the test criteria. Nevertheless, the test stabilized financial markets and the euro in mid-2010 and lifted the prospects for a eurozone ("eurozone" as used in this book refers to the geographic area in which are located the 16 members of the Economic and Monetary Union whose currency is the euro).

Along with the TARP allocation of bailout funds to the major banks, the Federal Reserve and the Treasury mounted two separate programs for relieving financial institutions and the economy of the burden of the mountain of troubled assets. These were mini steps, measures meant to build confidence. The Fed's Term Asset-Backed Loan Facility (TALF) advanced funds to potential investors for buying sick consumer securities (such as failing auto and student loans) and commercial real estate mortgages. The Treasury's Public-Private Investment Program (PPIP) sought out investors and offered them matching funds for retrieving toxic assets from financial institutions. These programs eventually seemed unnecessary as private investors got ready to pick up these assets amid reassuring signs of economic recovery in early 2010.

But the banking sector needed to be cleaned of its toxic assets before it could seek out profitable lending opportunities as the demand for loans picked up. The Federal Reserve devised a stress test for major banks that focused on two issues. First, the process would examine the assets in the banks' balance sheets and measure the banks' potential losses (net of their earnings) over a two-year period under the worst-case scenario of a severe recession. Second, the test would come up with the amount of capital each bank would need in order to achieve a tier 1 common equity capital ratio or a capital buffer equal to 4 percent of its assets.

I. The U.S. Banking Sector Stress Test and TARP Funding

The administration announced the stress tests for the largest 19 banks in February 2009. The announcement was met with doubts by everyone, including the regulators, the stock market, and the banking sector. Regulators disagreed on whether to make the results of the tests public. The stock market anticipated a dismal outcome from the exercise. Bankers feared that banks might stand to lose rather than gain from the test. Wells Fargo Chairman Richard Kovacevich described the test as "asinine."

But the Treasury's aim was to bring confidence back into the banking system. At the beginning of 2009, some investors and analysts felt that some banks would have to be closed or nationalized. It was critical to dispel that uncertainty. The concrete policy goal was to estimate the big banks' near-term losses and ensure that they had enough capital to withstand a severe recession. As a result, the banks would survive and so would the U.S. economy.

One specific fear was that the weak banks could pull down the strong ones. The tests, however, distinguished between the weak and the strong. In other words, it did not apply an across-the-board formula for assessing losses from subprime mortgage or commercial real estate loans in the banks' asset portfolios. Rather, each bank's balance sheet was examined separately for projecting individual losses, bigger losses at some and smaller at others. The weak participants would be shored up by taxpayer money if necessary. The results published on May 7, 2009, revealed a wide gap between the healthy banks and the not-so-healthy banks.

Stress Test Results

Among the 19 banks the Treasury stress test focused on were Bank of America Corp., Citigroup Inc., Wells Fargo, JPMorgan Chase, and Goldman Sachs, all giants, all considered too big to fail. They held two-thirds of U.S. banking sector assets. The number crunching was done by the Federal

Reserve, which deflected charges of a possible ploy on the part of the Treasury. More than 150 members of the regulatory agencies pored over the balance sheets of the 19 banks in order to gauge their capital adequacy, examined bankers' projections of their near-term survivability, and sought to sidestep surprises lurking in the bankers' books.

The purpose of the test was to determine the banks' need for capital backing based on their 2009 first-quarter balance sheet health and their projected losses in 2009 and 2010 in the event that the worst-case scenario, that of a severe recession, materialized. The results indicated that the banking industry was in better shape than anticipated. Nevertheless, Bank of

Table 2.1
Stress Test Results and Tarp Funding for 19 U.S. Banks

Banks Needing Extra Capital	Capital Required (based on capital actions and first-quarter results)	Projected Losses (in 2009 and 2010, assuming adverse scenario)	TARP Funds Received
Bank of America	$33.9	$136.6	$45
Citigroup	5.5	104.7	45
Wells Fargo	13.7	86.1	25
Morgan Stanley	1.8	19.7	10
PNC Financial Services	0.6	18.8	7.6
GMAC	11.5	9.2	5
SunTrust	2.2	11.8	4.9
Regions Financial	2.5	9.2	3.5
Fifth Third Bancorp	1.1	9.1	3.4
Keycorp	1.8	6.7	2.5
Banks with Adequate Capital			
JP Morgan Chase	$0	$97.4	$25
Goldman Sachs	0	17.8	10
US Bancorp	0	15.7	6.6
Capital One	0	13.4	3.6
American Express	0	11.2	3.4
BB&T	0	8.7	3.1
Bank of NY Mellon	0	5.4	3
State Street	0	8.2	2
Metlife	0	9.6	0

(Federal Reserve.)

America and Wells Fargo, which fared the worst with regard to their current capital adequacy, and eight others were asked to raise total equity capital of $74.6 billion as a buffer against their current risky assets. The other nine of the 19 received a reassuring nod of financial health regarding their current capital adequacy (table 2.1).

But how did these 19 banking giants rank with regard to the impact on their financial viability if the recession were to get worse? Bank of America, Citigroup, JPMorgan Chase, and Wells Fargo would fare worst, in that order, if the recession turned out to be severe. This suggested that they held toxic assets that would decline in value as the recession worsened. If they failed, they would have to shed assets, sell shares, and perhaps have the Treasury on board as a main shareholder. The healthy ones could access the public markets or convert preferred shares into common equity. Those that could not do either would have to turn to the Treasury or sell assets. Rising unemployment implied more mortgage foreclosures and increasing damage to these assets and bank balance sheets. In the meantime, all 19 of the banks received varying amounts of taxpayer-financed TARP support, led by Bank of America and Citigroup at $45 billion each (table 2.1).

Ben Bernanke, chairman of the Federal Reserve, declared on May 7 that the stress tests had been "comprehensive, rigorous, forward looking, and highly collaborative. . . . Undoubtedly, we can use many aspects of the exercise to improve our supervisory processes in the future." Not everyone agreed.

Independent Assessment of Stress Test Results

Neil M. Barofsky, the special inspector general who oversaw the bank bailout, declared a year later, on October 12, 2009, that the Treasury had made a few misleading statements and even unfairly disbursed funds to the biggest banks. Why did the regulators mislead the public by declaring that the earliest bailout recipients, among them Citigroup and JPMorgan Chase, were all healthy? Were the regulators really concerned about the health of the banks that received the first bailout (to be followed by the remaining amount later)? For example, why did Bank of America get $15 billion when Citigroup and JPMorgan Chase each received $25 billion in a single shot to be followed by more cash later? Shouldn't government officials have been more careful about expressing their rationale and undertaking their decisions? In a letter included in the Barofsky report, the Treasury said that any review of the announcements made a year earlier must be "considered in light of the unprecedented circumstances in which they were made."[1]

Despite the Treasury's brush-off, a few bailout numbers raised doubts. On the one hand, the loss rate for first-lien mortgages was set at 8.8 percent, whereas the loss rate for second-lien mortgages was calculated at 13.8 percent. On the other hand, the loss rate for commercial real estate holdings by banks at 8.5 percent seemed optimistic in view of the sector's disastrous condition. Tier 1 capital of banks included common and preferred shares. In the official viewing of the test results, most banks were adequately capitalized, although investors had fled earlier in the year. The government suggested that tier 1 capital backing in terms of common stock be at only 4 percent of risk-weighted assets. That implied a leverage of 25 to 1.

Implications of Bailout for the Treasury, the Federal Reserve, and the Banks

Despite the substantial TARP support, the Treasury and the Federal Reserve were not planning to take a hands-on role in the daily operations of the banks. The Treasury might monitor the management and replace a board member or a CEO. It would not, however, vet their business plans as it had done with Chrysler and General Motors. By contrast, the U.K. authorities took over the management of shareholdings in fully or partially nationalized banks such as Northern Rock and Royal Bank of Scotland.

Nationalizing the troubled U.S. banks, in my view, would have been a colossal mistake. It would have required spending hundreds of billions of dollars for taking over the major banks and managing them for years. It would have involved the bailout of bank creditors and financing the claims of counterparties to their holdings of derivatives and securities in bank portfolios. Why amputate a limb that could be saved with a strong medicine? In early March 2010, Lawrence E. Summers, White House economic advisor, concluded affirmatively about the decision: "Today with all of the major financial institutions having a market capitalization of more than a hundred billion dollars and the economy growing again, the judgment not to nationalize but to put an enormous emphasis on raising private capital looks to have been effective."[2]

The stress test combined with TARP funding was predicated on two expectations: first, that the banks would restructure their assets, get rid of the sick items, and generate adequate capital backing for the re-structured portfolio; second, that while this process gathered speed, the administration and Congress would speedily complete the new set of regulations aimed at forestalling the occurrence of a similar financial debacle in the future.

Asset Restructuring and Adequate Capital Provision by Banks

Banks needed to be adequately recapitalized against their loans (as lenders) so that they could survive a business downturn. As recently as mid-2006, the proportion of troubled loans was around 2 percent of total bank loans and leases. However, toward the end of March 2009, the FDIC reported that the fraction had risen to 7.75 percent of the total. Banks were going to have to sell off worthless loans in their asset portfolios as well as add to their capital cushions.

Banks had several ways of replenishing their capital base. They could convert preferred stocks into common stocks so that they could avoid paying dividends and add to their capital backing. They could also sell new common shares. Common equity was important because it remained for the shareholders if the bank was liquidated. At the same time, they could convert existing preferred stocks—which the Treasury had acquired in 2008 at the height of the crisis in exchange for TARP funding—into "mandatory convertible preferred" shares. More to the point, the preferred convertible stock counted toward the tangible common equity that served as a buffer against future losses. These shares could then be converted into common shares at the banks' initiative or at the regulators' discretion or within seven years. By holding on to preferred shares, the government remained a passive, hands-off investor.

All in all, TARP recipients had adequate alternatives for raising their capital backing against their risky assets. However, the bounty had strings attached to its availability.

TARP-Related Constraints

While Congress was debating the details of a regulatory framework, the administration imposed restrictions on the award of taxpayer-funded

12-16-09

(TOLES © *The Washington Post.* Reprinted with permission of UNIVERSAL UCLICK. All rights reserved.)

TARP dollars to the banks. These constraints related to compensation and hiring practices. Not only were salaries of top executives limited, but also additional payment to them needed to be made via restricted stock options. Congress added its set of measures, verging on the punitive, that barred TARP recipients from distributing bonuses to top executives in excess of a third of their compensation.

Occasionally the TARP-related guidelines were overlapping and confusing. Should companies pay 2008 bonuses according to the new rules, which went into effect in early 2009? Did the congressional rules apply only to senior executives or also to mid-level managers? The recipients of TARP bailout funds, especially the healthy banks, were motivated by self-interest considerations. Wouldn't it be smart to return TARP funding and escape the rules? The next section explores the banks' actions in this regard.

II. Big Banks on the Move

A few banks had stopped paying dividends to the Treasury by mid-June 2009 as they faced a shaky capital base, raising questions among some bankers and lawmakers. In their view, the Treasury oversight of taxpayer-funded assistance to the banking sector was not consistent and vigilant.

But also by mid-2009, the major banks' market resurgence was clearly visible. Some among them—JPMorgan Chase, Goldman Sachs, and Morgan Stanley as well as Barclays, Deutsche Bank, and Credit Suisse across the Atlantic—had recorded substantial profits from resurgent commodity and foreign exchange trading and from new debt and equity flotation. By contrast, Citigroup and Bank of America lagged behind.

Clearly, the well-capitalized banks were ready to shake off the government oversight that came with the TARP funding. But according to conditions imposed by the Treasury and the Federal Reserve, TARP funding could be returned only if banks had sold bonds that were not insured by the government. Banks could check in but it was a lot harder to check out from TARP. But the healthy banks were ready to shake off the captivity of the so-called Hotel Geithner, a tongue-in-cheek reference to Treasury Secretary Tim Geithner.

As early as mid-May, Goldman Sachs, JPMorgan Chase, and Morgan Stanley had successfully borrowed from the market without needing a government subsidy. They were ready to return to business as usual. In their view, compensation caps and other restrictions damaged their banks' competitiveness. They feared the portents of new regulations (under consideration by Congress) that promised to be more extensive than in the pre-crisis years. They swung for the fences from their boardrooms and their trading desks to entice their corporate clients and outcompete their weakened archrivals such as Citigroup and Bank of America.

On June 9, 2009, 10 large banks, among them American Express, Goldman Sachs, JPMorgan Chase, and Morgan Stanley, announced plans to return a combined $68.3 billion, a quarter of the TARP bailout. They were allowed to exit from TARP before they had cleared their balance sheets of their toxic assets and before Congress had put in place reforms aimed at forestalling a new crisis. The Treasury guidelines and decision making with regard to the return of TARP funding by banks were not always clear. In early December 2009, Bank of America won the Treasury's approval to repay its $45 billion TARP funding. As part of its exit strategy, the bank had acquired cash from the market by selling $19.29 billion in common stock. By contrast, Citigroup was asked to raise $20 billion in common stock for returning $20 billion in TARP cash to the Treasury. Wells Fargo would also need to drum up big bucks from the market if it desired to exit from the TARP trap. Citigroup was concerned that raising common equity from the market would dilute the value of its $100 billion in common equity. Both banks feared that they would be placed at a competitive disadvantage vis-à-vis Bank of America if they were not allowed to exit from the TARP door. The Treasury had the upper hand. Besides, it expected a total repayment to the tune of only $25 billion in 2009 and could use the extra cash for shoring up the finances of other units without having to approach Congress for fresh funding.

Toward the end of September 2009, $572 billion of the total allocation of $700 billion had been spent for rescuing banks (in the amount of $250 billion), the auto industry, and AIG. Was the bank bailout in the amount of $250 billion profitable? By early April 2010, the Treasury had made more than $10 billion on banks' repayments. Goldman Sachs and American Express paid dividends and ultimately a favorable price to the Treasury for repurchasing their preferred stocks, which they had given to the government in exchange for the bailout aid. By contrast, the Treasury expected to lose on its investments in the auto industry and smaller banks. The biggest loss-making ventures and an increasing drain on the Treasury's bailout activity continued to be Fannie Mae and Freddie Mac, as I posited in the previous chapter.

TARP was scheduled to expire by the end of 2009.

Terminating TARP: The Controversies

The Treasury could extend TARP as a safeguard against an unexpected downturn in the banking sector. Technically, the program could not end until the recipient banks had repaid the financial support to the Treasury. But some lawmakers worried about the program turning into a long-term subsidy to the banks. Indeed 39 Republican senators and one Democrat wrote to the Treasury Secretary to terminate TARP and use the returned bailout funding for reducing the federal debt, which was close to hitting its $12.1 trillion debt ceiling in late fall 2009. On November 17, 2009, Senator John Thane (R-SD) introduced a bill in the Senate that would prohibit Treasury Secretary Geithner from extending further TARP funding beyond December 31, although the legislation would allow Citigroup, General

Motors, and others to retain the $400 billion worth of handouts that remained with them. The remaining $300 billion would be returned to the taxpayers right away.

But Geithner informed lawmakers in early December that the government needed the funds until October 2010. Besides, it could use the remaining funds for creating jobs and helping small businesses. Republicans were opposed to recycling TARP funds for a jobs bill. Originally launched as an emergency measure for stabilizing the financial system, it was turning into "walking-around money" for mortgage modification, small business lending, and capital enhancement of small and community banks. The program had been devised as a loan program, and in the view of Republican members, the use of the funding for infrastructure buildup and aid to states would violate its original commitments. Among the least controversial and legally permissible was support for small banks scattered across the United States.

Among them were 8,000 banks that had been battered by the declining economy, housing foreclosures, and real estate crash. Let's examine their situation.

III. What About the Small Banks?

In the growth years of the early 2000s, small banks had borrowed from the market, extended loans to small regional businesses, and promoted commercial real estate. By mid-2009, they could not compete with the majors in attracting bargain-hunting investors who were focused on recapitalizing the big units. Many were forced to raise their capital base by selling their assets or making fewer loans. Between the start of 2008 and the end of March 2010, a total of 237 small banks had failed, and the number of "problem" banks as designated by the FDIC had been rising steadily for three years, from 252 at the end of 2008 to 702 at the end of 2009 to 775—roughly 10 percent of the U.S. banking industry—in the first quarter of 2010.[3] The problem banks could cost the FDIC billions of dollars and deplete its insurance fund, which protects household deposits.

When a bank fails and its deposits are guaranteed by the FDIC, the agency may take it over. In that case, the FDIC must pay the depositors (up to the legally maximum insured amount of $250,000 per depositor) and sort out the assets and liabilities of the failed bank. Alternatively, the bank may be bought by another bank, in which case the FDIC avoids the bailout costs, and the bank depositors and employees switch their allegiance to a new owner. The FDIC covers the costs of the bailout activity from the insurance fund to which the banking industry contributes. By the end of 2009, the FDIC fund was in the red, and the agency had to cover its impending losses in the coming months by ordering the nation's big banks to prepay their deposit insurance fees in the amount of $45 billion for the end of 2009, 2010, 2011, and 2012. The alternative of borrowing from the Treasury would have appeared politically controversial. "I do think that the American people would prefer to see an end to policies that looked to the federal balance sheet as the remedy to every problem," Federal Deposit Insurance Corporation Chairman Sheila Bair said.[4]

As 2010 unfolded, the FDIC saw an opportunity to collect cash from buyers of failed banks if the bank buyout was received favorably by the buyers' shareholders and if the deals turned out to be profitable. Indeed, the FDIC collected $23.3 million in December 2009 from New York Community Bank Inc., which had acquired AmTrust Bank, a Cleveland thrift institution that had failed. Within weeks of the deal, the shares of New York Community had rallied, and the FDIC profited from a financial provision inserted in the deal that entitled it to a fraction of the stock rally. In 2010, the FDIC would include such profit-sharing mechanisms in future auctions of failing banks across the country.

But small banks were slow in scrubbing their balance sheets of troubled assets. Those with less than $1 billion in assets faced a lengthy recuperation period in 2010 as they struggled to clean up the troubled commercial real estate assets in their balance sheets. However, FDIC officials signaled that they had enough cash on hand to bail out problem banks without having to levy new fees on the banking industry. At the same time, private investors had begun taking over troubled banks in early 2010, easing the strain on FDIC bailout resources. During the first quarter of 2010, the FDIC had lowered the amount of money it had set aside for bank rescue by $3 billion, the first reduction since the second quarter of 2007.[5] "We are seeing light at the end of the tunnel," Chairman Bair said in a May 2010 interview.[6]

The FDIC had to be innovative not only in collecting cash, but also in economizing in cash payments. In mid-2009, it let CIT Group go under even though the depositors' funds in CIT Bank were FDIC-guaranteed. In fact, CIT had received $2.3 billion in loans from TARP, but it had failed to raise cash from the bond market. In mid-July 2009, the FDIC turned down CIT's request for funding from its Temporary Liquidity Guarantee Program (TLGP). Why would the FDIC turn down this request? Wouldn't the

TLGP lifeline help CIT borrow? Probably not—its loan portfolio was already overburdened with loans to troubled businesses and its credit rating had plunged. And perhaps Washington policy makers and the financial system had moved on from the Lehman bankruptcy and the fear of an extensive bank debacle to signs of financial stability. CIT was left to sink or swim on its own. But in a country that has second chances, CIT bounced back from bankruptcy protection in December 2009 after clearing $10 billion in debt. It continued its search for a CEO amid the credit crisis, executive pay caps, and the overarching reach of government scrutiny. In early February 2010, John Thain, the former CEO of Merrill Lynch who was ousted by Bank of America during its Merrill takeover 13 months earlier, took a chance to restore his career from a fall from grace and revive CIT's role as a lender to small and medium-sized businesses.

The TARP-led implementation of the U.S. banking sector cleanup was fast, decisive, and open. It was also backed by the Treasury's readiness to advance bailout support to banks that had low capital backing relative to their problem assets. In contrast, EU leaders were slow in implementing a stress test for European banks for resolving these issues, as we see in the next section.

IV. EU Banking Sector Problems

The delay in mounting a U.S.-style stress test for EU banks arose from several directions, with a number of questions. Should there be a stress test at all? Which banks should be included? What criteria should be employed for assessing the capital requirements of the banks? In particular, should the balance sheets of the EU banking system be assessed for their holdings of the depreciating sovereign bonds of Greece, Ireland, Portugal, and Spain? In the U.S. stress test, the 19 too-big-to-fail banks were included in the test. Their collapse could stall the functioning of the U.S. financial system. Their capital inadequacy was assessed with respect to the onset of a severe recession, which would further damage the mortgage-based securities in their balance sheets.

The timing, coverage, and scope of the EU stress test were also influenced by the loan activity of the European Central Bank (ECB), which lent to eurozone banks as part of its easing of monetary policy. In particular, in the summer of 2009, the ECB had extended €442 billion ($563 billion) in one-year loans in a single liquidity operation to eurozone banks as emergency funding for a year. The ECB was motivated by quantitative monetary policy easing designed to encourage bank lending to businesses. A year later, on June 24, 2010, the banks were under obligation to repay these loans to the ECB. Just as the banks were scrambling to raise cash from the market, they were under mounting pressure to undergo a stress test. Their balance sheets would have exhibited fewer problems if they had been given an early warning of an impending stress test. The less-afflicted banks could have managed to borrow from the market and improve their cash provision for debt repayment ahead of the test. Clearly, much time was lost as European leaders dithered over the need for assessing EU banking sector health.

What indeed was the exposure of European banks to problem assets?

European Banking Sector Exposure to Problem Assets

According to a Bank for International Settlements (BIS) report, banks in the eurozone held nearly $1.6 trillion of government debt and credits to corporations and individuals in Greece, Portugal, Spain, and Ireland. French and German banks were exposed to the extent of nearly $1 trillion of these problem assets. The BIS did not identify individual institutions in line with its confidentiality rules.[7] Rather than publish information about the volume of their problem assets, the ECB released data about the aggregate adjustments eurozone banks needed to undertake in their balance sheets. Thus, from 2007 to 2010, eurozone banks were expected to write down €361 billion ($458 billion) from their accumulated holdings of loans and securities. They would be required to make an additional loan loss provision of €105 billion ($133 billion) in 2011.[8]

Clearly, eurozone banks were in critical financial condition. Even as banks made adjustments in their balance sheets via write-offs of non-performing debts, they needed to refinance their maturing bonds and borrow for the purpose (as I have indicated, they needed to repay the one-year loans from the ECB). In so doing, they competed with the government and corporate sectors for new bonds. Banks had also stalled in securitizing and packaging loans to investors. Without bond issues and securitization, banks failed to raise money to repay the ECB and to lend to companies and households. Interbank lending, which advanced loans to banks for overnight to a year, had dried up in May 2010. Banks hoarded cash in order to cover their debt obligations. In other words, if the financial markets were functioning and if banks could have borrowed freely from the market and from one another, they would have kept less cash as precautionary cover. But most of the eurozone's 3,000 banks found it difficult to access the interbank lending market. The financial markets had become dysfunctional.

In contrast to the United States, with stress test scrutiny followed by the required support to the big banks, EU leaders vacillated over lifting the cleanup of the banking sector to the top of their policy agenda. The next section discusses this.

V. EU Leadership Vacillation Over Banking Sector Cleanup

From early on, the issue of a banking sector cleanup had plunged European leaders into debating the uncertainties of a stress test and safeguarding individual country interests. Christine Lagarde, the French economy minister, raised procedural questions. Do we do the test by country? Do we do it at the same time? Do we publish only the criteria? Do we publish the criteria and the results?

By contrast, former German finance minister Peter Steinbruck did not plan to run a stress test on individual German banks. Even if he did, he would not publish the results. He did not want troubles for state-owned regional banks, known as *Landesbanken,* before the September 2009 general election. Of course, these banks were supported by the state governments that constituted the German federation. They had begun accumulating risky securities after Steinbruck had arranged a deal with the eurozone financial authorities in Brussels in 2001. The arrangement allowed state governments in Germany to continue supporting these banks for a specified period for loans provided by the banks to local businesses. In Spain as well, policymakers were reluctant to carry out stress tests on the 45 regional savings banks—*cajas*—that accounted for about half the assets of the Spanish banking sector. Occasionally, local politicians sat on the management and supervisory boards of these banks. During the Spanish housing and nonresidential construction boom of the late 1990s extending into the early years of 2000, these banks advanced loans on terms that bypassed strict commercial risk criteria.

European banking supervisors carried out stress tests on EU banks in 2009 without publicizing the results for individual banks. The exposure of the banks to problem assets—such as subprime mortgage-backed securities (similar to their U.S. counterparts) and the risky sovereign debts of troubled eurozone governments—was not revealed, although a few banks in Britain, Germany, and Spain were bailed out.

It was necessary to get to the bottom of the banking sector health in the EU and get detailed information about its balance sheet condition. After a prolonged delay, German authorities dropped their resistance to a stress test on June 16, 2010. Spain's central bank agreed to it, saying its stress test had indicated that Spain's commercial and savings banks had adequate capital reserves to deal with difficult growth scenarios.

However, how many of the 3,000 eurozone banks should be included in the test? What criteria should be specified for testing the health of their balance sheets? And should the results of the exercise be published? Was the German role critical in adopting the final design of the stress test that would be uniform for all of the problem banks? These questions, which were avoided in the earlier tests, are addressed in the next section.

VI. EU Stress Test: Design and Results

At the outset, the EU regulators needed to select banks that might adequately represent the assets of the banking industry. The EU-wide stress test in 2009 had included only 22 banks. On June 23, 2010, European officials announced preliminary details of a new test that would include an additional 60 to 120 banks. Some of the weakest German *Landesbanken*, but not the largest, would be included in the test. The tests would be conducted by national regulators, and the bank-by-bank results would be published in the second half of July. The Central Bank of Spain had stolen a march in the process, not only by announcing a merger of 39 of its 45 *cajas,* but also by pledging to publish the stress test results of all its banks.

As the stress test design began taking a final shape, a pressing issue arose related to the criterion for assessing the balance sheet viability of the banks to withstand a crisis. How might that crisis be defined?

Defining a Shock That Banks Might Face

What criterion should be adopted for measuring the stress on bank balance sheets? How severely would EU banks be affected if Greece, followed by Ireland, Portugal, and Spain, defaulted on its sovereign debt? That would be an extremely demanding test. How much cash would the affected banks need? The interim June announcement had said that the stress test would examine if the listed banks could withstand the shock of losses on government debt rather than an actual sovereign debt default in the eurozone. The debt default scenario seemed less plausible with the extension of a €110 billion ($140 billion) bailout to Greece followed by an announcement on May 10, 2010, of a €750 billion ($955 billion) rescue plan for a troubled eurozone economy. (Chapter 4 covers this in depth.) It was, however, necessary for European regulators to undertake a less stringent test by defining the shock criterion in terms of a loss in a bank's sovereign debt holdings.

Stress Test Criterion of a Sovereign Debt Default Shock

As the Greek sovereign debt crisis in the early spring of 2010 created fears of a sovereign debt default contagion from Greece to Ireland, Portugal, and Spain, the trading in government debts of these countries, which banks used as collateral for interbank lending, had come to a standstill. Eurozone government debts had opened up a hazardous link between government finances and the banking system. An exceptional action was necessary to unfreeze the government debt market. On May 10, the ECB stepped in to buy government debt. The ECB had broken a taboo. The American-style monetization of government debt of a member country experiencing fiscal woes was an extraordinary step in the ECB's 12-year history. In the view of German policy makers, there was a risk of inflation if the ECB released euros in exchange for government debt instruments that it acquired.

The relationship between the ECB and Germany was critical for sorting out details of the monetization role of the ECB and of the stress test design.

German Role in Stress Test Implementation

German policy makers' focus on inflation control and an independent monetary policy, which prohibited the ECB from monetizing the budget deficit of a member, were the founding principles of the monetary union and the adoption of the euro as a single currency by the 16 members on January 1, 1999 (chapter 4). The latter rule was broken when the ECB departed from its disciplined policy making and in May 2010 started purchasing Greek government debt from the 16 eurozone central banks and from eurozone banks in the secondary market. Of course, the ECB had promised that it would sterilize its sovereign bond purchases from these banks. The banks that sold their sovereign debt holdings to the ECB were required to place interest-bearing deposits with the ECB. In other words, the ECB would remove one euro from circulation for every euro it used to buy the sovereign bonds from banks. But increasingly, banks started keeping the cash they received from the ECB. They needed it for rolling over debts that fell due. The ECB pledge to offset its sovereign bond purchases with deposits from banks was not working. Having handed over significant amounts of cash to the ECB in May and mid-June, banks were refusing to cooperate. Why not impose a stress test that would reveal their vulnerability to their holdings of the sovereign debts of the default-prone countries? Besides, if these banks needed capital to cover their debt holdings, it should be provided by the member governments from their budgets rather than by the ECB. A stress test that revealed the possible loss in bank holdings of sovereign debts would provide a measure of such capital requirements.

The final word on the issue came from German Chancellor Angela Merkel: "Given the current uncertainty in financial markets, more transparency can restore trust. . . . But building trust will only work if every country also shows how it will handle the results, for example by recapitalizing its banks if necessary."[9] In other words, if banks held loss-making sovereign debts in their balance sheets and if they needed to be bailed out with extra funding, the cash should be provided by the taxpayers of the member country in which the banks were located. The TARP model should be followed for that purpose.

The final decision and details of the proposed test for European banks were announced in mid-July by the Committee of European Banking Supervisors.

Issues Raised by the Final Test Criteria

The test would include 91 European banks, which covered 65 percent of the EU banking sector and at least 50 percent of the banking sector of each member state. The test would examine the capital requirements of banks in case the country GDP underperformed EU predictions for 2010–2011 by 3 percent. The pass mark for adequate capital requirement set the tier 1 capital-to-asset ratio at 6 percent, whereas the U.S. stress test tier 1 capital-to-asset adequacy ratio was 4 percent. The criterion with regard to the impact of a debt default shock was defined with regard to a likely loss in the market valuation of country sovereign debt rather than an actual debt default. The likely losses, or haircuts, were set at 23 percent for Greece's sovereign debt, 14 percent for Portugal's, 12 percent for Spain's, and 10 percent for the United Kingdom's. The tests would be carried out by member country regulators, and bank-by-bank results would be published on July 23.

The primary issue related to the adequacy of reserves with the candidate banks: Would they be sufficient to cover the impact of a recession and of a decline in sovereign debt valuation?

According to analysts at Credit Suisse, the problem banks could need close to €100 billion ($127 billion) of fresh capital, of which €91 billion ($116 billion) would be claimed by the Spanish *cajas* and the German *Landesbanken*.[10] According to the ECB's president, Jean Claude Trichet, the capital-short banks should raise the funds from their retained earnings or borrow from the market or resort to emergency schemes of their government. The funding shortfall was expected to be manageable. As mentioned above, most European banks were hoarding cash. Besides, several countries had preexisting bailout mechanisms. Germany had a €50 billion ($64 billion) federal fund; Spain had a €12 billion ($15 billion) provision. And Greek banks could expect to be bailed out by a €10 billion ($13 billion) fund of the International Monetary Fund and the ECB.[11] In other words, the funding for banks would be country specific. Recapitalization must come from the member governments as German Chancellor Merkel had suggested.

Was the stress scenario more stringent with regard to a likely Greek debt crisis shock to bank balance sheets? What haircuts should they take for that possibility? The haircut in the proposed test of 23 percent for Greek debt holdings was low in view of the fact that Greek sovereign debt traded at a discount of 75 percent of its par value.[12]

Stress Test Results

A vast majority of the European banks passed the test in terms of the capital they would need in order to survive an economic recession and a sovereign debt valuation decline in their holdings. Only seven of the 91 largest European banks needed to raise more capital in order to deal with a recession or a sovereign debt loss in their holdings of Greek, Irish, Portuguese, and Spanish sovereign debts. A German bank already owned by the government, a Greek bank, and five Spanish banks failed the test. The capital shortfall of the seven failed banks, which did not meet a 6 percent tier 1 capital ratio, was $4.5 billion. By contrast, 10 of the 19 U.S. banks needed to raise $75 billion in new capital.

The tests were not transparent because they did not disclose the sovereign debt holdings of the banks. Six German banks that were included in the test did not provide breakdowns of their sovereign debt holdings. Nor were the criteria stressful enough because the discounts of sovereign debt were lower than suggested by the market valuations of the sovereign debts. Besides, most of the banks had capital ratios of 10 percent already. Questions arose: Was the commotion about the extreme vulnerability of the European banks to a sovereign debt crisis and a decline in economic activity overdone? Were the test criteria, especially with respect to the potential loss on sovereign debt holding, deliberately kept manageable?

Would the results restore confidence in the EU banking sector? The distressed banks would recover at varying speed. As I have noted, U.S. banks had returned their tax-financed TARP support to the Treasury within a year, although small banks across the country continued to be monitored and supported by the Federal Deposit Insurance Corporation. Financial markets chose to take a wait-and-see attitude following the European banking sector test results as financial analysts wondered about the transparency and stringency of the test design. Was it ultimately much ado about nothing?

A pressing issue in the context of the stress test exercise related to the continuing role of the ECB in acquiring member country sovereign debt in its assets. Was the ECB overstretched in its acquisition of such assets? Did it also need a stress test? Let's take a look.

VII. ECB Balance Sheet Assessment

The ECB's acquisition of the sovereign bonds of eurozone countries with unsustainable budget debts starting in early May 2010 raised worries about the ECB's ratio of capital to troubled assets. Was the ECB itself highly leveraged? The Federal Reserve, too, had acquired Treasury bonds and subprime mortgage securities of Fannie Mae and Freddie Mac and flooded the U.S. economy with monetary emission. It raised doubts about the Fed's ability to get rid of these troubled assets and soak up the excess dollars. (I discuss these issues in the next chapter.) Was the ECB placing itself in a similar situation by acquiring the sovereign debts of the troubled economies of Greece, Ireland, Portugal, and Spain?

ECB sovereign bond purchases of these governments worth €16.5 billion ($20.9 billion) in mid-May had tapered off to negligible amounts by mid-July. Were the ECB to continue acquiring problem assets, including sovereign bonds, its capital-to-asset ratio could become unmanageable. The combined balance sheet of the 16 central banks of the eurozone and of the ECB was sending danger signals with assets at €2,150 billion ($2.72 trillion) and capital at €77.9 billion ($99 billion) at the end of June 2010. That suggested a leverage of 28 times. Of course, the ECB could expand its monetary base without triggering inflation, which was at an annual rate of less than 2 percent at that time. How did the combined leverage of assets to capital of the ECB and the 16 eurozone central banks compare with that of the Federal Reserve? The Fed had accumulated Treasury bonds in the amount of $300 billion as the federal budget deficit escalated during 2009. But its assets of $2.2 trillion by February 2010 consisted of acquisition of subprime mortgages of Fannie Mae and Freddie Mac and of AIG. (The next chapter provides details.) However, on April 1, 2010, the Federal Reserve started selling its problem mortgage assets as they began attracting private investors in a recovering U.S. economy. In early August, the sale was halted as the "uncertain" U.S. recovery needed quantitative easing, and the Fed converted the proceeds from the sale of maturing mortgage securities in its balance sheet into long-term Treasury bonds. It managed to alter the structure of its assets while keeping the size unchanged at that point.

Would the ECB be able to maneuver a shift in its asset portfolio and get rid of the problem assets in its balance sheet at its own timing and discretion? Would it have to wait longer? The answer depended on the prospects for eurozone recovery in 2010. They had moved down as the sovereign debt crisis in the economies of the southern periphery required severe cutback of budget spending in Greece, Ireland, Portugal, and Spain. German authorities also imposed lower budget spending. The ECB mid-year forecast for eurozone GDP growth for 2010 was 0.7 to 1.3 percent. The German economy's robust July-August recovery, led by exports, could push the overall eurozone growth to the higher level of the forecast. In view of the moderate growth forecast, the ECB decided to continue with quantitative monetary easing at least to the end of 2010. It would provide unlimited three-month loans extending to the end of the year so that banks could meet their financing needs. The bank also kept its benchmark interest rate at the low 1 percent and declared its intention to continue intervening in the government bond market without providing exact details. Indeed, worries over government debt resurfaced once more in early August. The spreads on Greek, Irish, Spanish, and Portuguese government bond yields over their German equivalent widened. Investors raised the cost of insuring against the likelihood of these governments defaulting on their debts. In September, the ECB bought short-dated Irish government bonds in a bid to stabilize worries in financial markets about the credit-worthiness of these bonds. It would seem that managing eurozone monetary policy constitutes a more aggravating challenge for the ECB as a lifeguard in choppy seas than U.S. monetary policy execution presents to the Federal Reserve.

The Federal Reserve had persistently declared, starting in December 2008, that the low 0 to 0.25 percent federal funds rate, at which U.S. banks met their overnight funding needs, would continue for "an extended period of time." It also undertook quantitative policy easing by acquiring long-term Treasury bonds in July 2010 when the U.S. recovery prospects appeared "uncertain." However, unlike the ECB, the Federal Reserve and the Treasury were keen to induce private investors into acquiring toxic assets from banks. Two programs, each mounted by the Federal Reserve and the Treasury Department, began operating in 2009. The next section talks about those programs.

VIII. TALF and PPIP

In March 2009, the Federal Reserve introduced the Term Asset-Backed Loan Facility, initially with a view to encourage consumer lending by investors who would buy the sick consumer securities involving autos and student loans. TALF was later extended to include commercial real estate mortgages. Toward the end of October 2009, the Treasury introduced the Public-Private Investment Program, in which it would match, dollar for dollar, a private investor's bid to pick up unwanted mortgage-backed securities from banks and financial institutions.

TALF and New Loans

The TALF program, backed by generous funding of $1 trillion from the Fed, initially included new student loans and auto financing. In June 2009, it was extended to include the so-called commercial mortgage-backed securities (CMBS). CMBS, which involved malls, for example, could be lucrative because discount retailers in these malls continued attracting price-sensitive customers. A revival of retail sales would help the mall banks offload such CMBS languishing in their bank portfolios. How did the program work?

Assume that a mortgage raised by mall owners Westfield Group during 2004 was sliced and repackaged by the mortgage issuer and sold to a bank where, by 2008, it turned up as a toxic asset in the bank portfolio because mall customers had disappeared. A bargain-hunting investor targets the asset (defined as CMBS) and seeks a loan from TALF for which he qualifies because a shopping mall is solid collateral. The investor extends a loan to Westfield Group, enabling it to refinance its mortgage and expand its business as sales pick up.

The TALF program was calculated to clear up the mountain of similar commercial mortgage-based securities involving hotels, shopping centers, and office buildings. As before, auto loans, credit card debt, and student loans qualified for the program's loan facility. The prospective investor's eligibility for a TALF loan depended on the value of the collateral he could offer to TALF, which was funded by the Fed.

Hedge funds were eligible as likely investors, but they were expected to take a higher share of potential losses when buying CMBS. They could take out the TALF loans for up to five years, but the haircuts they were expected to incur could be substantial.

Toward the end of 2009, investors' reliance on TALF backing in order to buy bonds backed by consumer loans was declining. Indeed, buyers had begun using their own cash for buying troubled bonds backed by auto and student loans and credit card debt. Traditional investors wanted to make their own deals on terms they felt comfortable with rather than rely on cheap loans from the Federal Reserve that demanded appropriate collateral. The switch to non-TALF deals was heartening because the program with regard to consumer loans was scheduled to end in March 2010. As for cleaning up CMBS, the TALF contribution was minuscule. The commercial real estate loans raised by developers and construction firms during the boom years of 2004–2007, estimated at $3 trillion, were too large to be refinanced via TALF funding.

TALF had stolen a march on the Treasury's PPIP via an early start and a relatively bigger bang.

PPIP and Matching Treasury Funding

By early October 2009, PPIP was set to rescue a tiny fraction of the tainted mortgage-based assets at the initiative of five investment firms that would retrieve assets worth $12 billion from bank portfolios. The Treasury would match the amount with its equity investment and credit and share the profits with the private investors in the event the investments turned a profit. Asset managers, it was hoped, would raise cash from investors and use the additional capital plus the taxpayer-funded loans from the Treasury to buy up to $1 trillion in toxic assets from banks. Banks would use the cash for extending loans to businesses. Instead of offloading their subprime securities at throwaway prices, banks bought additional securities in the hope that they could sell them later at a profit as their valuations went up in the market. The Treasury's initiative of launching a program in the belief that small beginnings could facilitate the process of cleansing banks of their unsalable holdings had misfired.

In the end, TALF and PPIP would get minor footnotes as misdirected initiatives, the former for seeking to help commercial property owners with their mortgage payments and the latter for helping banks offload their subprime assets. The Federal Reserve and Treasury gambits were off the mark.

3

Is the U.S. Economy on the Mend?

By early 2009, U.S. policy makers put in place a threefold agenda, which included a stress test of the Wall Street banks, a substantial fiscal stimulus, and continuing monetary easing by the Federal Reserve.

The banking sector investigation via a stress test of the 19 too-big-to-fail banks in May 2009 (discussed in chapter 2) provided a reassuring signal with respect to their balance sheets. In the months ahead, the issues relating to the regulation of the financial sector were finally sorted out. The process involved vigorous bargaining among lawmakers in Congress and active lobbying by Wall Street bankers. Congress passed the Dodd-Frank Wall Street Reform and Consumer Protection Act on July 14, 2010. It was signed by President Obama on July 21 and awaited precise rule writing by regulators of the mandated requirements (chapter 6 covers the details in depth).

Around that time, in mid-2010, the state of the banking sector, the federal budgetary situation (extending beyond the set of stimulus and job creation measures), and the monetary policy stance of the Federal Reserve provided mixed signals and raised continuing debates regarding the efficacy of the policy measures from five perspectives.

First, the too-big-to-fail Wall Street banks had repaid their TARP bailout funding and returned as active financial players in the securities, commodities, and currency markets, but they had held back from extending credit to businesses for reviving the economy. Banks around the country, some of them carrying subprime mortgages, failed to extend loans to small and medium businesses that could provide job opportunities to the unemployed.

Second, the federal budget deficit at 10 percent of GDP in 2009 was necessary to fill the gap in household and business spending, but it posed a staggering medium-term challenge of bringing it under control substantially and soon enough.

Third, throughout 2009, the Federal Reserve had emphasized that inflation was not a major concern of its monetary policy management. It had kept the federal funds rate at a maximum 0.25 percent. However, in late February 2010, it raised the discount rate (at which banks borrow from the Fed) from 0.50 to 0.75 percent. That step represented a slightly higher cost to banks of borrowing from the Fed rather than the beginning of an exit strategy from the Fed's steadfast easy monetary policy. Indeed, the Fed's policy stance in late July showed significant concern over the economy's uncertain recovery and especially over the weaker-than-expected producer price data in May and June, which some analysts feared might initiate a price deflation. On August 10, the Fed decided to reinvest the proceeds from the fully mature, expiring mortgage-based securities on its balance sheet in purchases of long-term Treasury bonds. Such purchases in specified amounts represent a definite injection of liquidity in the economy. By contrast, variations in the federal funds rate or the discount rate change the money supply at the discretion of market participants. The Fed signaled its readiness to undertake more quantitative easing if the economic outlook were to deteriorate further in the second half of 2010.

Fourth, U.S. real GDP, boosted by a slower inventory decline by businesses, grew at an annualized 5 percent in the final quarter of 2009; 3.7 percent in the first quarter of 2010; and 1.7 percent in the second quarter. The declining trend raised questions about whether the recovery would lose its momentum in the second half of the year. At the same time, the economy's jobless rate at a high 9.6 percent of the labor force in July 2010 remained the major concern of policy makers. In mid-2010, the high jobless rate interacted with continuing home foreclosures and a weak housing market.

Finally, the recovering U.S. economy faced new uncertainties in July on top of a rise in unemployment benefits, a decline in home sales, and sluggish manufacturing activity. The home buyers' tax credit initiative and the cash-for-clunkers program for auto sales had been petering out. Fewer jobs, less income, and lower household spending held back the recovery momentum. At the same time, the significant export orders of recent months for U.S. goods had declined in June. A weak euro combined with sluggish demand from Europe (plagued by a sovereign debt and banking sector crisis) for U.S. exports affected U.S. growth momentum. Indeed, slowing recovery prospects around the globe, including in China, sent signals of weaker global performance and raised questions about the impact on U.S. growth prospects in the second half of 2010.

However, by the end of August, the U.S. economy showed signs of improvement. The private sector had added more jobs. The manufacturing sector index had moved up in August. Durable goods orders, excluding the volatile transportation component, had gone up. The producer and consumer price indexes had stabilized in July. Jobless claims had fallen. At that point, the likelihood of a double-dip recession had receded, but the prospects of a robust GDP recovery continued to be uncertain—the housing market was depressed, and the unemployment rate remained high, at 9.6 percent of the workforce.

Despite the array of formidable problems, the U.S. economy, among the developed global economies, had the potential to grow between 2 and 3 percent during 2010 with improving performance of consumer confidence, retail sales, and housing starts. The fiscal and monetary measures, in a trial-and-error mode that began in late 2008 and continued in 2009 and beyond, contributed to this recovery prospect as the year advanced.

These measures unfolded a controversial, but nevertheless an encouraging record that I trace here, beginning with the troubling features of the real economy that these policies were calculated to overcome.

I. Problems of the U.S. Real Economy

A recession is marked by at least two quarters of declining real GDP. The U.S. real GDP, quarterly figures at annual rates, had grown at an average of 3 percent for six years from 2002 until the end of 2007 when the current recession began. The annualized quarterly GDP growth rate slumped from 2.9 percent in the fourth quarter of 2007 to a low of −6.8 percent in the fourth quarter of 2008 (figure 3.1). Which specific component of GDP contributed to this staggering reversal of almost 10 percent in the size of the U.S. economy in a single year? National income accounting helps provide an answer. In the accounting exercise, GDP consists of consumption spending by households (C), investment outlays by businesses including new homes and net-inventory change (I), government expenditure excluding transfer

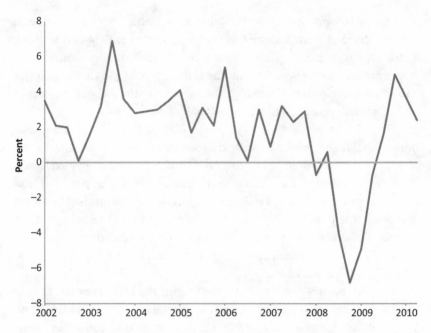

Figure 3.1.
Annualized Quarterly GDP Growth Rates. (Bureau of Economic Analysis.)

payments (G), and net exports (X minus M). Which of these four factors triggered the current recession that began in December 2007?

The escalating mortgage obligations that Americans could not fulfill in 2005, 2006, and going into 2007 pushed them into heavy indebtedness, home foreclosures, and declining home values. In a word, American consumers, who contributed more than 66 percent of GDP via consumption (C), were decidedly less well off. They spent less on household items, consumer durables, restaurant meals, and travel. As a result, consumer confidence (with 1985=100) continued declining and sank to its lowest level in mid-2009

Figure 3.2.
U.S. Economic and Financial Indicators: 2002–2010. (Federal Reserve; Labor Department; Bloomberg; Consumer Research Center.)

Note: Dow Jones Industrial Average data are from Bloomberg; inflation excludes the volatile food and energy items and is annualized monthly data. The Consumer Confidence Index with a base year of 1985=100 in the original data has been converted to a base of 2002=100.

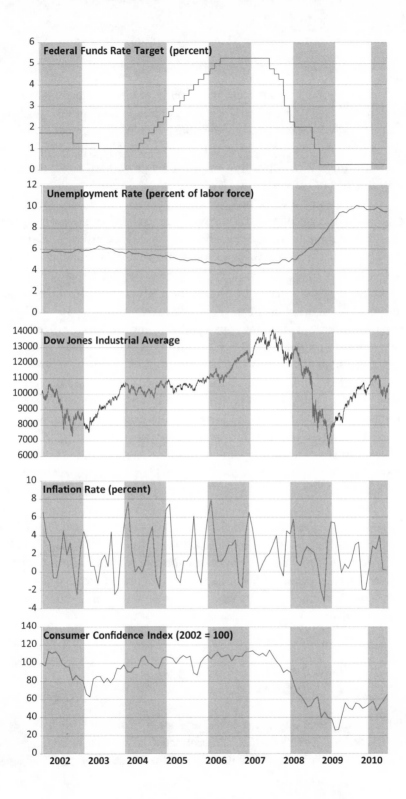

Federal Funds Rate Target (percent)

Unemployment Rate (percent of labor force)

Dow Jones Industrial Average

Inflation Rate (percent)

Consumer Confidence Index (2002 = 100)

(figure 3.2). In the first half of 2009, falling home prices had slashed household wealth by $1.5 trillion. In a reversal of their past pattern, Americans had started cutting back their consumption and begun saving. The impact of less consumption spending affected retail sales, manufacturing activity, and the services sector, which in turn began laying off workers. Cutbacks in consumption spending and its consequences triggered the recession and the first wave of worker layoffs.

The depressed state of the U.S. housing market was at the center of the rapidly declining economy throughout 2008 (coupled with worsening unemployment numbers) and the uncertainty with regard to the anemic prospects for its revival. As the unsold housing stock accumulated, home prices continued falling. Builders were constructing fewer homes and weren't hiring additional labor. The lagging construction sector was an additional contributory factor to the declining economy and rising unemployment triggered by falling consumption spending. Home prices had to stop falling in order for the U.S. economy to turn around and for the construction sector to register an upturn and hire more workers.

At the same time, small and medium-sized banks around the country, which held substantial mortgages, suffered losses on their balance sheets as these assets incurred knockdowns from low and declining home prices. Large Wall Street banks had accumulated subprime mortgage-based assets as well and held back lending to businesses. They needed to clean up their asset portfolios as they awaited signals of a reviving economy via household spending. In short, banking sector credit, which could spur investment (I) outlays and worker hiring by businesses, had plummeted in 2008. In the final quarter of 2008, the unemployment rate had moved to a high 7 percent of the workforce (figure 3.2).

Along with the high and rising unemployment rate, a related feature of the U.S. economy was a low inflation rate. Indeed, in the final quarter of 2008, the consumer price index had registered an annualized deflation rate of –1.38 percent (figure 3.2).

The Deflation Scare, Mounting Unemployment, and the Distressed Housing Market

Deflation occurred during the Great Depression in the 1930s: The price level moved down as activity stagnated. A protracted deflation via declining prices could cut into business profitability, deepen the recession, and raise joblessness. Indeed, the U.S. economy had moved into a low annual inflation rate of below 2 percent in 2009 and could continue that way in 2010. The successive reports of the Federal Open Market Committee (FOMC) that accompanied the easy monetary policy of the Federal Reserve via the federal funds rate decisions from mid-2008 until mid-2010 indicated that inflation was not a risk for the U.S. economy "for an extended period" (figure 3.2). Indeed, as the mid-year producer price index and manufacturing sector data turned out to be lower than expected, the Federal Reserve emphasized that it would consider further easing measures if the growth outlook weakened "appreciably." In the Fed's judgment, the pressures from the inflation hawks, who argued that the mounting budget deficits and the escalating money supply by the Federal Reserve would create inflation momentum, were not relevant. The Fed carefully watched the price movement and was intent on pursuing an easy monetary policy for the rest of 2010 supplemented by further quantitative easing announced on August 10 if necessary.

At the top of the Fed's concern was also the troubling unemployment rate (already a high 9.4 percent in May 2009), which interacted with continuing distress in the housing market via rising home foreclosures. Temporary hiring had improved in May but had deteriorated thereafter. The average workweek had dropped to 33 hours except in manufacturing. At the same time, the labor force was swelling because of a higher participation rate. Workers had postponed retirement in order to cope with their depleted finances. Second earners had also joined the labor market. But jobs were becoming scarcer. With rising unemployment, home foreclosures escalated in 2009 and continued in 2010 as the unemployed failed to meet their mortgage payments.

The twofold program of fiscal stimulus and monetary easing was launched with a view to checking the rising unemployment rate and helping subprime mortgage holders in an environment of low inflation. Two features of the real economy in the second half of 2009 provided hopeful signals that the U.S. economy could start reviving without an inflationary impact during the period. Indeed, the National Bureau of Economic Research has suggested that the recession, which began in December 2007, ended in mid-2009 (I discuss this issue later in the chapter).

Benign Growth Prospects in the Second Half of 2009

The U.S. manufacturing sector had substantial excess capacity. At the same time, the mid-2009 unemployment rate was high at 9.4 percent and was expected to rise. Both features represented the output gap between the economy's potential growth (with low impact on the price level) and its actual performance. The output gap persisted toward the end of the year. For the output gap to narrow, Americans must start consuming more, retail sales inventories must start declining, and banks must start lending to businesses in order for them to finance their investment spending.

The $787 billion stimulus funding legislated by Congress in early 2009 was calculated to make up for the shortfall in consumption spending by households and investment outlays by businesses. Let's take a look at the stimulus package and its impact.

II. Fiscal Stimulus

The American Recovery and Reinvestment Act passed by Congress in February 2009 approved domestic spending by the federal government (G) of $787 billion. About $288 billion was earmarked as tax cuts. The remaining $499 billion was aimed at renovating public buildings, weatherizing homes, creating community health centers, building new roads, and repairing old ones, all with the explicit goal of creating new jobs. Seventy percent of the funding was to be spent by September 2010. By the end of February 2010, the package had risen to $862 billion.

In my view, the fiscally financed stimulus was necessary in 2009, and it needed to continue in 2010.

The Stimulus Impact

Congress had also mandated that the stimulus funding of $499 billion for public works had to be spent wisely, equitably, and economically. Wouldn't the spending on tens of thousands of projects via hundreds of agencies create opportunities for waste and corruption? When Vice President Joe Biden raised this question in a memo to President Obama, the president promptly shot back a return memo, saying "do it." Joe Biden knew his way around a rotten pork barrel project. The states must scrub and clean their wish list of anything that appeared unnecessary or wasteful. A plan for straightening headstones in a military cemetery was scrapped, as was a request for a $10,000 refrigerator to house fish sperm in South Dakota.[1]

(Ingram Pinn / *Financial Times.*)

And even though more jobs are created when old roads are repaired rather than new roads are built, Kentucky, where 38 percent of roads were in poor condition, was spending 88 percent of allocations on new roads.[2]

There were other issues as well. How could the employment impact of the stimulus be measured?

Measuring the Employment Impact of the Stimulus

While the stimulus package was being debated, the White House Council of Economic Advisors had suggested that the funding would lift employment by 3.5 million jobs. The Council estimated the actual employment impact via the Keynesian multiplier. A 1 percent increase in government spending (G) would raise GDP by 1.57 percent. Furthermore, based on historical patterns, a 1 percent increase in GDP would cut back unemployment by 0.75 percent. Based on this method, the Council reported in early September 2009 that the stimulus had lifted employment to a level "slightly more than 1 million jobs higher than it otherwise would have been."[3] But then if worker productivity had gone up, the number crunching would be less accurate. Besides, extra jobs could have been created by monetary policy easing. Was it ever easy to construct a numerical counterfactual relating to the impact of the stimulus in the midst of turbulent times? Not to be deterred, the Congressional Budget Office, a nonpartisan agency that studies the impact of fiscal legislation on the budget for congressional members, announced in late August 2010 that the stimulus had added 4.5 percent to GDP growth in the second quarter of 2010. That is, GDP would have been smaller by as much as 4.5 percent in the second quarter of 2010 without the stimulus. That estimate should have lifted the spirit of Democrats contesting the November elections.

But didn't stimulus packages work elsewhere, in China and Korea, for example?

The Varying Cross-Country Stimulus Impact

The stimulus size in relation to GDP would influence income and employment creation. The U.S. package of $787 billion at 5.5 percent of GDP was close to that of Korea at 5 percent, but substantially less than the Chinese package at 15 percent. But the stimulus focus and implementation speed varied from country to country. The Korean stimulus was directed at reducing the corporate tax rate, evidently providing a targeted incentive to businesses to maintain their exports. The Chinese push, via loan provisions to state banks, was state-directed. It was intended to stimulate cash-fueled demand for a variety of consumer durables, including autos, and to finance massive infrastructure buildup. The German stimulus at 3 percent of GDP was similarly targeted to maintain consumption by providing citizens with cash that could be used for buying new cars in exchange for old ones.

A similar cash-for-clunkers program in the United States in July and August 2009, in which auto buyers received up to $4,500 for disposing of old autos in exchange for fuel-efficient new ones, lifted auto sales by 700,000 and slowed the continuing deterioration of the industry. The $8,000 federal tax credit for first-time home buyers helped revive home purchases (in the investment component of GDP) in the third quarter of 2009. Both items lifted U.S. GDP growth in the third quarter ending in September to an annualized 1.6 percent (figure 3.1). By all accounts, this impact was temporary with little relief for the deteriorating unemployment numbers. But by the end of November, fresh stimulus ideas knocked at White House doors. Why not pay Americans cash to weatherize their homes via a cash-for-caulkers program? That would create job opportunities for idled contractors and construction workers—but can weatherizing a home be as simple as buying a car? More ideas trickled in. Why not replenish the military equipment depleted in Iraq and Afghanistan and add a couple of army brigades as well?

The U.S. stimulus was designed to work via transfers to states that directed the cash toward discretionary project spending for roads, bridges, and energy infrastructure. The decisions required coordination and consultation among federal distributors, state recipients, local contractors, and project managers. The disbursement of $85 billion by mid-September amounted to a little over half of 1 percent of GDP with minuscule impact on employment.

Not surprisingly, President Obama was guarded in his assessment of the stimulus.

Mid-2009 Assessment of the Stimulus by the President and His Advisor

In a radio address on Saturday, July 11, 2009, the president provided a cautious viewing of the economic situation and asked Americans to be patient, arguing that the stimulus package was intended to work not in a few months but over two years. On the same day, Lawrence E. Summers, director of the President's National Economic Council, was decidedly somber in his assessment. "I don't think the worst is over. . . . It's very likely that more jobs will be lost. It would not be surprising if GDP has not yet reached its low. What does appear to be true is that the sense of panic in the market and free fall in the economy has subsided, and one does not have the sense of a situation as out of control as a few months ago."[4]

A week later, Summers gave a progress report on the stimulus package, saying it was timed to peak during 2010, "with 70 percent of its benefits to be distributed to local governments, businesses, and families in the first 18 months. We are on track to meet that time line." But he warned that high levels of consumer and business debt were going to "act as a drag on spending and growth for some time to come. That meant that the government must cushion the adjustment process by providing support, but for no longer than necessary," he added.[5] It was not clear if Summers saw the need for a second stimulus. In a mid-year survey of economists, the majority ruled out a need for extra stimulus. As for the American public, it doubted if the stimulus had helped create jobs. A year later, in the summer of 2010, President Obama had been traveling in populous states with a pro-stimulus message for skeptical voters who were set to participate in close, mid-term congressional elections.

Republican legislators in Congress and some policy analysts in academia and business also feared that additional stimulus would add to government spending and the budget deficit without making a significant dent on rising unemployment. Nevertheless, couldn't an easy monetary policy lift the declining economy and create employment opportunities? The next section explores this question.

III. Monetary Easing

On December 16, 2008, the Federal Reserve set the federal funds rate, the rate at which banks borrow overnight from one another, in the range of 0 to 0.25 percent. Since then, in nine successive meetings until August 11, 2010, of the Federal Open Market Committee, the Federal Reserve kept this short-term rate at the low December 2008 level (figure 3.2).

The Fed deliberately kept the federal funds rate at a near-zero level starting in mid-2008 through 2009 going into late 2010 in order to encourage consumer borrowing and bank lending. In effect, it released a flood of money into the economy by buying securities in the market in exchange for cash that it released. In addition, it also bought $1.25 trillion of mortgage-backed securities and $175 billion in agency debt of Fannie Mae and Freddie Mac. Toward the end of February, its balance sheet stood at a mammoth $2.2 trillion. Short-term Treasury bills, the traditional mainstay of its balance sheet, made a tiny fraction of its assets. On the liabilities side, commercial banks held $1.2 trillion in reserves at the Fed (figure 3.3).

Of course, the Federal Reserve could offer a higher rate than the current 0.25 percent on bank reserves if it wanted to entice banks to keep excess reserves with it. In December 2008, Congress had allowed it to offer an interest rate to banks on their reserves with the Fed. That offer would tie up the cash that banks would otherwise lend to their customers or other banks. By the same token, lifting the discount rate would also tighten the liquidity available to banks. The Fed raised the discount rate to 0.75 percent in February 2010 in order to curtail excessive borrowing by banks. Despite the discount rate hike, banks might choose to borrow from the Federal Reserve for their future investment plans and add to their reserves. The amount of borrowing would raise bank reserves and money supply in the economy. But the process would depend on the banks' discretion and

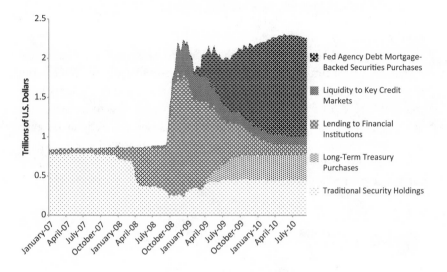

Figure 3.3.
Federal Reserve Balance Sheet: January 2007–September 2010. (Federal Reserve.)

needs. In lifting the discount rate, however, the Federal Reserve did not send a signal that it was ready to depart from its long-held policy of keeping the federal funds rate at a low 0 to 0.25 percent and switch to a tightening monetary policy.

On top of monetary policy easing, the Federal Reserve employed other measures in 2009 for stimulating the economy.

Monetizing the Government Debt and Acquiring Mortgages

In March 2009, the Fed initiated its plan to buy Treasury bonds worth $300 billion and monetize the government debt. It kept the timing and composition of these purchases at its initiative. As I have noted, it had also acquired mortgage-backed securities and Fannie Mae and Freddie Mac mortgages. Such direct quantitative infusion of cash from the Federal Reserve to companies would also raise their bank reserves, but it differs from the voluntary accretion of reserves when banks borrow from the Federal Reserve. In the current crisis, its balance sheet had more than doubled in relation to its recent history, from $8.74 billion in

August 2007 to $2.18 trillion by the end of 2009, and finally, to $2.2 trillion in February 2010 (figure 3.3).

Beginning in November 2009, the Federal Reserve sent four cautionary signals while continuing with its 0 to 0.25 percent interest rate policy. The signals were intended to convey to financial markets the Fed's understanding of the need for a timely exit strategy and its readiness to implement it at a moment of its choosing. As mentioned earlier, the Federal Reserve sent a reverse mini signal on August 10 when it announced its decision to start reinvesting up to $200 billion in annual proceeds from maturing mortgage-backed and agency securities into long-term Treasury bonds.

Four Cautionary Monetary Policy Signals

First, in the FOMC meeting in November 2009, the Fed announced that it would continue buying securities for the next five months. However, it placed a ceiling on its holding of the agency debt of Fannie and Freddie at $175 billion and of mortgage-based securities at $1.25 trillion, to be reached by the end of the first quarter of 2010. The financial markets, in the Fed's judgment at that time, showed signs of improvement. Therefore, it would taper off its acquisition of agency debt (such as of Fannie and Freddie) and commercial paper. It would also fold its arrangements of currency swaps with foreign central banks by February 1, 2010. (The currency swap with foreign central banks, with the Federal Reserve providing dollars in exchange for a foreign currency, was reinstated on May 8, 2010, following the announcement of a €750 billion [$955 billion] joint International Monetary Fund–European bailout plan for forestalling a possible sovereign debt default by some peripheral eurozone economies.) The Federal Reserve clearly distinguished between quantitative easing, which was to be discontinued in measured steps, and an interest rate policy of 0 to 0.25 percent, which would be continued for discretionary credit availability. Indeed, in the November FOMC meeting, the Fed was intent on combining the 0–0.25 interest rate with credit easing via increased demand for securities until April 1, 2010.

Second, in mid-December 2009, the Federal Reserve Bank of New York undertook reverse repurchase trials that could drain liquidity from the financial system. Had the Federal Reserve already begun an exit strategy for warding off inflation? An explanation was necessary. According to the New York Federal Reserve, these were only tests and did not involve actual operations of selling assets (such as Treasury securities) with an agreement to buy them back later at a slightly higher price. The tests represented "prudent advance planning" by the Federal Reserve and were not meant to convey an inference about the tightening of monetary policy.

Third, on December 28, it unveiled a rule change that would drain liquidity from the financial system without threatening the recovery while simultaneously heading off the threat of inflation: It planned to offer interest on reserves held by commercial banks for a prescribed period. In other words, it declared its intention to influence the $1.1 trillion of reserves held by banks over and above the amount required for their operational needs.

Finally, in February 2010, it raised the discount rate at which banks borrowed from the Fed to 0.75 percent from the earlier 0.50 percent. This minor discretionary credit tightening was supplemented by the start of a cautious quantitative reining-in from April 1: The Federal Reserve started selectively trimming its balance sheet and offloading mortgage securities in the market as it had announced in the November 2009 FOMC meeting.

Whatever its minor policy dances, the Federal Reserve was determined to stick to its focus of a 0 to 0.25 percent interest rate. As the final quarter of 2009 wound down, the financial and credit market showed signs of improvement, and the Dow Jones Average had crossed the 10,000 mark. But consumer confidence was low, and annual inflation measured by the CPI hovered below 1 percent (figure 3.2). At the same time, the unemployment rate in November was still high at 10 percent, having dropped by a mere 0.2 percent from October's 10.2 percent. More than three months later, despite the employment gain of 162,000 in March 2010 followed by 290,000 in April, the Federal Reserve would continue its low interest policy with a signal from Federal Reserve Chairman Ben Bernanke that it could stretch to the end of 2010. The resource slack was substantial, and inflation was subdued.

Indeed, in mid-2010, the producer price index from May to July had turned out to be lower and U.S. manufacturing data had proved to be weaker than expected. A hasty pullback from the easy monetary policy would not only smother the incipient recovery, but also perhaps drag the economy into deflation. At that time, Bernanke outlined measures before the Senate Banking Committee on July 21 that could ward off such a likelihood. The Federal Reserve could lower the interest rate it paid to banks on their reserves in order for the banks to lend rather than store the reserves with it. Next, rather than remove maturing mortgages from the Fed's balance sheet as announced earlier, the Federal Reserve would reinvest the proceeds or even make additional mortgage purchases. The Fed's announcement of August 10 to reinvest proceeds from maturing mortgage-backed and agency securities into long-term Treasury bonds would change the structure of the Fed's balance sheet holdings but keep their overall size at the $2.3 trillion level. In mid-September, the Federal Reserve was considering further measures for quantitative easing.

Even as the Fed continued decisively with its easy monetary policy aimed at reviving the economy and employment and fending off a likely deflationary downturn of the economy in the second half of 2010, Congress continued to be divided across party lines on the issue of budget allocation for the purpose. Of course, the TARP package of $700 billion and the stimulus funding of $787 billion were approved unanimously, but Republicans worried about the advisability of approving more funding aimed at relieving unemployment and its impact on the budget deficit. Occasionally, the market also sent mixed signals via yields on Treasury bonds about the inflationary potential of excessive budget spending. In the next section, we look at the concerns over the budget.

IV. Escalating Budget Deficit Concerns and Battles

By early June 2009, the sluggish demand for Treasury bonds and rising yields had inflation watchers worried (the prices of fixed-income Treasury bonds and their percentage yields move in opposite directions). The yield on the 10-year note had gone up to 4 percent at the start of June. The average rate for the 30-year, fixed-rate mortgage had risen from 4.61 percent at the end of March to 5.44 percent by the end of June. The rising yields had begun to send conflicting signals. Had the economy begun stabilizing? Had the credit market in general begun reviving? Had investors become risk prone, and were they moving into non-Treasury outlets? Or were they choosing to move away from Treasuries because they were worried that the ballooning government spending could drive inflation? If the projected borrowing of $10 trillion by the federal government over the next 10 years to cover its deficits were to materialize, it would crowd out loanable funds for private investors and raise interest rates in the future. Nor could foreign investors be counted on to finance these ballooning deficits. Did the higher mid-year interest rates reflect investors' concerns about future inflation, rising fiscal deficits, and the growth of national debt at a level not seen since World War II?

The actual numbers for 2009 revealed the start of a precarious fiscal situation. The federal budget deficit for 2009 of $1.4 trillion, at 10 percent of GDP, was the highest since the end of World War II when it had hit a staggering 21.5 percent. The national debt at $12 trillion amounted to 86 percent of GDP (figure 3.4).

Increasingly, the stimulus and deficit debates spilled into ideological concerns regarding the role of the government (G) in filling the gap in reduced business outlays (I) and consumption spending (C). On the one hand, ardent Keynesians, Nobel laureate Paul Krugman among them, argued in favor of a steadfast stimulus for battling the rising unemployment—let it spill right now into the federal budget deficit. On the other hand, Republican stalwarts vehemently supported appropriate tax cuts accompanied by budget spending cuts as a timely switch from the continuing stimulus and rising budget deficit, asking if the administration and the Treasury could manage to bring down the deficit forecast to 4.6 percent of GDP for the fiscal year 2013.

But why worry about that question now when the government, in the view of Keynesian pump primers, needed to fill up private spending cutbacks? The Keynesian stimulus would lift the economy from a downturn, generate extra income, prompt households to spend, and revive business investment. As a result of output and employment recovery, the burden of unemployment compensation would gradually diminish and tax receipts would materialize.

But when exactly would the sun start shining with gains in output and tax revenues? Could it happen with regard to the formulation of the budget for fiscal 2010 (starting on October 1)? Could the projected deficit for fiscal 2010 (ending on September 30, 2011) be less than 10 percent of 2009 GDP?

The Budgetary Challenges and Opportunities for Fiscal 2010

Continuing GDP recovery in 2010 would contribute to higher tax revenues at current rates than in the preceding year. But expenditures would continue to be higher. Persistent high unemployment would require continuation of the stimulus funding of $882 billion augmented from the original $787 billion of unemployment relief and tax credits for first-time home buyers. Immediate cutbacks in other budgetary outlays were unlikely. Lean military spending in Iraq would be offset by increased outlays for the

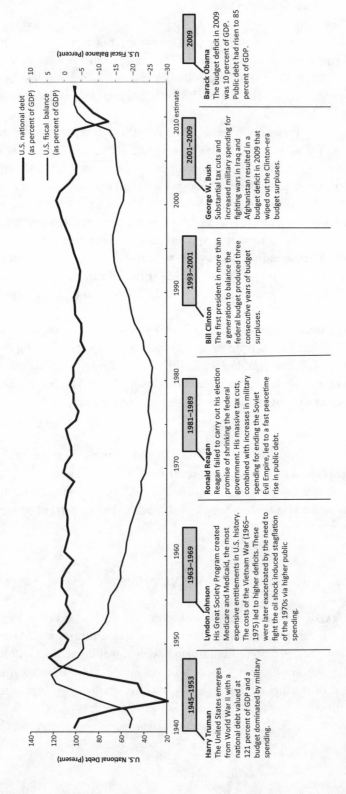

Figure 3.4.

U.S. Fiscal Deficit and Public Debt as Percentages of GDP. (Office of Management and Budget; Congressional Budget Office.)

Afghan war effort. Medicare cutbacks outlined in successive rounds of health care proposals would be countered by payments to doctors, hospitals, and insurance companies to manage the overhaul of the health care system.

Lifting tax rates and raising revenues with a view to managing the deficit had daunting problems. Budgetary planning must proceed without stifling the recovery. Besides, President Obama had promised in his election campaign that taxes on taxpayers with incomes below $250,000 would not be raised. Extensive tax cuts of the Bush presidency could be removed and taxes could be raised only for the higher income brackets.

What were the tax cuts of the Bush presidency?

Tax Cuts of the Bush Presidency

These tax cuts offered a window of opportunity because they were time bound. A U.S. Senate rule named after Senator Robert Byrd had stipulated that the tax cuts were to be temporary. The Joint Committee of the Congress on Taxation listed 113 tax provisions expiring as early as 2009 or 2010.[6] "Bush cut income tax rates, dividend tax rates, and the capital gains tax. He reduced the estate and gift taxes, expanded the earned income tax credit, reduced the marriage penalty, expanded the child tax credit, and allowed small businesses to deduct a more generous share of their expenses. . . . If you are married, have kids, have income, or run a small business, your taxes are in play this year."[7] In the budget exercise for fiscal 2010, the tax exemptions and credits could survive for those with incomes below $250,000. Beyond that, the marginal income tax rate and the dividend tax rate could move up and deductions could disappear. But the exact timing and trajectory would need to be carefully evaluated with regard to the political implications. Congress faced elections in November 2010. The entire House of Representatives, one-third of the Senate, and a few governorships were up for reelection. The election outcome was likely to erase the Democratic majority in the Congress.

Mindful of this, the White House came up with another idea at the start of 2010 with a view to raising revenues for the budget and placating the voters as well. Why not levy a tax or a fee on the banks that had unleashed the deepest recession in the economy since the Great Depression?

A Fee on the Big Banks

It was not clear what shape or size the levy on big banks would take. They had all repaid their TARP bailout, but the Treasury had incurred a loss estimated at $120 billion in implementing the program. At the minimum, a claw-back levy on the beneficiaries could recoup the loss whatever its size. But the levy needed to accomplish more than recover the TARP bailout loss. Shouldn't the loss include the 7 million jobs lost since the start of the recession? Besides, the impact of the levy, if imposed on bank assets and if made permanent, could arguably cut down the size of risk taking by the banking giants that had wreaked havoc on the livelihood of ordinary workers. Even if the cost of the levy is passed on by the banks to investors and customers, the ultimate impact could restrict their size.

Another idea under consideration by White House budget planners focused on taxing the profits of the big banks. They earned these profits not from lending to credit-strapped businesses, but from trading in commercial paper, currencies, and commodities on the basis of cheap financing from the Federal Reserve. A one-time tax windfall on the bonuses, which the resurrected banks planned to extend to their employees, was totally appropriate.

On January 14, President Obama put an end to the debates and doubts and unveiled his plan.

The $90 Billion Fee on the Big Banks

The $90 billion bank tax, appropriately dubbed the Financial Crisis Responsibility Fee, carried a strong admonition to the recalcitrant bankers and a tough pledge to recover the TARP cash that was spent to save them: "We want our money back, and we're going to get it." The fee of 0.15 percent would be levied over the next 10 years on bank assets net of their common stock and disclosed earnings. Banks around the country would pay a smaller fee, based on their net assets, than the Wall Street banking companies, among them Citigroup, JPMorgan Chase, Bank of America, Goldman Sachs, Morgan Stanley, and Wells Fargo. The proposed tax must be approved by the Senate.

That was a tough call. Treasury Secretary Tim Geithner faced questions from members of the Senate Finance Committee on May 4, 2010,

when he proposed the $90 billion levy on big banks. Senator Charles E. Grassley (R-IA), who was open to the notion, argued that it should be used for reducing the budget deficit. He invoked the familiar Republican siren song: "If a TARP tax is imposed and the money is simply spent, that doesn't repay taxpayers 1 cent for TARP losses. It's just more tax-and-spend big government while taxpayers foot the bill for Washington's out-of-control spending."[8] The proposal had support from outside. The International Monetary Fund called for a levy on big banks by the world's wealthiest nations to recover the costs of bailouts and rein in their excessive risk taking.

The fee could work as a political bounty in favor of the Democrats as they faced congressional elections in November 2010. The Republicans could oppose the tax and alienate the angry voters. They could side with the president and estrange the anti-tax activists. The bankers argued that the fee would constrain their lending potential even as surely they passed on its impact to bank customers and investors. Besides, the fee could be tax deductible. Investors shrugged off the levy, and bank shares inched up on Wall Street at the time of its initial announcement. Even the political gain in favor of the Democratic contestants in the November elections was an uncertain bet.

Amid the uncertainty of Democrats retaining their majority in Congress, the administration's budget worries posed the biggest challenge beyond 2010 with regard to its ability for managing a sustained deficit reduction in relation to GDP.

Although the medium-term scenarios of containing the deficit were frightening, they did not, in my view, detract from the short-term need for stimulating the economy in the midst of lagging business and consumer spending. Besides, the growing health care cost of an aging population rather than stimulus spending (which could taper off with a reviving economy) was expected to raise U.S. public debt to more than 108 percent of GDP by 2028. In particular, everyone worried about the long-term impact on the federal budget deficit of a federally funded health care plan.

Long-Term Budget Deficit Impact of the Health Care Plan

In its forecast of June 16, 2009, the Congressional Budget Office reported that the universal health insurance legislation would require additional federal spending of $1 trillion over 10 years. The president's pledge that the legislation would be deficit-neutral required cutbacks in Medicare and Medicaid disbursements and trimming of discretionary spending and defense. According to Summers, a reduction in health care cost by even a limited amount—1 or 1.5 percent a year—would make a huge dent in the federal budget deficit. By mid-May, the Senate Finance Committee had worked up options for new taxes on everything from employer-sponsored health care benefits and nonprofit hospitals to alcohol and sugary drinks. At the same time, the health care reform bill passed by the House of Representatives in early November 2009 would levy taxes on businesses and impose a new tax on personal incomes exceeding $500,000 on top of the burden they would face when the Bush tax cuts expired. Would these additional tax levies prevent the cost of the bill from spilling over the price tag of $1 trillion over 10 years? These health care costs constituted a policy nightmare and required a determined effort to deal with them in a systematic progression. How soon should it begin?

Rather than provide a hasty pullback, the president and his advisors focused on the incipient recovery and the persistent high unemployment rate, which was the critical element in their policy-making focus. The next section examines this.

V. Lagging Employment Recovery

Past experience showed that employment growth tended to trail behind GDP recovery from the start of a recession. For example, in the recession of 1981, which began in July, GDP had stabilized in six months, by January 1982, whereas employment had continued falling at a softer pace for 18 months and began recovering after January 1983 (figure 3.5). Similarly, in the 2001 recession, GDP had begun recovering in nine months, whereas employment began climbing up in December 2002 after a sluggish 21-month decline. By contrast, with the unemployment rate at 10 percent in November 2009, the lag (in months) of employment growth catching up with output recovery was calculated to be significantly higher than during earlier recessionary episodes. For example, in the current recession, which began in December 2007, GDP had continued declining for 13 months before it stabilized in January 2009, whereas employment continued falling for 22 months until its slight recovery by 0.2 percent in November 2009 (figure 3.5). More to the point, in both of the earlier recessions, GDP and employment declines during the recessionary downturn were softer than during the current recession. Although GDP could grow by more than 2 percent in 2010, the employment recovery would be fragile. The number of unemployed for more than six months at 6.7 million was nearly 46 percent of the unemployed. A monthly growth of 290,000 would take more than four years to fill the hole of steep job losses from 2008 to 2010. Congress had yet to show strong leadership and make good on its promise to pass broad legislation to boost employment. With most optimistic forecasts, unemployment toward the end of 2010 could be as high as 8 percent of the workforce.

The White House needed to mount a job recovery stimulus plan.

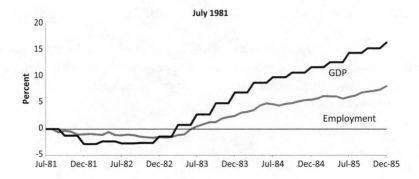

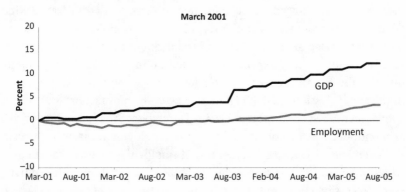

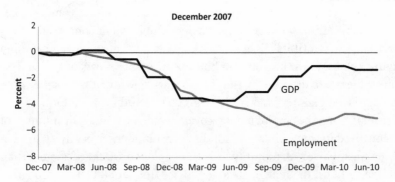

Figure 3.5.
GDP and Employment Recoveries During U.S. Recessions. (Bureau of Labor
Statistics; Bureau of Economic Analysis.)

Note: GDP is real annual growth; employment is percent of the labor force.

White House Job Recovery Plan of December 2009

Aware of the lagging employment recovery, the White House organized a job summit in early December with plans to unveil new proposals involving tax credits for small business hiring, more infrastructure spending, and tax incentives for promoting energy-efficient homes. Of course, the Labor Department had reported that the November unemployment rate had dipped to 10 percent with a job loss of only 11,000 workers and more temporary hiring at 50,000. Was November at last a turning point from jobs being cut to jobs being added? A single observation, however, does not make a turning point. Besides, 15.4 million Americans were still struggling to find jobs at that time. On December 8, the president suggested that some of the $200 billion that was left over from the TARP bank bailout program be used for the stimulus spending on job creation.

He was at his most eloquent and promised to alleviate the "continued human tragedy" of unemployment and create "the greatest number of jobs while generating the greatest value for our economy." His call raised hopes and prompted questions, the most pressing of which was: How much of the unused TARP funding of $200 billion, out of the $700 billion approved by Congress in late 2008, would be utilized? But TARP was a loan program for rescuing banks and not a slush fund that the administration could use without congressional approval. According to Republican Senator Mitch McConnell (R-KY), the Senate minority leader, "this violates both current law and the pledge we made that every dollar we got back would be returned to the taxpayer to reduce the national debt." The president shot back with reference to the legacy of "fiscal irresponsibility" under his predecessor George W. Bush. "These budget-busting tax cuts and spending programs were approved by many of the same people who are now waxing political about political responsibility." In the president's view, the desperate unemployment situation required an overpowering response here and now, without prolonged discussions on the source of the cash and its immediate impact on the budget.

By mid-2010, however, the political consensus in favor of additional spending to help the unemployed had begun to weaken. On June 24, the Senate turned down a White House package of jobless benefits and aid to the states, although the proposals had been trimmed several times. They were approved later after further bargaining and cost cutting.

"And I want the World's Greatest Boss mug back before I leave." (From *The Wall Street Journal*, permission Cartoon Features Syndicate.)

Delayed Support for Revenue-Short States and the Unemployed

U.S. state and local governments are required by law to balance their budgets, but as their revenues declined with the recession, they began running into deficits. State budgets were collapsing, with governments facing a collective hole of $112 billion in the fiscal year ending on July 1. They laid off teachers, police officers, firefighters, and public officials. Such retrenchment was uneven and was excessive in some states, such as California and Illinois. On August 4, two Republicans broke ranks and helped the Senate overcome the filibuster. By a vote of 61 to 38, the bill approved allocations of $26 billion to states for meeting their Medicaid payments and for preventing teacher layoffs.

At the same time, the extension of federal benefits to the unemployed through November 2010 would have cost about $40 billion. Aren't unemployment benefits a vital safety net that qualify as emergency spending? The number of people not receiving federal jobless benefits had swelled to 1.25 million by mid-2010. In a *Wall Street Journal*/NBC poll of 1,000 participants and 55 economists reported in July, 59 percent of the economists who responded said that if they were in Congress, they would vote to renew the extension of unemployment compensation for up to 99 weeks.[9] But a growing number of lawmakers, including some Democrats, were beginning to worry about the accumulating budget deficit. In their view, the allocation for unemployment benefits must be offset by reductions in the budget. "We have to stop spending money we don't have," Representative Jim Cooper (D-TN) said in one of the debates in the House. Besides, the unemployed must try harder to find a job. After much foot-dragging, Congress passed in August the administration's proposal for extension of unemployment benefits to the jobless.

The issue of which programs to support and which taxes to raise and which specific Bush-era tax cuts to adjust was increasingly debated among White House advisors and the legislators in the context of their impact on the budget deficit and on the November 2010 elections. Let's examine this.

VI. Which Tax Proposals? What Budget Numbers?

Some spending, such as on antiquated weapons systems and NASA's moon program, would be easy to cut. Indeed, on August 9, Defense Secretary

Robert Gates advanced a modest set of proposals for trimming the more than $700 billion annual defense budget by $100 billion over five years. His plans included reduced spending on contractors by 30 percent and removing part of the military command established during the Cold War–era confrontation with the Soviet Union. At 4.8 percent of GDP, defense spending exceeded all other U.S. discretionary programs combined. Representative Barney Frank (D-MA) would want the defense budget to be slashed by $1 trillion over 10 years. Many Republicans wanted cutbacks in various programs and personnel to remain in place. But cutbacks in subsidies to oil companies and to agribusiness, both with lobbying power, would be difficult to enact.

The biggest challenge lay in dealing with the Bush-era tax cuts, which were set to expire on January 1, 2011. President Obama wanted to retain tax cuts for the middle class only, with an annual income cutoff in the range of $250,000. It was not clear for what period. Several House Democrats wanted to extend the cuts for the middle class as well, but for a year or two only. Republicans and centrist Democrats talked about extending all the tax cuts. According to Senator Kent Conrad (D-ND): "As a general rule, you don't want to be cutting spending or raising taxes in the midst of a downturn."[10] According to the Congressional Budget Office, a one-year extension of the Bush tax cuts would cost the Treasury at least $115 billion. Clearly, Democrats would not want to tackle the issue of which tax cuts to extend for which groups and for what period until after the November elections.

While an increasing number of Democrats were expressing doubts about the wisdom of abolishing the Bush tax cuts, Treasury Secretary Geithner announced on July 22, 2010, that the tax proposals aimed at removing the Bush tax cuts for the wealthy would arrive on schedule. How high could the proposed taxes on the wealthy go? According to one report, the plan could lift the top income tax rate to 41 percent (from the current 35 percent), the top dividend rate to 39.6 percent (from the current 15 percent), and the estate tax to 55 percent (from the current 0 percent).[11] The increase in the top marginal income tax rate to 41 percent would hit the most profitable small businesses especially hard because they filed their earnings as personal income. But the wealthy, according to Secretary Geithner, tended to save more of the tax breaks than other groups. So raising their taxes would have a minimum impact on economic activity. And the Treasury needed the revenue. Former Fed chairman Alan Greenspan suggested in early August that all the Bush tax cuts should be repealed. He supported the cuts when he was Fed chairman because the budget was in surplus. He endorsed their outright repeal because the budget was in deficit and needed revenue.

Clearly the tax cut debate on the Bush tax cuts inside and outside Congress was getting polarized between the Republican demand that all the tax cuts be retained and the Treasury's position, supported by the administration, that the cuts for middle-income taxpayers be retained permanently. In my view, a timely and sensible middle ground would require retaining the tax cuts for a year in the middle of a fragile economy and reconsidering the issue a year later. Besides, would Democrats have 60 votes in the Senate, assuming a few defections from the party, to secure the approval of the administration's proposals before the November elections? If the Senate debates extended beyond November, the Democrats' numbers would be reduced, and they would need to compromise with Republicans for retaining some tax cuts of the Bush presidency.

Increasingly, as the November election primaries advanced and party leaders focused on election issues and prospects, the battles inside Congress over the pros and cons of the Bush tax cuts became a distraction. The Senate decided on September 23 to postpone a vote on the issue until after the election. In the final week, it was official: House Speaker Nancy Pelosi also capitulated and decided to avoid a vote on the issue before the election. Congress would tackle the Bush tax cuts after the election.

Amid the escalating tax and deficit debates, the White House Office of Management and Budget had announced its forecasts for the economy in late July.

What Growth Prospects? What Budget Deficit Numbers?

The budget deficit of $1.47 trillion for 2010 was estimated at 10 percent of GDP. The 2011 budget deficit was projected at 9.2 percent of GDP. These deficits would remain high. Real GDP was expected to rise by 3.1 percent in 2010 and 4 percent in 2011. The unemployment rate, which averaged 9.7 percent of the labor force in 2010, was projected to decline to 8 percent in 2012, but not fall below 6 percent until 2015. Finally, public debt was projected to rise from 63 percent of GDP in 2010 to 77 percent in 2020. These projections clearly reflected the economic advisors' belief that the economy must start growing and people must find employment ahead of deficit reduction. In any case, the deficit had a built-in feature to continue growing because of rising Medicare costs and the burden of Social Security and Medicaid, which exceeded the inflows of tax revenues for those programs. The public deficit debates, which focused on the stimulus and its apparent failure at creating additional jobs, overlooked this negative overload, a situation that the Obama administration had inherited. At a Democratic rally in Missouri in early July, President Obama referred to this Bush-era legacy: "They spent nearly a decade driving the economy into the ditch, and now they are asking for the car keys back."[12]

On the eve of the November congressional elections, Democrats faced the likelihood of losing their majority in the Senate. Republicans kept pounding on high unemployment and deficits without giving concrete alternatives, saying only to cut taxes and slash spending. As for the voters, they did not like unemployment, but they did not favor deficits either, and in their view, the stimulus had failed to bring about recovery and jobs. In the mid-July 2010 *Wall Street Journal*/NBC survey of 1,000 respondents and 55 economists cited earlier, 63 percent of the public and 70 percent of the economists agreed that Congress should focus on reducing the budget deficit even if it meant it would take longer for the economy to recover.[13] At the same time, the president's job approval rating had been falling, especially among independent voters he had won over in 2008.

Setting aside the negativity of voters, grounded in their concern with the twofold issues of persistent unemployment and a high budget deficit, the signs of improvement in the economy by mid-2010 need to be examined. How did the policy makers manage to lift the economy out of the most unnerving financial crisis since the Great Depression? The next section explores how their record might be assessed.

VII. The Overall Assessment of the Policy Record

The worst was over a little more than a year after the devastating impact of the financial crisis on the financial fortunes of U.S. banks, on the housing market, and on the state of consumer and business confidence. GDP had been recovering quarter by quarter from the end of 2008 until mid-2010 at an annualized rate exceeding 2.3 percent (figure 3.1).

In early 2009, the U.S. banking sector had to be fixed first. Wall Street, meaning the financial system, needed to be pulled out from the crisis impact ahead of Main Street, meaning the households and businesses. The restoration of the financial health of U.S. banks was correctly seen by the policy makers as a necessary precondition for the ability of the banking sector to initiate the recovery. It was the necessary first step, but not a sufficient one. Banks could borrow at low rates, but businesses were not ready to borrow from them. Instead, the big bank recovery was marked by banks reaping profits from commodities and securities trading. Americans also had to straighten out their budgets and pay off their debts before consumption demand, which constituted two-thirds of U.S. GDP, could pick up. As a result of the decline in consumer spending, businesses in the U.S. manufacturing sector laid off workers in massive numbers, ran down inventories, and developed excess capacity. But by early 2010, U.S. manufacturing, supported by recovering retail sales and a pickup in exports, had begun moving ahead, although the construction sector, residential and nonresidential, lagged behind.

I weigh in positively on the policy makers' record from the perspective of the stress test of the too-big-to-fail banks and of the stimulus aimed at lifting job losses. Both policy decisions were undertaken in early 2009. At that time, the severity and persistence of high unemployment interacting with home foreclosures, lagging consumption, and weak bank lending to businesses required the injection of government pump priming. Without the stimulus, the unemployment, in my view, would have turned out to be higher and the growth recovery weaker.

However, by mid-2010, the decisions with regard to the budget deficit needed to be combined with explicit signals and concrete proposals about how it might be systematically reduced. By that time, the administration and the Treasury needed to begin acknowledging that the deficit carried a staggering medium-term challenge for them that they were ready to deal with via a combination of appropriate spending cutbacks and carefully devised tax relief. That was a clear message from the public and from the majority of policy analysts and economists. Federal Reserve Chairman Bernanke gave a positive nod to a continuation of the Bush-era tax cuts of 2001 and 2003, saying: "In the short term, I would believe that we ought to maintain a reasonable degree of fiscal support—stimulus—for the economy. There are many ways to do that. This is one way."[14] Indeed, till mid-2010, the policy decisions of the Federal Reserve with regard to a timely and adequate exit from the easy monetary policy were on the mark.

However, the weak performance of U.S. manufacturing in July 2010 sent a discouraging signal with regard to the ongoing recovery and the likely onset of a double-dip recession. In early August, the Federal Reserve reacted with a modest quantitative infusion of cash into the economy by

(By permission Bruce Plante, Tulsa World Planteink.com.)

investing the proceeds of maturing mortgage securities in its portfolio in long-term Treasury bonds. It stood ready to undertake further quantitative monetary easing.

But let's see if the economy was indeed heading toward a double-dip recession in July 2010.

VIII. The Likelihood of a Double-Dip Recession in the Second Half of 2010

The Philadelphia Federal Reserve's index of manufacturing activity fell from 8.0 in June to 5.1 in July. Manufacturing was growing, but not fast enough to create many jobs. The Labor Department data of the producer price index (PPI) showed a larger-than-expected decline of 0.5 percent from May to June. Copious spare capacity in manufacturing could keep the PPI trend low for the foreseeable future. The housing sector, marked by continuing foreclosures and uneven recovery of new home sales, also remained in a limbo. The unemployment rate at 9.6 percent of the workforce masked the staggering effective unemployment rate of 17 percent. Fewer jobs implied less earnings, reduced consumption, and depressed retail sales. Businesses in manufacturing and service sectors awaited decisive signals from consumers before they would expand, seek out bank loans, and hire more workers. U.S. banks, flush with cash estimated at $1 trillion, were ready to start lending to businesses.

Amid this internal, wait-and-watch uncertainty in mid-2010, continuing U.S. economic recovery faced fallout signals from the eurozone debt crisis earlier in the year and, in particular, from the declining demand for U.S. exports. In late July, the encouraging balance sheet health of EU banks following the stress test results (discussed in the previous chapter) stabilized the euro. But following that positive outcome, eurozone recovery prospects were modest. They were driven by export-led Germany, whereas the noncompetitive peripheral economies in the eurozone's southern areas lagged behind. Outside the eurozone, Britain posted slower growth prospects. So did China, with a revised, lower growth forecast for the third quarter. This discouraging growth scenario in the major global economies reduced the likelihood that U.S. recovery in the third quarter could be pushed forward by a rise in exports. President Obama's agenda of doubling U.S. exports in five years faced hurdles at the start.

With the downsizing of the recovery momentum, could the economy move into a double-dip recession starting in July?

The impact of the financial crisis in 2008, the economy's recovery in 2009, and the uncertainty about its continuation in the second half of 2010 resulted in interesting guesswork as to which letters of the alphabet could best capture the shape of the recovery. The uncertain state of the recovery in July raised the likelihood of a double-dip recession and a restoration of the letter "W." Could that happen?

Which Letter of the Alphabet?

In terms of the engaging alphabetical formulation of the recession impact and the subsequent recovery stretching into 2010, which of the four letters—V, L, W, U—could best capture the process?

First, did the U.S. economy sink and rise like a sharp V or did it stagnate during the recession at the bottom of a slippery U-shaped bathtub?

According to a provisional assessment of the Business Cycle Dating Committee of the National Bureau of Economic Research, the economy

seemed to have reached the bottom of the recession in terms of several indicators in mid-2009. Annualized real GDP growth rate from quarter to quarter shows a V trajectory with the bottom hitting in the second quarter of
2009 (figure 3.1). It dropped from a high of 2.9 percent in the fourth quarter of 2007 to a low of –6.8 percent in the fourth quarter of 2008, rising to
a still low –0.7 percent in the second quarter of 2009. It had climbed up to
5 percent in the fourth quarter of 2009. The year-on-year monthly percentage decline in industrial production in January 2008 had reached its bottom
in mid-2009, after which it had moved up until March 2010.[15] The trajectory
is V-shaped. In another version, the year-on-year monthly percentage decline in retail sales had hit the bottom somewhat earlier, at the end of 2008,
but had decisively moved up (after a short decline) in mid-2009[16] (figure 3.6).
These indicators suggested a V-shaped recession from the end of 2007 until
mid-2009, ruling out both a stagnating U and an L.

But having moved up decisively in terms of these benchmarks, would the
economy take a sharp dip in the second half of 2010 and turn into a double-

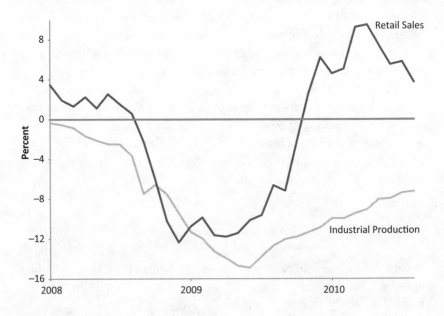

Figure 3.6.
Year-on-Year Monthly Percentage Changes in U.S. Production and Sales: 2008–2010.
(Federal Reserve; U.S. Census.)

Note: The data is seasonally adjusted and in constant prices.

dip W? From mid-June through July, the recovery was on track, although it showed a few signs of slowdown. Across most U.S. regions, manufacturing, transport, services, tourism, and retail sales continued to increase, but residential and commercial real estate markets remained weak. But the signals were conflicting. The slowdown in economic recovery contrasted with strong corporate sector earnings in August.

Indeed, several features of the U.S. real economy combined with improving performance elsewhere, especially in China, ruled out the occurrence of a double-dip recession in 2010. The manufacturing sector index, from automobile production to furniture making, had gone up from 55.5 in July to 56.3 in August. It had risen in China as well. Durable goods orders, excluding the volatile transportation component, had risen by 2 percent in August. The U.S. private sector had added 235,000 jobs from June to August. Jobless claims had declined to 473,000 in the week ended August 21, 2010, down from 651,000 in March 2009. The Labor Department reported that the PPI had risen by 0.2 percent in July compared with a 0.5 percent decline in June. The consumer price index also had inched up. And in a behavioral shift, banks had started lending to businesses toward the end of August.

According to the *Wall Street Journal*/NBC poll, 64 percent of the economists said that the economy would get better over the next 12 months, whereas only 33 percent of the general public expected the economy to improve. Economists, on average, saw the odds of a double-dip recession at 20 percent.[17] Why not leave the alphabets aside? In my view, the economy's pace would pick up in the final quarter of 2010. It would certainly not be so strong as to require an inflation-fighting exit strategy from the Federal Reserve. Nor would it generate more than the budgeted revenues for the Treasury, which must await the post-election resolution in Congress over the Bush tax cuts. More to the point, the growth prospect is unlikely to lift the unemployment rate to 8 percent by year-end from 9.6 percent in August 2010. More than any other consideration, the U.S. unemployment rate would continue to figure as a strategic input in the policy decisions at the highest level.

The U.S. economy decisively stepped out of the Great Depression and its ravaging consequences following World War II. No such decisive push awaits it this time.

4

Global Recovery Prospects
North America and Europe, Asia, and South America

Everyone agreed that the financial crisis originated in the United States. France's President Nicolas Sarkozy provided a sophisticated version of its onset by attributing it to the out-of-bounds Anglo-Saxon liberalism, whereas Germany's Chancellor Angela Merkel commented on the spendthrift Americans damaging the welfare of the thrifty Germans.

In reality, low interest rates beginning in 2001, combined with slack regulatory supervision, prompted Americans into excessive borrowing for home ownership. As interest rates gradually moved up, subprime mortgages began accumulating beginning in 2005. The crashing valuations of mortgage-based assets held by U.S. financial institutions crippled their lending potential. By the second half of 2009, U.S. GDP growth had revived and consumer spending had edged up, but new home prices had failed to move up in the midst of continuing foreclosures. The April 2010 unemployment rate of 9.9 percent continuing at a high 9.6 percent in July raised doubts about the resuscitating impact of the record stimulus package approved by Congress in early 2009. In the second quarter of 2010, U.S. GDP growth recovery had slowed amid falling consumption, a slowing manufacturing sector, and declining exports.

Across the globe, the impact of the crisis and the pace of GDP recovery varied among groups of countries. Despite the mid-2010 growth setback and a halting revival of banks' lending to businesses, the U.S. economy was estimated to record positive real GDP growth between 2 and 3 percent in 2010.

By contrast, the 16 member countries of the Economic and Monetary Union (EMU), which comprises the European states whose common currency is the euro, showed signs in early 2010 of a near-stalled recovery in the eurozone. (EMU membership increased to 17 when Estonia became a member on December 31, 2010.) The severe debt crisis in Greece threatened to destabilize eurozone banks with a likely default by the Greek government of the sovereign debt that they held. The significant budget deficits of other member countries, among them Ireland, Italy, Portugal, and Spain, required cutbacks in their budget spending amid declining economic activity. The fears of a debt default contagion added to the urgency of stabilizing the finances of these peripheral economies via resource transfer from a common EMU fund. A substantial rescue package of €750 billion ($955 billion), conditioned on appropriate budget-tightening by member countries, was announced on May 10, 2010. The results of the stress test of eurozone banks published on July 23 also sent reassuring signals to financial markets about their balance sheet health. The eurozone economy had emerged from the grim possibility of its breakup as the value of the currency stabilized in mid-2010. Eurozone member banks, however, lagged behind in extending credit to private businesses, although the European Central Bank (ECB) had kept the interest rate at a low 1 percent beginning in March 2009. The area's GDP growth rate was forecast at less than 1 percent for 2010.

Outside the EMU, low prospects of GDP growth in 2010 pervaded in Britain and several members of the European Union, including Hungary and the Baltic states of Latvia and Estonia. The Northern European countries of Denmark, Norway, and Sweden, which are outside the eurozone, were better poised, with a 2010 GDP growth forecast varying from 1 to 2.7 percent. Despite these countries' heavy export dependence, which affected their recovery prospects, a solid record of budget surpluses, a healthy banking sector (except for a manageable exposure of two Swedish banks to nonperforming loans by borrowers from Baltic countries), a nonexistent housing boom (unlike in Britain), and a flexible currency (the Danish krone, however, is pegged to the euro) gave them extra maneuverability in lowering the impact of the crisis. Outside Europe to the east, Russia awaited uncertain growth recovery as its policy makers sought to resuscitate the banking sector and awaited revival of oil and commodity prices amid policy makers' loud rhetoric on modernization and diversification of the economy. Widespread fires in the western part

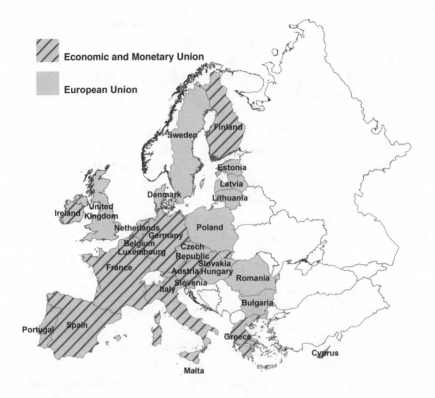

Economic and Monetary Union (Eurozone) and European Union. (AND International Publishers N.V. 2008. Europe Countries [polygon] Redlands, California, USA: ESRI.)

of the grain-growing region, which damaged the grain crop, were set to lower the 2010 growth prospects. A less uncertain 2010 recovery outlook awaited Ukraine.

In contrast to Europe and the post-Soviet zone, Asia presented solid GDP growth prospects for 2010, led by China, India, South Korea, Malaysia, and Indonesia. Indeed, Asian economies faced inflationary buildup and exchange rate appreciation as foreign capital began moving in their territories. The sole exception was Japan as its policy makers sought to fight deflation amid a precarious gross public debt to GDP buildup of nearly 200 percent and also to maintain export recovery amid a rising yen.

The major South American countries, among them Argentina, Brazil, Chile, Colombia, Mexico, Argentina, and Venezuela, conveyed 2010 growth prospects varying from 2 to 5 percent except Venezuela with a forecast exceeding –2 percent. Brazil and Chile led the group with a steady reduction in their budget deficits and inflation rates in a stable political environment. In both countries, the improvement in these macroeconomic indicators contrasted with lagging performance in this regard in Argentina, Colombia, and Mexico, all dealing with political uncertainties. Policy makers in Mexico also struggled with the impact of a sizable decline in remittance inflows from the United States and the continuing hold of drug cartels on the leaders' policy maneuverability. Venezuela, the South American basket case, represented extreme features of political authoritarianism and economic mismanagement.

Clearly, the 2010 GDP recovery prospects varied from one set of economies to the next, from the United States to Europe and from Asia to South America. Despite the variations, an analytical framework based on major variables can explain the differing crisis impact on a country's growth prospects in 2010.

In addition to banking sector health and export dependence as factors affecting crisis *origin,* the speed of recovery in 2010 would depend on the capability of policy makers to launch a stimulus package and design its orientation. Persistent budget deficits in the pre-crisis phase spilling into 2009 in several EMU-member economies required that their budgetary spending be cut back in 2010 amid declining economic activity. At the same time, while the U.S. and EU economies mounted their 2010 policy initiatives in an environment of low inflation, significant current inflation limited the size of the stimulus package and the adoption of easy monetary policy in India and Russia.

Among the global economies struggling to revive in 2010, Iceland deserves special treatment as a poster child waiting to explode into a financial, economic, and political collapse. Let's look at the policy lesson to be drawn from the brief history of a country wanting to live way beyond its means.

I. Why Did Iceland Fly Too Close to the Sun?

"There is no mystery about how it happened."[1] Beginning in the late 1990s, privatized Icelandic banks went on a borrowing spree from foreign banks, which sent its economy into an unprecedented boom. Inflation soared, and the krona, its currency, strengthened as short-term capital inflows supported a huge current account deficit. High interest rates, calculated to rein in inflation, attracted speculative capital inflows. The equity firms linked with the banks bought retail and real estate businesses in Britain and Denmark with short-term credits. Icesave Bank, managed by Reykjavik-based Landsbanki, went overboard and received deposits from more than 300,000 British and Danish depositors. The borrowing binge of the three large banks was way out of proportion to the tax base of the small island economy and the lender-of-the-last-resort capability of its central bank.[2]

A dizzying combination of shocks toward the end of September 2008 created a policy paralysis in Iceland. The foreign exchange market stopped functioning. The stock market collapsed. The three banks were nationalized. The government resigned in late January 2009, leaving behind a trail of unresolved debt payments by banks to foreign depositors, which threatened the status of its sovereign debt. Indeed, more than a year later, Iceland voters rejected a deal in March 2010 to repay Icesave debts to British and Danish depositors amid anger that taxpayers were being penalized for the mistakes of greedy bankers. The Icesave dispute obstructed Iceland's access to international finance until a breakthrough agreement with the International Monetary Fund (IMF) in April promised a go-ahead for release of the blocked funding of an IMF loan to Iceland. That promised a revival of the island's shattered economy.

Elsewhere, the recovery prospects in the United States (discussed in chapter 3), Europe, Asia, and South America clearly depended on the speed with which policy makers formulated and adopted measures amidst varying problems operating in their financial sector and the real economy. Let's examine Europe first.

II. EU and EMU Recovery Prospects in 2010

The challenges that European leaders faced in combating the crisis impact and reviving their economies varied significantly between the larger group of the 27 EU members and the smaller group of the 16-member Economic and Monetary Union whose single currency is the euro.

A brief history of the EMU's formation is instructive in bringing out the handicaps of a monetary union operating without tight fiscal coordination among members. The dream of European leaders a generation ago of creating a common European geographic space faced unraveling as the impact of the global financial crisis within the EMU degenerated into an unmanageable debt crisis in Greece, which threatened to spill into neighboring Portugal and Spain.

EU-EMU Background

The formation of the European Union starting in the 1950s and, later, of the Economic and Monetary Union was pushed by successive European leaders who believed that the integration of countries located in the European space would help them operate under liberal economic and political arrangements. The financial crisis brought into the open the accumulated burden of the structural inflexibilities and the hangover from the illiberal political legacy in some member countries. Thus, Greece, Portugal, and Spain not only battled the consequences of the nonmarket rules under which their economies functioned under prolonged dictatorships, but also the desires of their working classes to improve their living standards upon joining the European Union. The former constrained their competitive performance vis-à-vis EU members to the north and the latter imposed excessive burdens on their budgets.

By the same token, members of the former Soviet bloc in Eastern and Central Europe also continued dealing with the double whammy of their businesses seeking to escape their noncompetitive, nonmarket background and their governments trying to shake off the budgetary burdens of the entitlements that their citizens received under socialism. In a word, some members of the expanding European space carried historical burdens that had decidedly negative implications for their economic performance and fiscal management.

Leaders of the European core—France, Germany, Belgium, the Netherlands, Luxembourg, and Italy—who envisaged the enlargement were aware of these concerns and sought to impose membership criteria. The financial crisis laid bare the hazards of a monetary union in which economic decisions with regard to fiscal management operated under rules that fell far short of automatic resource transfers to needy members, as should be the case in a fully operating political union, like the United States and India. Just as the U.S. financial crisis set in motion urgent action from the top for an overhaul of the grossly inadequate regulatory environment, the crisis in Europe called for a revision of EMU arrangements that (as I describe below) would eventually facilitate entry of members from the larger, expanding European Union.

EU Enlargement and EMU Creation in 1992

The process of EU enlargement was far from smooth. France's President Charles de Gaulle had opposed British membership, fearing U.S. influence via Britain in European decision making. Increasingly, the enlargement was driven by political rather than economic considerations. The three Mediterranean countries, Greece, Portugal, and Spain, had ceased to be dictatorships in the 1970s and needed to be part of Europe in order for them to consolidate their nascent democracies. France's President François Mitterrand had opposed their entry on grounds that they were economically unprepared. The disintegration of the Soviet Union in late 1991 and the end of the Cold War created demands from eight Eastern and Central European countries for joining Europe so that they could escape Russian domination. The Maastricht Treaty of 1992 defined the criteria of the rule of law and a functioning market system for their entry. The existing members placed restrictions on travel and job-seeking rights by citizens of the new Eastern Europe members. The treaty also formally converted the European Economic Community into the European Union.

Any European country can qualify for EU membership provided it fulfills the criteria established in 1993 by the European Council in Copenhagen: It must have a stable democratic government and a functioning market economy. Its institutions must implement the rule of law and protect minority rights.

While the process of EU enlargement moved forward, plans were also taking shape for a closer integration of EU members that adopted a common currency and that fulfilled five convergence criteria specified by the Maastricht Treaty. An aspirant's financial system must be compatible with the European system of central banks. Its inflation rate must be within 1.5 percent, and its interest rate must be within 2 percent of the corresponding rates in three member states with the lowest rates. It must reduce its budget deficit to below 3 percent of its GDP. Its exchange rate must be within specified limits as well.

Eleven EU members that met the convergence criteria joined the proposed monetary union, and the euro was launched on January 1, 1999. By 2009, the membership had increased to 16. The ECB, headed by Jean-Claude Trichet, sets EMU monetary policy. The individual governments manage their own fiscal policies. The Maastricht criteria of 1993 requires that members maintain their inflation rate below an annual 2 percent, their budget deficit as a fraction of their GDP at less than 3 percent, and their public debt at 60 percent of their GDP.

The creation of the EMU raised hopes as well as concerns. On the one hand, a common currency would reduce currency exchange fees, set common standards for price comparisons, spur foreign investment, promote competition, and raise growth and employment. On the other hand, concerns arose regarding restricted labor mobility across country borders, the loss of the policy option of varying the exchange rate, and the lack of fiscal consolidation among EMU members. Amid these handicaps, the ECB managed monetary policy (which I describe below) by setting the interest rate for the entire zone, whereas policies relating to adequate fiscal stimulus for averting crisis severity were established and implemented by individual members. In particular, Franco-German differences on the size of the stimulus implied that policy implementation on this critical recession-fighting instrument lacked U.S.-style speed and uniformity for the zone.

Eurozone Monetary Policy

In contrast to its U.S. counterpart, the ECB was slower in reducing the interest rate and cleaning member banks of dubious assets. After the collapse of Lehman Brothers in September 2008, the ECB lowered its lending interest rate, but not fast enough. Again, between June 2007 and the end of April 2009, ECB lending had risen to 16 percent of eurozone GDP, higher than the Fed's 14 percent of GDP, but the Federal Reserve had moved faster in its discretionary lending activity via reduction in the federal funds rate. The Fed had also released massive amounts of cash via quantitative acquisition of mortgage-backed securities. It was not until June 24, 2009, that the ECB undertook quantitative monetary easing by extending unlimited euro loans for one year (at its policy interest rate of 1 percent) to 1,100 eurozone banks for unlocking the credit crunch. It was the single largest operation in its 17-year history. But unlike the Fed, which acquired Treasury bonds, the ECB had avoided acquiring member-country government bonds and monetizing its debts (until May 2010, as I discussed in chapter 2).

These early policy restrictions, self-imposed, arose from several considerations. The Economic and Monetary Union was not yet a political union that could convert the eurozone into a single nation-state such as the United States. Were the ECB to monetize a given member's debt, it could be seen as being indifferent to the fiscal travails of another member. More to the point, it must not blur monetary and fiscal decision making. It was in charge of the EMU monetary policy and not a member's fiscal decision making except to require that each member target inflation at an annual rate of 2 percent of its GDP and budget deficit at 3 percent of its GDP. From that perspective, the ECB was bound by rules that were at loggerheads with the severity of the financial crisis. At the same time, the overpowering constraint in adopting a U.S.-style fiscal expansion arose from an initial Franco-German split on this issue.

Franco-German Split on Stimulus Adoption

According to Chancellor Merkel, today's fiscal and monetary excess would bring tomorrow's regrets. This warning demonstrated the German chancellor's awareness of German history with hyperinflation as well as her frustration with U.S. profligacy. More to the point, it reflected her concern that a misguided policy initiative would take away the prosperity that Germans had realized under her leadership (prior to crisis onset). It would damage German economic growth, which had been running at an annual 2.3 percent between 2006 and 2008 and had absorbed 2 million workers, slashing unemployment to 3 million workers. Besides, the government under her leadership was set to balance the federal budget by 2011. These imperatives came into conflict later in working up a German bailout contribution for alleviating Greek budget woes.

In view of this background, the anti-crisis program from German policy makers' perspective had to be tailored to German requirements despite the fact that the economic situation was dismal. A mid-year Organisation for Economic Co-operation and Development forecast put the 2009 contraction of the German economy, highly export dependent and the world's third largest, at 6.1 percent, in contrast to the eurozone's 4.8 percent drop. Despite the forbidding forecast calling for a sizable fiscal stimulus, German legislators passed a constitutional amendment that prohibited the federal government from running a counter-cyclical deficit (over and above the normal structural deficit) of more than 0.35 percent of GDP from 2016 onward. But that was in the future. Here and now, the lawmakers passed a stimulus package that was tailored for keeping workers in jobs and boosting consumption spending. It combined tax cuts with additional spending on subsidies and a popular per-worker bonus of €2,500 ($3,180), which encouraged Germans to scrap old cars and buy new ones. As a result, in the second quarter of 2009, the German economy registered consumption growth, quite unlike the situation in the United States.

Clearly, the size and orientation of the stimulus calculated to maintain jobs and consumer demand were motivated by the (forthcoming) September 2009 parliamentary elections. In the end, the post-election German budget deficits (including the stimulus) at nearly 4 percent of GDP in 2009 and 6 percent in 2010 exceeded the Maastricht requirement of 3 percent. The actual deficits turned out to be significantly higher than Chancellor Merkel's forbidding strictures at the recession onset. Ultimately, the German policy approach resembled that of the French leadership. President Sarkozy and Finance Minister Christine Lagarde had argued early on that the crisis-induced deficits should be treated differently from the deficit limit of 3 percent of GDP imposed on EMU member countries by the Maastricht criteria of 1993. In any case, the budget deficits of the major EMU members were lower than that of the United States, at 10 percent of its GDP in 2009.

By the end of 2009, the EMU (16 countries) unemployment rate had risen to 9.5 percent of the workforce, up from 9.3 percent in April. The ECB had in the meantime announced that it would keep its interest rate constant at 1 percent despite signs of the deepest recession to hit continental Europe since World War II. In the ECB's policy maneuvering, a lower interest rate would not induce banks to borrow and augment their reserves voluntarily and jumpstart lending to businesses. A quantitative cash infusion via unlimited, one-year euro loans to member banks was necessary. Uncertainties remained, however. With a quantitative monetary policy carrying the burden of a eurozone revival, could the generous mid-year offer by the ECB of unlimited loans to eurozone banks accomplish the task? Could it be sufficient to revive eurozone economies until the banks managed to clean up their losses? The holdings in eurozone banks of the sovereign debts of some of the peripheral economies, including Greece, dampened the prospects of a credit crunch thaw via bank lending in the zone (chapter 2).

Greek budget deficits, which had been accumulating from the pre-crisis years, had begun escalating in 2009. They created fears of sovereign debt default by the government; they sent contagion signals of similar default likelihood by the governments of Portugal and Spain. They damaged the stability of the euro. Let's take a look at Greece's budget crisis.

III. Greek Budget Crisis

EU leaders faced a momentous decision when they gathered in Brussels for a summit on February 11, 2010, as Greek bond prices plummeted, their interest rate spread widened to 4 percentage points over German bonds, and Greek civil servants marched in the streets of Athens to protest a curtailment of the gravy train. Britain, France, and Germany, three EU stalwarts, faced an urgent task of working up an appropriate bailout for Greece without signaling that it would end up as a Trojan horse for the rest of the affected economies. A more difficult test for the rescue would require the imposition of budget slashing requirements for the bailout recipients. Moral hazard had appeared in the eurozone in a different guise. How stringent could the conditionality be for the budget-busting offenders? More to the point, where would the resources for the rescue come from?

The imploding Greek situation drove EMU members into a flurry of announcements and negotiations that sought to aid the Athens policy makers and ensure that the impact of a weakening euro did not affect the balance sheets of EMU banks, which held Greek sovereign debt, and ultimately halt the economic recovery of the eurozone. While the Greek policy makers scrambled via successive budget exercises to rein in government spending on public sector employees and support to pensioners, Chancellor Merkel openly opposed working up a rescue package for Greek bailout. She had a point. The next supplicant could be Portugal with its significant budget deficit, followed by Spain. Ireland had taken quick steps to cut back some public spending. Even the issue of Greek policy makers seeking credit from the IMF, an EMU outsider, could not be resolved in time. The uncertainty spilled into vigorous and divisive debates on the future of the euro and of the EMU itself and the urgency to strictly monitor and implement budgetary policies more cohesively in the entire zone. Without such effective disciplining of the eurozone fiscal regime, the European Central Bank's role of devising and implementing monetary policy would become difficult and the policies would remain ineffective.

The Imploding Greek Crisis and the Search for a New EMU Paradigm

Indeed, in early May 2010, the budgetary woes of Greece had catapulted the eurozone into the most severe crisis since its creation. The challenge of

Greece within the EMU was formidable and exceptional. Its estimated budget deficit of 12.7 percent of the GDP in 2009 went with net public borrowing of 86 percent of the GDP. By contrast, Ireland and Spain with 12.2 and 9.6 percent budget deficits had 25 and 33 percent of public debt–to–GDP ratios.

The Greek government's budgetary management was marked by an unusual combination of public sector corruption, imaginative doctoring of fiscal data, and massive tax evasion. The budget deficit, which hit 12.7 percent of the GDP, was financed by heavy reliance on foreign purchases of government debt. The ensuing debt crisis threatened to spread to Portugal and Spain as investors dumped Greek sovereign debt. The origin of the crisis in these peripheral European economies raised doubts about the effectiveness of the norms that were laid down when the euro was introduced in 1999. As I have suggested, these low-cost economies were expected to compete with the higher-cost eurozone suppliers to the north by raising worker productivity and tightening their fiscal belts during the good times. Instead, having joined the EMU in 2001, the Greek policy makers expanded their budgets during the prosperous years lasting until 2007, adding employees to government rolls even as tax receipts declined. The government of Spain also had accumulated massive debt as it financed an American-style housing boom that collapsed as recession hit the economy in late 2008. Portugal and Ireland were not far behind in racking up their budget deficits and accumulating public debt.

On the weekend of May 9, 2010, the EMU core came to the help of the southern periphery by announcing a €750 billion ($955 billion) rescue package, having realized that the separate bailout for Greece of €110 billion ($140 billion) of a week earlier was clearly inadequate. The financial market was not convinced that the latter could effectively prevent a default of Greek sovereign debt.

The European Financial Stability Facility of €750 Billion

Larger than the $780 billion plan legislated by the U.S. Congress in early 2009 to relieve the impact of the financial crisis on the U.S. economy, the "shock and awe" package of €750 billion ($955 billion) was 8 percent of the eurozone GDP. Although the initial details were fuzzy, the European Financial Stability Facility (EFSF) was divided into three parts: the largest, €440 billion ($559 billion), would be funded via a special-purpose vehicle guaranteed by the participating EMU states; another €60 billion ($76 billion), under the authority of the European Commission for emergency balance of payments support, would come from the EU budget; and finally, €250 billion ($318 billion) would be contributed by the IMF. The EFSF would be headquartered in Luxembourg with a life span of three years. It would be run by Klaus Regling, a former head of the economic and financial division of the European Commission. The cash would provide loan guarantees and credit, with some of the initial cash coming from the IMF. The European Central Bank would buy the sovereign debts of the overly indebted governments in explicit contradiction of its previous policy stance of American-style monetization of euro member government debts (these acquisitions were gradually tapered off by the end of July). The Federal Reserve opened a swap facility that would provide dollars in exchange for euros.

How did the euro react to the international efforts at stabilizing its value? After an initial surge above $1.30, it slumped back to around $1.27. The bailout plan required Greece to slash the budget deficit to less than 3 percent of its GDP by 2014 from the current 13.6 percent. The spending cuts were stretched over a longer period and the Greek government was not required to restructure its debt. Soon thereafter, the two-year yield on Greek government bonds slipped from around 18 to 8 percent, restoring investors' confidence in their worth.

The rescue plan raised more debates about the tardiness of the eurozone's big players, among them Germany and France, and about their policy differences.

Franco-German Debates Surrounding the "Shock and Awe" Rescue Plan

Chancellor Merkel emphasized in her policy pronouncements that the euro and the eurozone must remain stable, but her notion of stability rested essentially on disciplined management within each country that would rule out cash transfers from the better-off German taxpayers to the not-so-well-off participants in Southern and Eastern Europe. In its extreme version, mooted by the popular German newspaper *Bild Zeitung,* the European Union cannot be converted into a "transfer union." The Merkel government defended its position by arguing that the special-purpose vehicle of €440 billion ($559 billion), which would provide funding to cash-strapped members, would come from national governments and not from an EU fund.

The French interpretation of the €440 billion ($559 billion) special-purpose vehicle, which was backed by eurozone government guarantees, was the opposite of the official German view of the arrangement. President Sarkozy welcomed the provision as a historical turning point that, in his view, had succeeded in rewriting the rules of the eurozone's operation. Indeed, it would provide funding for relieving unsustainable pressures of a member's macroeconomic imbalances. In the French view, coordination must go beyond each member's budgetary situation and fiscal rules. The French president was also pleased with the Americanization of the ECB in its readiness to monetize a member government's debt and the entry of the IMF as a provider of significant cash in the bailout.

The announcement of the bailout was followed by budget-cutting plans by Greece, Spain, and Portugal as preconditions that qualified them for accessing the rescue funds. In the north, Germany led the way for fiscal austerity, which was taken up by France and Italy as well. At the G20 June 2010 summit, the European leadership position on budgetary discipline presented a sharp contrast to the contrary view of Treasury Secretary Tim Geithner's emphasis on government spending for pulling an economy out of recession. The EMU fiscal cutbacks followed by the positive assessment of the banking sector via a stress test in late July (discussed in chapter 2) dispelled the gloom-and-doom scenario of early 2010. The precarious economic and financial eurozone situation bordering on a breakup at that moment seemed similar to the one that compelled Benjamin Franklin to come up with the admonition to the 13 American colonies: "We must hang together. Else, we shall most assuredly hang separately."[3] By the end of July, the dire forecasts relating to the survival of the euro as a common currency were instead replaced by encouraging assessments of a 2010 GDP growth forecast for the eurozone of around 1 percent.

Of the major EU economies, the post-election Conservative-Liberal coalition government leaders of Britain outside the eurozone had deliberately chosen to keep away from active participation in salvaging the euro. They were too preoccupied with rescuing the British economy from the ruinous impact of the financial turmoil. Indeed, Britain was the first to be a severe crisis casualty in Europe, the first to mount a vigorous stimulus package and banking sector cleanup, and the first to undertake a severe austerity program via budget cutbacks following the defeat of the Labor government under Gordon Brown in May 2010. Would it be the first to revive? The next section examines Britain's situation.

IV. Reviving Britain

How could Britain crawl out of a recession that in early 2009 was marked by an unemployment rate of 7.3 percent and the weakest bank lending to businesses since 2000? The thrifty British were also saving more and pushing the savings rate as a share of personal disposable income to 4.8 percent in the fourth quarter of 2008 from a low of 1.6 percent in the fourth quarter of 2007. How could the economy revive without more spending, which would be financed by more bank lending?

What went wrong with British banking, which early on had the reputation of being a safe, even stodgy business?

Britain and the United States:
No More Siamese Twins Under Cameron-Clegg

With the entry of American banks in Britain in the early years of the twenty-first century, British banks lowered their guard in order to compete with American banks, took risks, and traded in mortgage-backed securities. The biggest casualty was the Royal Bank of Scotland, which was partly nationalized. At the same time, the government of Prime Minister Gordon Brown began undertaking speedy and massive deficits in order to stimulate the economy. As in the United States, this undertaking ran the threat of high inflation and the emergence of a significant public debt–to–GDP ratio. "The right way of thinking about New York and London is that they are Siamese twins. They were the same institutions doing the same things with the same set of regulations. . . . If regulation is transformed in London, it is because of what the U.S. does. The U.S. will say, 'You are to follow us.' We now have no regulatory autonomy."[4]

That said, until the defeat of the Labor government, Britain was a heavily taxed, severely regulated country in which government accounted for about half the workforce and half the economy. Britain's public finances were burdened by massive peacetime deficits, despite heavy taxation unmatched in peacetime. The budget relied heavily on revenues from the value added tax on consumption and from corporate taxes, especially on profits of financial businesses. The collapse of government revenues of the British Exchequer was far out of proportion to even higher output declines in recession-hit eurozone economies. In view of the new Cameron-Clegg Conservative-Liberal coalition, it was time to slash the budget spending and the deficit and depart from the American-style expansionary fiscal stance. The June 2010 budget set across-the-board cuts, to take place over the next five years, of 25 percent in all government departments. Tens of thousands of government workers faced job loss or a wage freeze and potentially sharp pension cutbacks. The Siamese twins, Britain with a budget deficit of 11 percent of its GDP and the United States with 10 percent, had parted company in mid-2010. Although the U.S. budgetary policy was still tied to high spending, Britain had embarked on an austerity program.

Would the austerity measures of the June budget to be implemented over five years push Britain into a severe recession? In the second quarter of 2010, the economy had grown at a seasonally adjusted annual rate of 4.5 percent. The recovery was led by the service sector (accounting for 75 percent of the GDP), the construction sector (in the biggest quarterly rise since 1963), and a moderate growth of manufacturing. In the second half of the year, however, as spending cuts and tax increases were set to dampen consumer confidence, the growth rate could turn out to be lower as a result of lower consumer spending.

Unlike the uncertain 2010 recovery in Britain, Denmark, Norway, and Sweden, outside the eurozone, signaled better prospects. A solid record of budget surpluses gave their policy makers more freedom in extending tax relief to households and businesses without getting into unmanageable budget deficits. Norway, unlike Britain, had built one of the largest sovereign funds in the European Union from its oil revenues. While the Danish krone was linked to the euro, the Swedish and Norwegian policy makers could vary their exchange rates for promoting their exports. Toxic subprime mortgages that afflicted British banks were generally absent. The impact of nonperforming assets in Swedish banks arising from loans to Baltic borrowers was manageable. Sweden and Denmark experienced GDP growth declines of 5 percent in 2009. The GDP growth forecasts for 2010 ranged from a low 1.5 percent for Denmark (the same as for Britain) to 3.5 percent for Sweden. Norway lagged behind both with a forecast of 1 percent.

This overview of the crisis impact and recovery prospects in the United States (outlined in the preceding chapter), Britain, the Scandinavian subset, and the EMU members facilitates their ranking in terms of crisis severity and recovery possibilities, examined in the next section.

V. Crisis Impact and Recovery Prospects in the North American–EU Group

The group banking sector carried varying and heavy burdens of over-leveraged bank balance sheets, including worrisome sovereign bonds in German and French banks. At the same time, the high unemployment rates in the United States–EU subset (except in Canada) called for government-financed stimulus as private household and investment spending declined. In the United States, the decisions relating to the banking sector investigation, the sizable government stimulus, and the continuing monetary policy easing by the Federal Reserve were swift and significant despite the controversies they promoted. By contrast, policy initiatives in the EU subgroup were slow and conflicting. They lacked the drive to clean up the banks. The woeful fiscal mismanagements in the southern countries in the eurozone, including Greece, Portugal, and Spain, damaged its recovery prospects and threatened the stability of the euro. The bailout package of May 2010 therefore required that these countries undertake fiscal austerity. All the eurozone members exceeded the Maastricht requirement of a budget deficit cap at 3 percent of the GDP in 2009 and posted worrisome ratios of public debt to GDP. France, Italy, and Germany announced plans in June for budget cutbacks in order to fulfill these requirements. Britain, outside the EMU, had stolen a march with an awesome austerity budget to be implemented over five years with a view to cutting back a bloated public sector.

There was, however, one saving grace for the entire North American–EU group. The low annual inflation of around 1 percent allowed the Federal Reserve, the Bank of Canada, the Bank of England, the ECB, and the Scandinavian central banks the policy option of keeping their interest rates at their year-end low rates in early 2010.

The crisis impact for 2009 and the recovery prospects for 2010 in terms of GDP growth for North America (including the United States and Canada), seven EMU countries, and three Scandinavian countries are presented in figure 4.1. North America—the United States and Canada—remains at the top in terms of 2010 GDP recovery, whereas Germany, France, the Netherlands, Britain, Sweden, and Denmark form an intermediate cluster with Italy and Spain at the bottom of the EU subset. Britain, Germany, Italy, and Denmark suffered a GDP growth decline of 5 percent in 2009. The ranking of countries from top to bottom is based on a visual screening of the actual 2009 and projected 2010 GDP growth rates. The

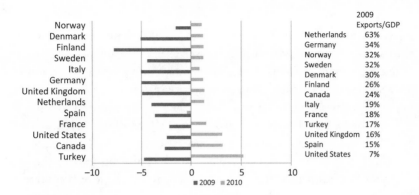

Figure 4.1.
Crisis Impact in 2009 and Recovery Prospects for 2010: GDP Growth Rates—North America and Europe. (International Monetary Fund.)

relative positioning will change as more recent 2010 GDP forecasts become available, but the group ranking of North America at the top and Spain at the bottom is likely to remain intact. (The Spanish economy was hit hard with a crumbling construction sector, which had ballooned in the pre-crisis years.)

To the east of Britain, France, and Germany in the EU, the Eastern Europe EU members, except Poland, were also hit by the globalization of financial turmoil, but for reasons that differed from those of the European stalwarts. Let's take a closer look at the Eastern European countries.

VI. Eastern Europe, the Baltic States, Russia, and Ukraine

Banks in some of these economies, including the highly export-dependent Baltic economies of Estonia, Latvia, Lithuania, and Hungary, had borrowed heavily from hard currency banks in order to lend to exporting businesses during their pre-crisis growth phase. Hungary and Latvia, both export dependent and each holding significant loans in its banking system from Swiss and Swedish banks, had also resorted to IMF credit financing. Estonia was equally troubled, but did not resort to the IMF credit option. Instead, the government implemented an austerity program, which resulted in heavy labor layoffs. In 11 regional economies, local banks had borrowed 60 percent of their cash requirements from foreign banks. Some banks in

Sweden went into severe financial stress because Latvian banks could not repay the loans to their Swedish creditor banks. Some Swiss banks encountered repayment problems from over-leveraged Hungarian banks. In Hungary, the ruling Fidesz Party, which swept into power with an unprecedented two-thirds parliamentary majority in April 2010, chose to favor populist policies over fiscal discipline. The finance ministry refused to enforce the budget deficits required by the IMF credit facility. The likely defaults of corporate and household foreign currency loans increased as the Hungarian currency continued declining against the euro in the second quarter of 2010. By contrast, banks in Poland had kept away from relying on foreign loans and had also kept away from excessive mortgage financing for home ownership by households. With the crisis onset in late 2008, the credit flows from Polish banks to businesses of the pre-crisis phase had tapered off in 2009. However, EU-financed infrastructure projects countered the drop in private business investment, and the $20.6 billion IMF financing in reserve promised to supplant the cheap credit flows of the pre-crisis expansion phase. Poland's GDP growth in 2009 was bolstered by domestic consumption, and continuing GDP recovery in 2010 was set to put Poland as the top performer among Eastern and Central European economies.

Further to the east and outside the European Union, recession-hit Russia and Ukraine faced sluggish recovery prospects for 2009 and 2010.

Russia and Ukraine

The spectacular annual GDP growth of Russia at 7 percent from 2000 to 2007 was based on the booming oil, natural gas, and commodities prices in world markets. As these prices collapsed, the Russian economy faced a depressing scenario. Its budget surplus was estimated to move into a deficit of 8 percent of its GDP in 2009 as taxes from oil export earnings plummeted. The ruble continued to decline throughout the final quarter of 2008 as foreign investors fled, and nervous holders of ruble assets dumped them following the brief Russian-Georgian war of August 2008. The foreign exchange reserves of the Central Bank of Russia totaling $600 billion were used to support the ruble. The state-owned Vneshekonombank supplied cash for bailing out Russian oligarchs (who had borrowed from foreign banks). Russian domestic banks, which faced nonperforming loans of up to 20 percent of their total assets, needed cash infusions as well. The March 2009 stimulus package of $90 billion (at about 5.5 percent of its GDP), announced by Prime Minister Vladimir Putin, was used for supporting the hard-hit auto industry and the unemployed, whose numbers had reached 9.5 percent of the workforce by mid-year 2009. By that time, the ruble and the stock market had stabilized, but manufacturing output had declined by 16 percent in June compared with a year earlier. The Russian central bank, unlike the Fed and the ECB, faced a massive constraint in its expansionary policy stance as it battled an annual inflation rate of 10 to 11 percent in 2009. A high concentration of large enterprises in the natural resource sector, including energy, also posed policy challenges to the leadership for diversifying the economy. In a forthright assessment in early September 2009, President Dmitri Medvedev described Russia as "a raw-material-based, corrupt economy." Despite that discouraging testimony, foreign capital had begun to trickle into Russia by late 2009 in order to profit from the high interest rate of 9 percent and improving economic prospects as oil prices started moving up. As a result, the ruble had started gaining strength in relation to a dollar/euro basket. For countering the speculative inflows, the central bank sold more rubles in the foreign exchange market and cut the discount rate by half a percentage point. As 2010 advanced and oil prices moved up, the macroeconomic indicators, including the GDP growth rate, the budget deficit, and the unemployment rate, showed steady improvement. The GDP growth rate will be adjusted downward as the impact of the prolonged heat and fires in western Russia on the grain harvest is estimated.

In terms of the framework adopted here for analyzing crisis onset and recovery prospects, Russia had everything wrong. Its banking sector had tainted, nonperforming assets; it was dependent on exports, but particularly on oil and natural gas for budgetary revenues and growth recovery. Finally, its high inflation limited the government's adoption of a sizable stimulus.

The Ukrainian economy, with troubled banks, heavy export dependence on steel products, and high inflation, faced an additional impediment of a long-standing political feud between President Viktor Yushchenko and Prime Minister Julia Timoshenko, each angling for victory in the January 2010 elections. The infighting tested the conciliatory diplomacy of the IMF, which had extended a credit of $16 billion to Ukraine. Viktor Yanukevich, a problem-solving, hands-on politician who became president

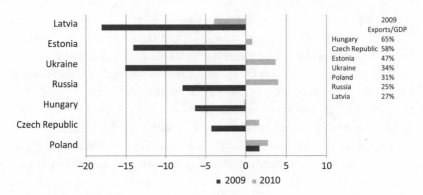

Figure 4.2.
Crisis Impact in 2009 and Recovery Prospects for 2010: GDP Growth Rates—Eastern Europe, Russia, Ukraine, and the Baltic States. (International Monetary Fund.)

following the election, promised to focus on the declining economy, work with the IMF, and, above all, work with the Russian leadership.

Figure 4.2 records the 2009 GDP growth rate decline and 2010 performance prospects of five Eastern European economies, Russia, and Ukraine. Russia, despite 2009 turmoil and modest 2010 prospects, ranks ahead of Hungary, Ukraine, Estonia, and Latvia at the very bottom. Poland could actually emerge as the leading performer of the group.

The latest IMF forecast reported that the developed global economies would record a modest recovery in 2010, but the emerging market economies of Asia, led by China and India, would return to resurgent growth and improve their positive performance of 2009. This is examined in the next section. I include Australia and South Africa among the Asian group in order to minimize the number of group classifications.

VII. Resurgent Asia

Had the Asian moons decoupled themselves from the planet west? Were they dancing to autonomous tunes? The major exception among the big Asian players was Japan, which sent a depressing signal of 1.8 percent GDP growth for 2010.

Japan

Following the lost decade of the 1990s, the Japanese economy posted a robust recovery from 2002 to 2007, primarily as a result of surging demand for Japanese goods from China, the United States, and East Asia. The export growth had ballooned from a modest annual 4 percent in the decade beginning in 1992 to almost 10 percent annually from 2002 to 2007, comparable to Germany's. At the same time, consumption growth during this latter period grew at an annual 1.1 percent a year, higher than in Germany, but staggeringly lower than in the United States.

The drastic fall in exports, estimated at 40 percent in the first half of 2009, slashed Japan's GDP by 6 percent in 2009, the sharpest drop since 1945 and the highest among developed countries. The policy makers' response was swifter and deeper than in the lost decade of the 1990s and in the slow-moving eurozone. Prominent Japanese companies, among them Toshiba, Sony, and Toyota, promptly laid off part-time and temporary workers. The stimulus package of $162 billion at 5 percent of GDP, combined with reviving export demand and depleted inventories, was expected to slow the economy's contraction. However, the gross accumulated debt of the government, pummeled by years of extravagant spending, had reached 180 percent of GDP, the highest among developed countries. The public debt, domestically held, nevertheless represented gross mismanagement of government finances under the prolonged, half-century tenure of the Liberal Democratic Party. The electoral victory of the Democratic Party of Japan on August 30, 2009, raised hopes for a different fiscal agenda under its direction that must displace Japanese bureaucrats from the role of fiscal policy making. Along with voters in Britain and Australia (in late August), the Japanese electorate had seized the opportunity, opened up by the financial crisis, of installing a new government. The leadership battle for the prime minister's post dragged on into mid-September 2010 when the Democratic Party elected Naoto Kan as prime minister on September 14. The next day, Japanese monetary authorities intervened in the foreign exchange market, bought dollars in exchange for yens, and lowered the currency, which had moved up to a 15-year high against the dollar during the year as risk-averse currency traders bought yens in increasing amounts. Japan thus became the first practitioner of currency intervention among the developed global economies afflicted by the financial crisis.

Japan was hit by massive export contraction and continued to battle deflationary pressures, an excessive cumulative public debt, and the need for reining in the exchange rate of the yen in order to promote its exports. These problems posed extreme challenges to the problem-solving capabilities of the new government. It was, however, spared the financial trauma of the Anglo-American type of an over-leveraged banking sector. So were India and the East Asian economies, but China developed worrisome symptoms of a residential and nonresidential property bubble in mid-2010 that was supported by excessive bank lending. The recovery prospects of the Asian economies varied, with a resurgent China striding ahead of India in growth performance for 2009 and growth forecast for 2010, although Chinese exports had fallen by 20 percent in the first six months of 2009 from a year earlier, and 20 million Chinese workers had headed from coastal cities to their distant villages.

China and India

On July 16, 2009, the Beijing National Bureau of Statistics reported that the Chinese economy had grown by 7.9 percent in the second quarter compared with a year earlier. The strong performance was driven by a massive stimulus package consisting of infrastructure buildup and support for consumer spending on autos and other items. This was steered via lending by state-owned banks to the tune of $1 trillion through June 2009.

This resurgent strategy was supported by successive surpluses in the state budget and a low inflation rate, both providing a cushion against fears of excessive buildup of public debt and an immediate ringing of inflationary alarm bells.

Nevertheless, the dangers of nonperforming bank loans and a speculative rise in property prices, both Chinese hallmarks of a thriving economy, had begun to creep up. A number of state companies had also employed over-the-counter derivatives and made bets on movements of commodity prices and foreign currencies with disastrous impact on their finances. The state-owned Assets Supervision and Administration Commission of the State Council (SASAC) would provide legal support to some companies that wanted to break their loss-making oil derivative contracts with foreign institutions. As 2010 advanced, the central bank introduced measures for reining in a property boom financed by bank loans. Some funds received by banks for stimulating the economy in early 2009 via infrastructure development had instead been diverted by the recipients into residential and nonresidential property. Bank regulators imposed stricter oversight over bank lending. They required a 50 percent down payment on second home purchases and mandated stress tests for identifying and restricting banking sector loans that were repackaged and sold by banks to special trust companies as investors. Loans valued at nearly 2.4 trillion yuan ($358 billion), which were repackaged into mortgages, turned into subprime assets with the investors wallowing amid unsold residential housing and nonresidential real estate in Chinese cities. China had developed a housing bubble with unoccupied property, insolvent construction companies, and distressed investors of mortgages.

In contrast to China, the impact of the crisis on the Indian economy via a likely cutback in exports was limited as a result of the unintended consequences of the inner-directed, import-substituting growth strategy of almost four decades. The Indian economy was less dependent on foreign capital inflows. Foreign exchange restrictions encouraged Indian businesses to borrow from state banks, which held 70 percent of bank assets. The banking sector as a whole was too conservatively managed and overregulated to consider advancing loans for reckless property ownership.

Indian policy makers, however, faced a high budget deficit and a persistent inflation rate running at an annual 6 percent. Their stimulus package, directed at lifting rural living standards and employment enhancement, pushed up the budget deficit to 6 percent of its GDP from April 1, 2009, to March 31, 2010. Nevertheless, in an early November 2009 policy decision, the Reserve Bank of India kept the interest rate constant for fear that lifting it (in order to contain the inflationary pressures) would attract more short-term capital and push the exchange rate of the rupee further. By contrast, China's adoption of a massive stimulus under the backdrop of a continuing record of budget surpluses and a low inflation rate put China ahead of India in the growth trajectory in 2009 and beyond.

Apart from China and Japan, and India in South Asia, the situation with regard to 2009 GDP decline and 2010 recovery potential in several East Asian economies had common features.

East Asia in 2009 and 2010

The East Asian tigers, among them Indonesia, Korea, and Malaysia, export dependent like China, were hit by the recession, but they were spared the severity of its impact by prudent banking sector management, healthy government finances, adequate foreign exchange reserves, and low inflation, allowing their policy makers an adequate fiscal stimulus and easy monetary policy. Indeed, all of them faced significant portfolio capital inflows toward the end of 2009. At the same time, a low renminbi[5] damaged the competitiveness of these economies in export markets (I discuss this issue at length in chapter 7). Similar also was the impact of the speculative capital inflows in these economies, which confronted their policy makers with the double whammy from neighboring China and distant investors. In 2010, they continued facing the challenge of preventing their appreciating currencies from damaging their export performance.

Australia, in the Asian subgroup, had managed to avoid a major impact on its macroeconomic health from the financial crisis. Its GDP growth forecast was 3.1 percent for 2010. The mid-2010 unemployment rate of 5.1 percent was low. The budget deficit at about 3 percent of its GDP was to be converted into a surplus by 2013. The annual inflation rate of about 3 percent needed a moderately tight monetary policy. The central bank had started lifting interest rates way ahead of other countries in East Asia. The major worry was managing the economy's trade dependence on China, which was a major importer of the country's mineral resources. A slowing Chinese economy with a stalled construction sector created uncertainties about the country's trade balance and growth prospects. Australian investors, mining-driven entrepreneurs, and the mining companies that oppose a new tax on their operations would welcome the liberal-conservative Tony Abbott taking charge of the government following a close parliamentary election on August 21, 2010.

A different foreign dependency problem affected the growth prospects of South Africa, which depended on significant inflows of foreign investment to cover its economy's current account balance; it was forecast at a negative 5 percent of its GDP for 2010. The budget, with a deficit of 6.2 percent, and the consumer price index at an annual 5.2 percent were worrisome as well. The most troubling macroeconomic policy issue for the government was a persistent high unemployment rate among the black majority, at 25 percent of the workforce.

Although the Asian economies were all poised to bounce back from the recession earlier than the developed West, their long-term prospects for reduced export dependence and increased domestic consumption (except in India) called for a combination of suitable management of their exchange rates and provision of liberal pension and social security benefits, which would induce their households to save less. It is not clear if the current financial crisis provided such a lesson for the emerging Asian economies, China among them, of a gradual decoupling from the West and of softening their financial and trade globalization.

In the meantime, how does the Asian group perform in terms of 2009 GDP growth and 2010 recovery prospects?

Asia in the Lead

The GDP growth in 2009 and recovery prospects for 2010 for several Asian economies, with China and India at the top and Japan at the bottom of the entire Asian group, are recorded in figure 4.3. Indonesia, Malaysia, and South Korea, in that order of diminishing 2010 GDP growth rate, dominate Australia and South Africa with a forecast of about 2 percent.

Next we look at the remaining group of emerging economies, in South America.

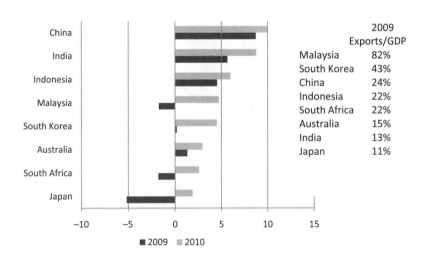

Figure 4.3.
Crisis Impact in 2009 and Recovery Prospects for 2010: GDP Growth Rates—Asia, Australia, and South Africa. (International Monetary Fund.)

VIII. South American Group Ranks Just Below Asia

Except Mexico and Venezuela, the sampled South American economies (figure 4.4) suffered minimal impact on their GDP growth rates in 2009. Except Venezuela, they were set to grow from 2 to 5 percent in 2010.

Brazil and Chile held out prospects of a robust recovery in their GDPs, both nearly 5 percent in 2010, just below China and India in Asia. Their policy makers had managed to bring their budget deficits and inflation rates within manageable limits on the eve of the crisis onset, and their exports were diversified and also less dependent on the U.S. market. Indeed, toward the end of 2009, they had started attracting portfolio capital flows that tested their central banks' monetary policy maneuverability: A lift in the interest rates for stemming inflationary pressures would attract more capital inflows. Brazil imposed a 2 percent tax on capital inflows in equity and bond markets. Mexico was hardest hit in the subgroup, with a GDP growth rate of –6.5 percent in 2009. Its export-to-GDP ratio of 32 percent in 2009 implied a heavy export dependence on the U.S. market. At the same time, the remittance inflows from Mexican immigrants also declined drastically in 2009. Mexico, so near the United States and a NAFTA member as well, awaited a swift U.S. recovery. Venezuela, an economic outlier with a

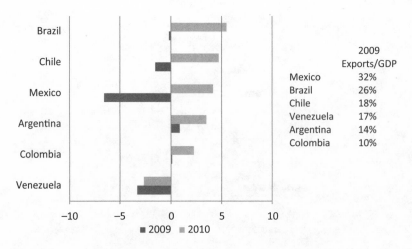

Figure 4.4.
Crisis Impact in 2009 and Recovery Prospects for 2010: GDP Growth Rates—South America. (International Monetary Fund.)

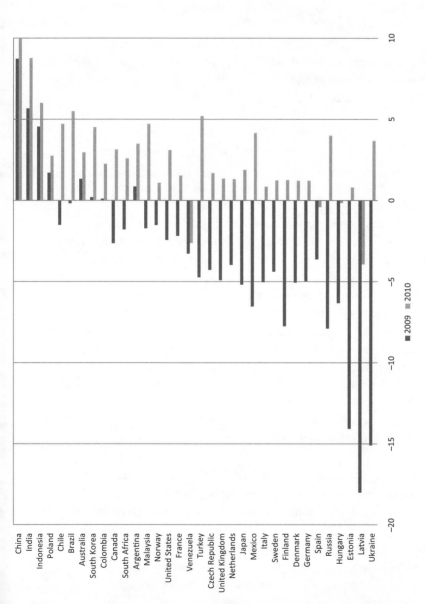

Figure 4.5.
Crisis Impact in 2009 and Recovery Prospects for 2010: GDP Growth Rates—Global Ranking. (International Monetary Fund.)

high unemployment rate of 9.2 percent of the workforce and a growth forecast of about –3.5 percent for 2010, was reduced to an explosive mix of political authoritarianism and economic mismanagement with escalating corruption and crime.

The above cataloguing of the selected economies in the four groups provides their overall global ranking (figure 4.5) from the best to the worst performers in terms of their 2009 GDP growth performance and 2010 GDP growth prospects.

IX. Country Ranking and Analytical Framework

Emerging Asia (which includes Australia and South Africa for lack of an alternative subgroup) is the top performer, followed by the South American group. The developed economies of the United States, Canada, and several EU members rank below the emerging markets of Asia and South America. Among the worst performers are Italy, Spain, Hungary, Estonia, and Latvia in Europe.

The group ranking in descending order of crisis impact and growth prospects and the positioning of a given country within a group will change with continuously updated data and expanded sample size. However, the analytical framework underlying the ranking of groups of countries in figure 4.5 will remain intact.

Analytical Cataloguing of Crisis Features and Growth Prospects Across Countries

The crisis symptoms suggest that financial globalization had gone beyond short-term capital flows into cross-border banks and businesses, which had marked the last decade of the twentieth century. Financial globalization in its early twenty-first-century incarnation involved the acquisition by global banks of structured credit instruments that originated in mortgage-based assets of dubious values in the United States. The resulting financial meltdown and the recession in the United States in the final quarter of 2008 continuing into 2009 also led to a chain reaction of plummeting exports and GDPs among the affected countries.

The varying impact of the process across groups of countries offers the following analytical cataloguing.

First, economies with significant export orientation faced grim recovery prospects in 2010 if their banks were excessively exposed to subprime mortgage-based securities (Britain), hard-currency borrowing (Iceland, Hungary, and Latvia), or sovereign debts of heavily indebted governments (Germany). The presence of toxic, mortgage-based securities and of hard-currency-financed assets in bank portfolios and the acquisition by banks of troubling sovereign debts required a banking sector cleanup without which banks could not begin lending. By contrast, despite heavy export dependence, countries with less banking sector exposure to such assets (Malaysia, South Korea) experienced a less recessionary impact. Banking sector cleanup was not a necessary precondition for their economic recovery.

Second, specific features of export dependence, such as excessive reliance on a commodity (oil in Russia and finished steel in Ukraine), inhibited a crisis-affected country's revival from a sharp recession.

Third, a pre-crisis budget surplus history combined with low current inflation (China in contrast to India) allowed policy makers the choice of a substantial stimulus package. Despite low inflation, however, the eurozone recovery was impeded by the pre-crisis government overspending in some economies (Greece, Portugal, Ireland, and Spain), which required budgetary austerity amid weak economic prospects. The pre-crisis budget situation of an economy, combined with current inflation, affected policy makers' ability to undertake adequate stimulus.

Finally, a decisive argument relating to the emergence of the crisis points to the flow of savings to the United States from export-surplus, net savers (China, Germany, and Japan, in particular), which kept interest rates low and created a housing boom and a subprime mortgage crisis in the United States. Should the United States, therefore, start saving more and China start saving less? Although the policy implications of correcting the United States–China saving imbalances differ for each country, the decision making in both will be marked by tortuous political considerations and difficult economic calculations (these issues are discussed in chapter 7). It will extend beyond the recovery, at a varying pace, of the crisis-battered economies from North and South America to the European Union, going east to Ukraine, Russia, and Asia.

5

Hedge Funds and Derivatives, Credit Default Swaps, and Rating Agencies

As the financial crisis intensified toward the end of 2008, most U.S. banks discovered that their balance sheets were loaded with near worthless assets. The hedge fund managers operating in their proprietary divisions had acquired them by employing over-the-counter derivatives and credit default swaps. They often used high-frequency trading, flash orders, and dark pools. These instruments and activities, routinely featuring in the voluminous commentaries of Wall Street aficionados and financial journalists, frequently leave outsiders, among them some economists, in the dark about the exact meaning of these newfangled financial vehicles. Shouldn't these activities be explained from the get-go so that their role in the gathering financial storm can be clearly brought out for an economics student who is a Wall Street outsider? How can appropriate regulations be devised without a precise ranking of the problems they pose for the financial system? They clearly represent the indispensable innovative drive that is part of the fiercely competitive realm of global finance. They nevertheless need to be regulated selectively and prudently on the basis of a clear understanding by the lawmakers of the dangers they pose to the financial system.

To begin with, what are hedge funds? Aren't they risky and complicated investment vehicles for ordinary investors? Did they contribute to the financial crisis? Should they be regulated? How? The first section discusses the answers to these questions.

I. Hedge Funds

Hedge fund managers hedge against fluctuations in currencies, interest rates, and commodity prices. Amidst the enormous volatility of the stock markets, commodity prices, and currency valuations, a hedge fund operative can make money overnight if he is on the right side of the bet. In other words, during sharp swings of a market, an astute hedge fund manager is supposed to separate the performance of a given share from the aggregate. The overall market may be in a bull phase, but a given share may signal a decline, creating profitable opportunities from short selling (which I explain later in this chapter). A successful hedge fund manager takes risks for his investors rather than drift with market bulls or bears. "When Alfred Winslow Jones set up the first [hedge fund] in 1949, he had the goal of disaggregating individual share performance from market movements. . . . But the industry seems to have forgotten what hedging was all about as equity bull markets led to a ferocious appetite for ever-increasing performance and a disregard for risk."[1] From 2002 until late 2007, the hedge fund business had expanded from about 4,000 funds and $700 billion in assets to almost 8,000 funds and $2 trillion in assets.[2]

Did U.S. hedge funds with a global reach contribute to the financial crisis? They did occupy a special status. Before the crisis onset, U.S. hedge funds did not need to register with federal regulators. Their transactions were not subject to oversight. They were a secret corner of Wall Street because their activities were not required to be transparent. As partnerships, hedge funds were allowed to pay taxes on their earned income over time as "carried-interest tax."

Hedge funds, however, do face a major restriction. They are not routinely available to mom-and-pop investors. The Investment Company Act and Securities and Exchange Commission (SEC) rules restrict hedge fund investment opportunity to "sophisticated investors" with more than $1 million in assets or individual income exceeding $200,000 in each of the last two years.[3]

Although hedge funds cannot freely compete for clients, they compete in other ways. Like banks and mutual funds, hedge funds actively lobby Washington legislators and contribute to their campaigns. Hedge funds have websites in which they seek to educate the public about their activities.

Hedge funds are here to stay despite their massive losses in 2008. Indeed, their comeback in 2009 suggests that firms with appropriate risk management can reap huge returns by identifying assets with low volatility and low association with a volatile equity market. Nevertheless, they need to be regulated so that they do not expand into oversized actors such as Long Term Capital Management, which threatened to bring down the entire financial system and had to be bailed out in September 1998. The regulatory guidelines of the Dodd-Frank Wall Street Reform and Consumer Protection Act (Dodd-Frank Act), signed into law in 2010, would require hedge funds to disclose their investment portfolios to a regulator; they would also be compelled to maintain higher capital requirements as a safeguard against over-leveraging their risk and becoming systemic threats. The lawmakers did not open them up for investment by ordinary citizens who can choose the safer investment option of mutual funds.

Hedge fund managers use derivatives. Let's take a look at what they are.

II. Derivatives

Derivatives involve buying and selling of currencies and stocks, commodities, and securities. Derivatives are instruments that "derive" their value from a deal with a counterparty. Over-the-counter derivatives (OTCs) trade in private deals rather than openly on a stock exchange as stocks do. (Only a fraction of stock trading takes place on exchanges such as the New York and London stock exchanges.) Occasionally, banks act as brokers in organizing these transactions—because they have access to prices and trading volumes, they have enormous clout. As brokers, they negotiate deals with pension funds and hedge funds that have money to buy securities. The banks commit to offer a price for a security to these potential buyers and charge high fees in opaque, mutually collusive deals.

Here is a nonfinancial OTC example. Alpha Airlines chooses to place a substantial order for oil for a future date with an oil supplier because it expects the price of oil to fall. (By contrast, if the airline has substantial oil reserves, it may contract to sell them at a future date to a buyer if the airline expects the price of oil to go up.) The oil supplier is the counterparty to the deal. (With Alpha as the oil supplier, the buyer is the counterparty.) This is an OTC deal whose price and volume details are known only to the contracting parties. Alpha, however, suffers a drastic passenger decline and defaults on the contract, leaving the oil supplier with the oil, which it may not be able to sell to an alternative customer. (Alpha's customer may not be able to pick up the oil, leaving Alpha with the oil reserve.) Similar deals may involve buying and selling of currencies and securities. A large number of such deals can pose a systemic risk if pension funds, for example, have acquired subprime mortgages in the false hope that these mortgages are financially solid.

The volatility of the dollar against major global currencies in the past two years has created opportunities for speculators of OTC currency trading back and forth from the greenback. For example, the nearly yearlong period from March 2009 until early 2010 represented active speculative trading against the dollar. During this phase, currency traders profited from a massive carry trade from the dollar into other currencies. They borrowed dollars at a near-zero interest rate and converted them into higher-interest-bearing nondollar assets. Therefore, the dollar fell against the euro, the yen, and several Asian currencies during this period.

The risk sentiment of currency traders, having initially worked in favor of the dollar and against the euro, settled in favor of the euro sometime later. In early 2010, as the Greek sovereign debt crisis threatened to spread into the neighboring, financially vulnerable economies of Portugal and Spain (also with significant budget deficits), the euro declined against the dollar as the financially stable EMU members to the north, among them Germany and France, dithered over working up an adequate bailout package for the potentially default sovereign debts of these peripheral economies. Until May 7, when the rescue plan was announced, the global financial markets remained overly risky as currency traders worried about the worth of the Greek, Portuguese, and Spanish sovereign debts held by French and German banks. OTC trading in euro remained risky until that point. The euro, however, moved up against the dollar and stabilized as a result of the rescue package and the late July stress test of several EU banks. OTC traders bet in favor of the euro.

Figure 5.1 shows that the notional value of all OTCs had ballooned from $80 trillion at the end of 1998 to a staggering $684 trillion in mid-2007. Of the total, interest rate swaps had increased from $36 trillion to $357 trillion (figure 5.2), and during that same period, foreign exchange contracts had swelled from $18 trillion to $63 trillion (figure 5.3). The numbers raised concern about whether the bet makers had sufficient margins to cover their transactions in case they faltered.

Shouldn't OTCs be subjected to regulation?

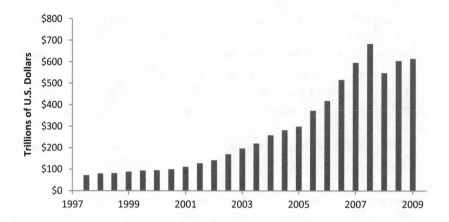

Figure 5.1.
Total Outstanding Notional Values of Over-the-Counter Derivatives. (Bank of International Settlements.)

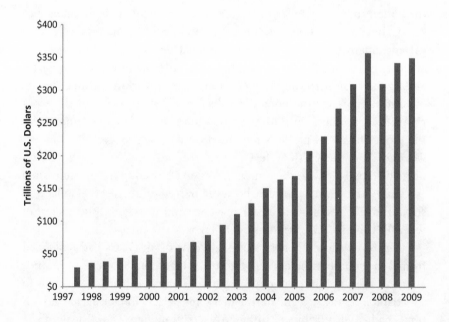

Figure 5.2.
Total Outstanding Notional Values of Interest Rate Swaps. (Bank of International Settlements.)

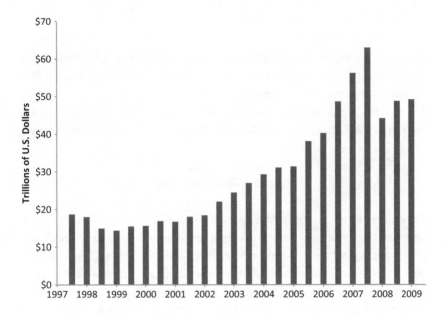

Figure 5.3.
Total Outstanding Notional Values of Foreign Exchange Contracts. (Bank of
International Settlements.)

The 150 pages of draft proposals submitted by the Treasury to Congress in June 2009 sought to regulate OTC trading by splitting it into standardized and customized contracts (discussed at length in chapter 6). The former would be traded on regular exchanges, whereas the latter would be privately traded. The division could prove to be arbitrary. Should foreign exchange swaps be excluded from the regulation? Should nonfinancial companies such as electric utilities and airlines be exempted from the requirements to use clearinghouses? Central clearing would imply that these companies must put up higher *cash* collaterals (such as U.S. Treasury bonds) against their derivative trades, whereas currently, banks required them to use less liquid collateral. "We would not want . . . hedge funds, financial firms, or other investment funds . . . [to] be able to evade the clearing requirement," declared Gary Gensler, chairman of the Commodity Futures Trading Commission, at a House Financial Services Committee hearing.[4] SEC officials voiced similar concerns. The Treasury's call that all OTC transactions be standardized and openly traded on a central clearing platform and their details made public faced opposition from bankers as the Senate debated the financial reform bill in mid-May. The Dodd-Frank Act empowered regulators to devise rules for subjecting derivative operatives, among them hedge funds, to careful scrutiny by clearinghouses. Derivative traders would be required to trade on exchanges and also keep adequate collateral against their trading volumes.

Credit default swaps, which contributed to the financial turmoil, are derivatives with inherent destabilizing features. Let us see how they work.

III. Credit Default Swaps

Credit default swaps seek to cut back risk on bank loans or on mortgage assets held by a financial unit (for example, an insurance company) by slicing and repackaging the riskiest and selling them to investors. These buyers pay a premium to the sellers, who would bail out the investors if the packaged securities went into default. The earliest credit default swaps were arranged by JPMorgan in December 1997. The dollar value of outstanding credit default swaps had gone up from $6.4 trillion in December 2004 to $58 trillion in December 2007 (figure 5.4).

As the housing boom gathered momentum, the mortgages undertaken by Americans were repackaged by the original issuers and sold to investment and commercial banks, hedge funds, and pension funds. Un-

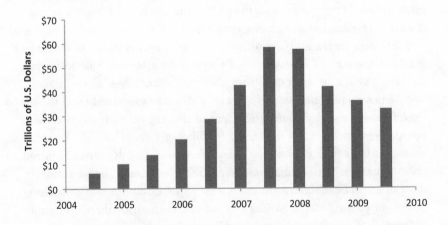

Figure 5.4.
Total Outstanding Notional Values of Credit Default Swaps. (Bank of International Settlements.)

like stock trading, these credit default swaps—like derivatives—were private transactions between two parties and were not regulated by a government agency. American Insurance Group (AIG) had traded its mortgage-based securities to investors as credit default swaps. It needed $182 billion in support from the Treasury and the Federal Reserve, the latter of which acquired these securities in an unusual—indeed, almost historic—operation for the Fed.

This is a good time to take a look at the rating agencies. Why couldn't these agencies, among them Standard & Poor's, foresee the demise of Lehman Brothers *before* it went under in September 2008 and the collapse of AIG *before* it was rescued by the Treasury and the Federal Reserve?

IV. Where Were the Rating Agencies?

"We rate every deal," a Standard & Poor's analyst wrote in a 2007 e-mail message that was later disclosed by the SEC. "It could be structured by cows and we would rate it."[5]

Despite this bombastic claim, the credit ratings turned out to be flawed for three reasons. First, the rating agencies were paid by the issuers of the securities they evaluated rather than by the investors who relied on their evaluations and undertook investment decisions. The agencies were driven by the interests of the issuers rather than by the prospective earnings of the investors. Next, the assessments they provided were protected by the First Amendment's free speech guarantees. As a result, investors could not sue them for their faulty judgments, just as editorial writers cannot be taken to court for providing an informed guess about a likely event or a weather forecaster be hauled before a judge for predicting sunny skies when the weather turned out to be cloudy. And finally, the rating agency structure was dominated by a few stalwarts, namely Standard & Poor's, Moody's Investor Service, and Fitch Ratings, although a few small entrants had also ventured into the rating business.

What was the way out? Perhaps the rating agencies should be paid by risk-taking investors rather than by the issuers of bonds and securities. Could the free speech guarantee be abolished as well? On both these counts, lawmakers seemed hesitant to scrap the old arrangements. Nevertheless, as investors began picking up securities, new rating firms financed by investors and encouraged by the SEC began to appear starting in early 2009. Indeed, the SEC adopted a ruling in late September 2009 requiring that information about a structured financial security provided by its issuer to a rating agency of its choice be given to all rating agencies. The information would not be released to the public, but its availability to all rating agencies would create a level playing field.

Ultimately, congressional legislation went beyond the SEC ruling for preventing a repeat of the exuberant AAA ratings of questionable securities that were picked up by hedge fund investors and money managers.

Legislative Proposals for Reforming Rating Agencies

A 2006 law empowered the SEC to investigate the agencies, but SEC inspection hadn't been effective in curbing the reckless rating pronouncements of Standard & Poor's, Moody's, and Fitch, the three issuer-paid giants that controlled 85 percent of the securities market. Congress was not ready to overhaul the structure from top to bottom and replace it with a fee-financed, independent agency as proposed by Senator Christopher Dodd (D-CT). The proposal would once and for all do away with the conflict of interest problem of the current arrangements, in which issuers of bonds and securities paid rating agencies for their assessments. Ultimately, the Dodd-Frank Act required greater oversight of the agencies and more disclosure of their procedures. Investors, among them pension funds, would be allowed to file lawsuits against the agencies and claim damages for their negligence.

The earliest ruling passed by the SEC, as the stock market dived to a low reading of 6,600 in November 2008, related to the widespread practice of short selling, which we look at next.

V. Short Selling

Traders profit from short selling in a declining securities or currency market. It involves precise timing and accurate guesswork with regard to stock prices. A trader will instruct a broker (for payment of a fee) to borrow shares from their owner with the promise that the trader will return them to the owner at a precise date in the future. If the trader expects the stock price to fall, he sells the shares to an investor at the current, higher market price. If the stock price declines, the trader buys the shares from the market at the lower price and returns them to the original lender. His profit arises from the original high price at which he has sold the borrowed shares to the investor and the lower price at which he buys the shares to return them to the original lender. If the market moves up, however, he will incur losses.

The practice of short selling goes as far back as the seventeenth century. It contributed to the violent dive in the Dutch tulip market. It certainly contributed to the Great Depression. But did it lead to the sharp decline in the U.S. stock market in the final quarter of 2008? The SEC banned short selling on 799 financial stocks from September 19 until October 2. The agency feared that some companies might go out of business if stocks declined to excessively low levels. But the stock market was pummeled by a variety of factors, among them the negative impact of the toxic, subprime mortgage assets in U.S. banks. On the one hand, despite the SEC ban, financial stocks continued tumbling in the final quarter of 2008. On the other hand, the ban may have reduced the volume of stock trading via reduced liquidity without influencing the declining trend.[6]

But the SEC was determined to regulate the securities market and prevent short sellers from dumping shares at cut-rate prices. On February 24, 2010, it approved a rule in a narrow 3-2 vote along party lines. The rule would allow short selling if a group of stocks declined at least 10 percent in a single day and if the price of the sale exceeded the highest bid price nationally. The rule was expected to take effect in six months.

Three months later, on May 19, 2010, Germany's Chancellor Angela Merkel dropped a bombshell by announcing a unilateral ban on naked short selling in Germany.

German Ban of May 19, 2010, on Naked Short Selling

The ruling by Bafin, the German regulator, applied to Germany's 10 most important stocks, eurozone sovereign bonds, and credit default swaps. Traders were not allowed to sell these instruments if they had not borrowed them or made arrangements to borrow them. For example, Deutsche Bank would not allow an investor to acquire via a broker a stock or a sovereign bond in its balance sheet for short selling unless the broker had first arranged to borrow the stock from the bank. In announcing the ban, the chancellor said to the German parliament: "It is a question of survival. The euro is in danger. If the euro fails, then Europe fails. If we succeed, Europe will be stronger."[7]

Was the German leader swinging at a straw man? Was credit default swap (CDS) trading (in sovereign euro bonds) active in Frankfurt as it had been (with regard to subprime mortgage securities) in London and New York during its heyday toward the end of 2008? Did German financial institutions own significant amounts of Greek, Spanish, and Portuguese sovereign bonds? German institutional creditors accounted for a lion's share of European banks' total exposure to Greece at $272 billion, to Portugal at $242 billion, and to Spain at $852 billion. As for German CDS exposure, it was not big enough to matter. Bafin had declared on March 8, 2010, that evidence of speculators using CDS for trading in Greek sovereign debt was missing.

The unilateral German move perhaps was driven by political considerations. The chancellor needed the German parliament to approve Germany's contribution to the €750 ($955 billion) billion bailout announced on May 10. A tough preemptive positioning would dispel public perception that Germany was outmaneuvered, especially by France, into agreeing to the rescue of eurozone's weak economies. The German ban, which took effect on May 19, 2010, would extend till March 2011.

The SEC ban, by contrast, had lasted two weeks.

Beyond rating agencies and short selling, the SEC regulatory drive extended to three related issues with regard to stock trading. Examined in the next section, these issues involved high-frequency computerized stock trading, flash trading of stocks, and anonymous trading venues known as "dark pools."

VI. High-Frequency Trading, Flash Orders, and Dark Pools

High-frequency traders can access share order flows on their electronic trading platforms milliseconds before the wider market. As a result, they score an advantage over retail investors, who are less tech savvy. High-frequency trading (HFT) has benefits. It reduces the likelihood of human error by automating millions of complicated trading entries. By the same token, the application of a "fat finger" on a wrong key can magnify the impact of the error, as may have happened when the New York Stock Exchange dived precipitously on May 6, 2010, before sharply turning up a few minutes later.

Short of creating such a market-shattering event, high-frequency traders can outsmart their competitors by using their lightning-fast, computer-based trading for figuring out their rivals' price limits. Their speed enables them to take advantage of price spreads. In the process, they manage to extract minuscule amounts of profits via trading limited numbers of company shares between trading platforms at supersonic speed.

In the current decade, HFT has grown in the United States from an estimated 30 percent of the daily volume of stock trading to nearly 70 percent in 2009. Among the leading HFT platforms, BATS Trading and Direct Edge, both private, compete with New York Stock Exchange (NYSE) Euronext and Nasdaq OMX. Needless to say, HFT has been adopted not only by U.S. exchanges, but also by European venues, among them Chi-X Europe, Turquoise, and the European branch of BATS. Proprietary trading desks at major investment banks have also emerged as prominent HFT players.

Although HFT has grown in the equity market, it has lagged behind in the $6.9 trillion U.S. Treasury market. Big traders in the U.S. Treasury bonds have maintained their market share because, having embraced HFT technology, they have prevented large institutional investors from accessing the two big electronic trading platforms—ESpeed and Brokertec. Until Treasury bond trading is carried out on a common platform, it will lag behind the dominant role HFT plays in equity trading.

HFT clearly marks a massive technological advance. Trading on the floor of a stock exchange is old-fashioned and outdated. Computerized systems need constant upgrading to keep ahead of the pack so that share transactions can be executed speedily. HFT players, among them banks, have also provided liquidity in the U.S. equity market. As the latest phenomenon in outsmarting competitors via a technological advance, HFT is here to stay, requiring all equity players to keep up with these advances.

In fact, NYSE Euronext, the parent of New York Stock Exchange, is constructing a state-of-the-art computerized exchange site 30 miles outside London, in a hangar-shaped building large enough to accommodate three football fields. In adjacent halls, it will accommodate computer servers belonging to trading firms and banks in order for them to bring their orders to the exchange's matching engine.[8] Traders have to be located close to exchanges so that they can undertake high-frequency trading. But the co-location of exchanges and servers raises questions: Can small traders with shallow pockets gain access in such facilities? Will these facilities lack transparency? Will some servers get better access to certain locations in a data center?

Stock brokers and dealers currently report their transactions to the SEC, but the agency needed to track down large market participants in order for it to assess the impact of these large trade volumes on the market. In mid-April 2010, the SEC adopted new rules with a 5-0 vote for precisely identifying large traders and requiring them to report the very next day the price and volume data of transactions requested by the agency. A firm or an individual whose transactions in exchange-listed securities equal or exceed 2 million shares or $20 million in any calendar day or 20 million shares or $200 million in any calendar month is defined as a large trader.[9] Large traders must self-identify within three months and broker-dealers within six months of the final adoption of the rule.

More worrisome to the SEC, however, is the practice of flash orders.

Flash Orders

HFT computers scan billions of bits of market data for trading opportunities that may exist for mere fractions of a second. Suppose Alpha Pension Fund wants to diversify its equity holding by undertaking a stock purchase and contacts the trading desk exchange operator at Omega Bank. The exchange operator at Omega trading desk must ensure that he can carry out his client Alpha Fund's purchase order at the lowest price. Having received Alpha Fund's stock purchase order at a specified price, the exchange operator finds that an exchange offers the stock at a lower price; he will flash the price information to a few select traders a split second before sending it to the market, thus giving those traders an opportunity to trade at a favorable price for their clients. When used properly, flashing ensures that an investor such as Alpha Pension Fund acquires equity via an exchange operator at the best available price.

The opportunity of getting price information in a fraction of a second before the wider market also allows the high-frequency trader in Omega Bank to make a tidy profit via a flash order if he manages to acquire a sneak preview of share order flows and their prices on another exchange. A less favorable outcome for the Alpha Pension Fund is also possible. The Omega trading desk operator can buy up all the stocks at the better price and force the Alpha client to trade with him at a less favorable price. Having secured the price information, the Omega trading desk may even choose to reformulate the original contract with Alpha with a view to making a profit on a revised deal.

Any investor can acquire advanced HFT technology and place flash orders. Indeed, retail brokers, institutional investors, and investment firm proprietary desks have participated in the process over the years. Currently flash orders comprise 3 percent of total stock flows, and they are likely to increase. They can, however, be speculative, add to market volatility, and damage the operations of risk-averse investors who focus on steady and predictable returns. The regulators face a tough technological choice. If HFT is allowed, can flash orders, which it facilitates, be prevented?

By contrast, a clear regulatory case can be made for prohibiting the secretive trading venues known as dark pools.

Dark Pools

No investor should be prevented from accessing information about share quotations that some electronic trading venues may deliberately refuse to make public. These "dark pools" restrict open access to information about buy and sell data that should be available to all equity traders. They resemble nonstandardized, over-the-counter derivatives because a few electronic trading networks match buyers and sellers anonymously and effectively restrict entry. Dark pool operators reveal their trading information only ex post facto. Until then, potential investors remain in the dark about the liquidity and size of their trading operations.

Do dark pools mark an advance in stock trading? In the traditional arrangement, "block desks" at big firms help institutional investors complete big trades. These desk managers make phone calls to other big investors and traders and commit a firm's capital for inviting participation in the trade by these potential investors. High-speed computerized trading systems slice up such big orders. They also reduce trading costs, and they can reduce the risk of undue impact on the market from such big-volume, market-moving orders, provided the new proposal of the SEC for tracking large traders is implemented. Dark pools, which use these computerized systems, handle about 9.2 percent of U.S. stock trading, and the percentage is expected to rise.[10]

It would seem that the activity of stock trading has been overtaken by fast-moving technological innovations that confound the regulatory capabilities of policy makers who must decide between promoting or prohibiting new engineering products. In testimony on September 23, 2009, before the House Financial Services Committee, Paul Volcker,

"Let's never forget that the public's desire for transparency has to be balanced by our need for concealment."

(© Robert Mankoff / The New Yorker Collection / www.cartoonbank.com.)

Federal Reserve chairman from 1979 to 1987, had the following sugges-tion: "Maybe the best reform we could make is have a big tax on financial engineers so that they can't make up all these new things quite so rap-idly; because it's this highly complex, opaque financial engineering that gave a false sense of confidence."[11]

The SEC has proposed monitoring high-frequency trading and banning flash orders and dark pools because they create a two-tiered, inequitable market. High-frequency traders can access trading possibili-ties more quickly; as a result, they can submit or cancel their trading bids faster than long-term investors. There is also a strong case for opening up access to dark pools. The SEC has suggested that dark pools should dis-play their orders publicly if they handle at least 0.25 percent of a stock's daily volume.

Defenders of dark pools oppose the proposed regulations and argue that the regulations are motivated by the desire of stock exchanges to avoid healthy competition. "Additional disclosure requirements for dark pools would be like forcing investors to play poker with their cards face up."[12]

The policy deliberations and public debates on high-frequency trading, flash orders, and dark pools acquired renewed vigor following the stock market crash of May 6, 2010. Let's take a look.

VII. "Flash Crash" of May 6

On the afternoon of May 6, 2010, the Dow Jones Industrial Average fell 1,000 points within minutes and recovered equally fast. Some shares fell to as low as a penny before recouping their losses. Did the "flash crash" result from a computer error? Was it a technological problem? Did it result from a regulatory loophole? Could it have been human error?

Stock exchange officials and regulators agreed readily on measures to prevent another market plunge and awaited the probable causes of the May 6 episode following an inquiry. In the participants' opinion, the differing rules among the stock markets for temporarily halting or slowing transactions in individual stocks exacerbated the decline. Currently, a market-wide circuit breaker system records the movement of the Dow Jones. However, the New York Stock Exchange is the only exchange that operates with circuit breaker levels for individual stocks. Under the NYSE system, when a stock hits a circuit breaker level of "liquidity replenishment point," the exchange stops its electronic trading, and that particular stock goes into a slow operational mode. The brief interval allows a designated NYSE trader to specify an order at an alternative price. During the May 6 "flash crash," the NYSE implemented the current rule and forced some trading to migrate to alternative, less liquid outlets and worsened the situation. For example, Procter & Gamble stock was traded on the NYSE floor at $56 while it could be bought for $39.37 on Nasdaq, which continued to operate electronically.[13]

How might a crash similar to that of May 6 be prevented? The circuit breaker level for an individual stock for every exchange should be similar. According to the new SEC plan set to start in mid-June and operate for six months, circuit breakers on individual stocks of all exchanges would simultaneously kick in and prevent trading in these stocks if the stock price moved by 10 percent or more in a five-minute period.

In the meantime, technicians of the SEC and the Commodity Futures Trading Commission continued poring over more than 25 gigabytes of data to figure out what went wrong on the afternoon of May 6, 2010, when a stock traded at "$40 one minute, a penny the next, and $39 the next minute."[14] On October 1, the two regulators announced that the crash happened because Waddell & Reed Financial, a mutual fund located in Overland Park, Kansas, was hedging against the risk of a market downturn. It used powerful computer algorithms for selling 75,000 futures contracts worth $4.1 billion within 20 minutes in an electronic transaction that would normally take five hours. Many of the contracts were bought by high-frequency traders who subsequently began to sell them aggressively when they realized that they had bought excessive futures positions. The high-frequency buying and selling, which lasted several minutes, wiped nearly $1 trillion off the value of U.S. shares on May 6. The federal regulators, however, declared that the high-speed transaction, although unusual, was legitimate.

High-frequency trading, flash orders, and dark pools raise challenges for regulators who must steer them in desirable directions without altogether banning them. The regulatory problem with these activities arises from the fact that they tend to be opaque and noncompetitive. Stock trading deals transacted via flash orders and transmitted to a limited number of clients, especially in dark pools of participants, raise issues of nontransparency and noncompetitiveness. Rather than ban these activities, regulators need to prescribe legal norms and investigative procedures for dealing with the potential for abuse. The SEC's evolving regulatory standards are a step in the right direction.

The regulatory agencies have also embarked on the momentous task of formulating rules with regard to the activities of hedge fund managers, derivative users, and rating agencies. The assignment of converting the legislative guidelines of the Dodd-Frank Act into explicit rules will perhaps prove less demanding than the actual task of implementing the rules. The regulatory staff will need to act as vigilant watchdogs and combine legal expertise with technical know-how in order to stay ahead of the activities of risk-prone deal makers in the financial sector.

6

U.S. and EU Regulatory Proposals
How Strict? How Cooperative?

Early in June 2009, Mervyn King, governor of the Bank of England, had emphasized the need for a sound regulatory system for dealing with the global financial crisis in these words: "The costs of this crisis are not to be measured simply in terms of its impact on public finances, the destruction of wealth, and the number of jobs lost. They are also to be seen in the lost trust in the financial sector among other parts of our economy."[1]

Equally concerned, the chairman of the Senate Banking Committee, Christopher Dodd (D-CT), presented to the committee on March 15, 2010, his bill for overhauling the U.S. financial system with an ominous warning: "The stakes are far too high and the American people have suffered far too greatly for us to fail in this effort. . . . This legislation will not stop the next crisis from coming. No legislation can, of course. But by creating a 21st-century regulatory structure for our 21st-century economy, we can equip coming generations with the tools to deal with that crisis and to avoid the kind of suffering we have seen in this country."[2]

The U.S. regulatory proposals sought not only to restore the broken financial system, but also to prevent the recurrence of similar destructive episodes in the future. Public trust in the financial sector, a tough call, could follow in time.

Two landmark pieces of congressional legislation for overhauling the U.S. regulatory framework of eight decades were introduced, one by Representative Barney Frank (D-MA) on December 18, 2009, in the House of Representatives and the other by Senator Dodd on March 15, 2010, eventually for consideration by the Senate. These proposals, passed by the House and the Senate, were debated in the joint Senate-House conference committee, where after vigorous debating and some horse trading, they were adopted in the early hours of Friday, June 25, 2010, and presented to Congress for its approval. Designed to ward off the next financial crisis, the Dodd-Frank Wall Street Reform and Consumer Protection Act was signed by President Barack Obama on July 21. It was hailed as the most sweeping overhaul of the financial system since the Great Depression.

The legislation was pushed by the president and Democrats in Congress and represented almost 18 months of fierce congressional debates along party lines and of intense lobbying by Wall Street bankers. As the Dodd-Frank proposals made their way through the legislative process, they sought to tackle five regulatory issues.

First, how can excessive risk taking by financial institutions—among them, bank holding companies, investment banks, and insurance companies—be reined in? Second, how can the newfangled financial instruments—among them, over-the-counter derivatives and credit default swaps—be regulated? Third, how can consumers as holders of mortgages and credit cards be effectively protected? Fourth, should these regulatory functions be concentrated in a single agency or spread among several regulators? Finally, how can the rules be made uniform across global agencies so that regulatory similarity and open access to participants in a given activity, such as insurance provision and derivative trading, can be ensured?

Before discussing their detailed provisions and their ultimate configuring at the hands of U.S. lawmakers, I provide a general outline of the relevant issues and a flavor of the energetic debates and the intermittent legal provisions that drove the decision making. These relate to the capital adequacy requirements (including the series of Basel Committee norms) by the too-big-to-fail banks; the inflammatory issue of bankers' compensation; restrictions on the ultra-advanced instruments, such as over-the-counter derivatives and credit default swaps that bankers employ for leveraging their financial choices; and finally, the likely contours of the Consumer Financial Protection Agency proposed by President Obama for safeguarding the interests of American consumers.

The regulatory momentum in the European Union relating to these issues was slow and dissonant, although EU leaders were aware that the existing regulatory arrangements called for a review and revision. The helter-skelter EU process was further affected by the Greek sovereign debt crisis, which took a serious turn in early 2010. It demanded the urgent attention of EU leaders and stretched their negotiating maneuverability and resource capabilities for rescuing Greece and the vulnerable economies of neighboring Portugal and Spain. The regulatory stance of the leaders of Germany—which, as the strongest economy, was called upon to contribute a lion's share of the rescue package—was stricter than that of France and Britain.

Ultimately, the Basel Committee's capital requirements were softened and their application to the 27 participating countries postponed until 2018. In early July, the European Parliament imposed strict rules on bonus payments to bankers, but the European Commission, the rule-making body, signaled a softer stance on rules with regard to nonfinancial over-the-counter derivatives. The EU approach on regulating hedge funds operating in the region represented the regulators' concern for safeguarding them from the overly competitive U.S. counterparts. Overall, the EU regulatory progression, in contrast to the decisive U.S. approach, was slow; it reflected the problems faced by the regulators of devising a consensus among 27 EU members that lacked the political cohesiveness of a nation-state.

The reform of the banking system, described in the next section, formed the core of the U.S. regulatory proposals.

I. The Structure of the U.S. Banking System

The U.S. banking system consists of commercial banks, investment banks, and bank holding companies. They differ with regard to the regulatory arrangements that seek to limit their excessive risk taking.

Commercial Banks, Investment Banks, and Bank Holding Companies

U.S. commercial banks receive deposits from households and businesses and extend loans to them. These banks are required to keep adequate cash reserves for covering their deposit liabilities, which are guaranteed, up to a limit, by the Federal Deposit Insurance Corporation. The banks can access the Federal Reserve's emergency lending facilities.

Investment banks raise capital by selling stocks and offering private equity to investors in exchange for a stake in their company. They trade stocks and bonds as well as commodity and currency options in order to make profit. They alert companies about profitable mergers and acquisitions and advise them about the timing and size of public offerings.

Unlike commercial banks, they cannot borrow from the Federal Reserve. As a result, they are not subject to the Fed's prudential regulatory oversight. The major difference between U.S. commercial banks and investment banks arises from the manner in which they are regulated: U.S. commercial banks are required by law to keep adequate capital backing against their deposit liabilities. Investment banks are monitored by the Securities and Exchange Commission (SEC) for ensuring the adequacy of their self-monitoring devices. These banks trade in securities in order to make a profit, but the securities market can be volatile.

Investment banks were not alone in undertaking outlandish risks. Concerns about regulating the insurance business became active when American Insurance Group (AIG) needed a bailout of $180 billion in September 2008. Its over-leveraged noninsurance financial unit, which had undertaken risky investments, needed a quick and massive rescue. An insurer needs to keep adequate capital, a solvency margin, in order to forestall unexpected losses in its investments and surges in claims by its clients, for whom it holds insurance policies. The solvency margin must also cover the activities of its noninsurance business. At the same time, these solvency requirements must be uniform for cross-country insurers, such as MetLife Inc., in order to prevent a systemic crisis. A meeting of the International Association of Insurance Supervisors held in Taiwan from June 24 to June 26, 2009, began deliberating these issues in the hope that they could be sorted out in a few years, sooner than later.

With the passage of the Gramm-Leach-Bliley Act of 1999, investment banks could acquire commercial banks as well as insurance companies and become bank holding companies. In late September 2008, Goldman Sachs and Morgan Stanley, until then investment banks, were allowed by the Federal Reserve to convert their banking and financial operations into bank holding companies. Both sought financial strength and funding access by accepting stricter Fed oversight. Both joined the top guns in the exclusive list of about 50 U.S. bank holding companies, among them Bank of America, JPMorgan Chase, Citigroup, and Wells Fargo.

Over time, these bank holding companies, among them the leading financial conglomerates, had become too big to fail. The 10 largest financial institutions held 10 percent of U.S. financial assets in 1990. Their share was greater than 60 percent in 2008 at the onset of the financial crisis. They also took excessive risks because they were inadequately regulated as they operated with complex credit instruments.

Too-Big-to-Fail U.S. Banks

In short, the financial crisis was marked by excessive risk taking by large global banks that combined investment and commercial banking under a single holding umbrella. Its destructive sweep raised the question of whether these banks had become too big. They were so big that they could not be allowed to fail without having a destructive impact on the U.S. financial system. A primary reason for the emergence of such banking giants in the United States was the abolition in 1999 of the Glass-Steagall Act of 1933 (officially called the Banking Act of 1933), which separated banks either as commercial banks or investment banks according to their business, allowed the Federal Reserve to regulate interest rates on savings accounts in banks, and prohibited a bank holding company from owning a financial company. All of these provisions were repealed. The Federal Deposit Insurance Corporation, which guaranteed customers' deposits with commercial banks, was spared the legislative scalpel.

Over time, U.S. bank holding companies' proprietary divisions (which I define later) began trading complex assets, such as credit default swaps, that were backed by shaky mortgage-based securities. Among the large holding companies, these assets turned out to have inadequate capital backing.

How can the recurrence of the destructive impact of the too-big-to-fail U.S. banks, which underestimated the risks of their contaminated assets, be prevented?

Reining in Big Banks

First, how much capital should these banks be required to keep as cushions in relation to their risky assets? How high should such prudential management enforcement go? Wouldn't excessive backing cut into bank profit? If banks borrow short term and invest in hard-to-sell, nonfungible assets, they should be made to hold more capital. They should also follow pro-cyclical capital backing by holding more capital in good times in order to be able to absorb losses in lean times.

The need for safe capital backing was acknowledged even before the onset of the current crisis. The Basel Committee on Banking Supervision, consisting of central banks and supervisory agencies of 10 countries in 1988, created the Basel I Capital Accord in that year. The accord set forth an international definition of the minimum amount of capital that banks should hold in order to cover their risky assets. The details are presented in the next section.

II. Basel Committee Capital Requirements

The accord defined tier 1, or core, capital to include shareholder equity and declared reserves of banks. Tier 2, or supplementary, capital included all other capital items, such as bank investments and long-term (maturity of five years or more) bonds held by banks as creditors. Next, the committee classified assets according to their risk levels. For example, gold and government securities of the U.S. Treasury and the Organisation for Economic Co-operation and Development carried zero risk.

By contrast, an unsecured loan (not covered with adequate collateral) made by a bank to a nonbank would require 100 percent capital backing by the bank. Overall, the Basel I Accord of 1988 required a capital provision by banks at 8 percent of their risky assets. This original design was later replaced by Basel II, which modified the calculation of risk weights.

The U.S. capital adequacy ratios prescribed by the Federal Reserve on the eve of the current crisis modified Basel I norms and added another leverage-capital requirement.

Federal Reserve Capital Requirement Guidelines

These leverage-capital requirements accounted for the off-balance-sheet exposure of U.S. banks to the newfangled credit instruments of credit derivatives involving currency and commodity contracts. Under these rules, a bank holding company must hold a tier 1 capital ratio of at least 4 percent, a combined tier 1 and tier 2 capital of at least 8 percent, and an additional leverage ratio of at least 4 percent in order to be adequately capitalized against counterparty risks in bank assets. When U.S. banks received Trouble Asset Relief Program (TARP) bailout funding, the Treasury defined tier 1 capital to include bank equity of common and preferred stock.

As the crisis unfolded, the pronouncements on bank capital requirements became more stringent. Alan Greenspan, former Fed chairman, recommended a mandatory backing provision of 15 percent. Ben Bernanke, the current chairman, told the House Financial Services Committee on October 1, 2009, that such a cushion was necessary not only for preventing possible losses in banks, but also for penalizing them for becoming too big to fail. In other words, they should be required to save themselves out of their own ready cash rather than with taxpayers' money.

The Basel Committee, currently composed of central bankers and regulators from 27 countries, got into the act as well. It proposed new norms of capital adequacy for possible adoption by banks in 2010 when the impact of the crisis would settle down.

Basel Committee Provisional Rules on Capital Adequacy for Possible Adoption in 2010

On December 14, 2009, the Basel Committee put forward, in an ambitious 82-page report, a set of standards that would ensure banks keeping sufficient cash and liquid assets to enable them to surmount future financial turmoil.

The report provided definitions and rules. The definitions related to capital adequacy, overall leverage, and crisis-combating liquidity ratios. First, the capital adequacy, tier 1 capital would have to consist only of common shares and retained earnings. And banks must disclose these components of capital to ensure the transparency of the capital base. This provision seemed to rule out Bernanke's proposal for bonds that a bank could convert into contingent convertible (CoCo) common stocks if its capital adequacy ratio came under pressure. According to Basel standards, these CoCo bonds would constitute a questionable hybrid capital backing.

But capital adequacy was not all. Beyond that requirement, the committee also introduced a *global* leverage ratio that would take into account counterparty risks in a bank's assets. The fulfillment of the *overall* leverage ratio of equity to assets implied that banks must build up countercyclical capital buffers by setting aside reserves in good times that they could use in bad times.

Even that was not enough. What safeguards must banks undertake in order to survive a crisis without a taxpayer bailout and what safeguards would resolve the moral hazard issue? According to the committee, banks must keep enough cash and easy-to-sell assets to be able to continue functioning during a 30-day financial crisis.

In a wait-and-see attitude, the Basel Committee said it would analyze the likely impact of these standards on bank balance sheets during 2010, then issue detailed requirements at the end of 2010, and gradually phase them out by 2012 as the global financial situation improved. In other words, it did not want to overreact as a global financial watchdog by prescribing capital requirements that could smother the financial recovery. The final norms of capital requirements (discussed later in the chapter) were announced by the committee in September 2010.

Returning to U.S. regulators, the next question beyond capital adequacy in bank balance sheets consisted of sorting out too-big-to-fail bank bailouts in extreme circumstances without creating issues of moral hazard. If banks undertake hazardous risks and if they are bailed out by taxpayers, they successfully pass the moral obligation of their rescue to outsiders. The next section talks about how such morally hazardous behavior can be prevented.

III. Big Bank Bailouts and Moral Hazard

Where does one draw the line in bailing out too-big-to-fail banks? Should the bailout process focus more on larger, interconnected banks out of concern that their failure would have a disproportionate impact on the financial system as a whole? This raised the question of a bailout strategy. Paul Volcker, former Fed chairman and member of President Obama's group of economic advisors, suggested early on that commercial banks, which held public deposits, deserved to be rescued in extreme circumstances. Bernanke, however, noted that banks should be prevented from becoming too big to fail to begin with. They could be required to hold contingent capital. The bonds they sold for raising cash would automatically turn into common stock if they faced trouble. This provision would expose bondholders to more risk because as holders of common stock (instead of bonds), they would be the last to be paid from bank assets. Banks would cease to be too big to fail. In early 2010, Volcker would propose, with President Obama's backing, the Volcker rule (discussed later in the chapter), which would involve a virtual breakup of bank holding companies.

The U.S. Treasury and the House Financial Services Committee (under the chairmanship of Representative Barney Frank) proposed less severe legislation that would create a resolution authority for winding down a too-big-to-fail company on the verge of collapse. The Treasury could identify a large interconnected company as systemically risky, and the Federal Reserve could force such a company to sell divisions. If that failed, the government could seize it, dismiss the directors, and wipe out the shareholders. The proposed legislation would give the Federal Reserve the authority to force a firm to sell or transfer assets or terminate activities if its size or scope directly or indirectly threatened financial stability. Rather than break up all bank holding companies as suggested by the Volcker rule, the House Financial Services Committee proposed to dissolve only those too-big-to-fail units that could be identified as financially risky.

In sum, these proposals (excluding the Volcker rule) related to limiting the size of banks by requiring them to keep the correct amount and appropriate kind of capital for covering their risky assets. They also sought to break up too-big-to-fail companies that were on the verge of a financial breakdown. Such companies should be required to self-immolate for their extravagant risk taking, rather than be saved with taxpayer bounty. The Wall Street Reform and Consumer Protection Act (hereafter the House Financial Regulatory Reform Bill) passed by the House of Representatives on December 18, 2009, contained provisions for dealing with these issues.

One issue surfaced prominently as the process of establishing regulatory provisions moved forward: How far should the provisions go in preempting risky behavior by Wall Street bankers and in protecting U.S. taxpayers from future bailouts of too-big-to-fail banks? How could the profligate bankers be prevented from going overboard without unduly curtailing their entrepreneurial energy and risk taking in the interest of promoting American business? What did Lloyd Blankfein, the Goldman Sachs CEO, mean when he declared that he was doing "God's work"? Was he undertaking productive financial transactions in order to revive the economy by greasing the wheels of commerce and trade? Having been bailed out by the taxpayers, didn't Goldman Sachs take advantage of the Fed's easy money policy and accumulate profit by trading in currencies and commodities? Did such activity provide anything beneficial to the unemployed?

Was it productive to the U.S. economy in a recession? Shouldn't such financial units be reduced in size and forced out of the habit of excessive risk taking and habitual entitlement? Millions of Americans faced the traumas of lost jobs and foreclosed homes and pondered the unequal impact of the financial meltdown. Why should the financial wizards receive sumptuous bonuses while ordinary mortals took the consequences of the economic fallout the beneficiaries of those bonuses had themselves unleashed? Perhaps fate would mete out adequate punishment to those who had ruined them. But Americans didn't want to rely on fate to deal with future offenders. Americans wanted to rely on laws and regulations.

On January 22, 2010, President Obama announced proposals, formulated by Volcker, that sent tremors through Wall Street bank holding companies such as Goldman Sachs and JPMorgan Chase. They could borrow money from the Federal Reserve and accept retail deposits just as commercial banks do. But they must, therefore, separate their proprietary and private equity operations from commercial banking. The next section takes a closer look at these proposals.

IV. The Volcker Proposals

What are these proprietary trading activities and private equity holdings that the Volcker rule sought to decapitate?

Proprietary trading involves deal making by bank traders in stocks and bonds, currencies, and commodities via derivative contracts or other instruments *with the bank's own money*. Banks employ multiple desks of traders who undertake proprietary trading solely with a view to making profit. The traders may also undertake these transactions on behalf of a bank's client, in which case the client's cash would finance the deal. The distinction between proprietary versus nonproprietary trading may turn out to be ambiguous, but generally, bank traders would tend to be more careful and less prone to risk taking with a client's cash. Goldman Sachs and Deutsche Bank earn a significant share of their profits via proprietary trading.

A private equity unit in a bank holding company may track an equity deal and represent a company that is offered for sale. It may facilitate an initial public offering or a subsequent equity or debt transaction. Equity trading by bank holding companies involves in-depth market research and trading expertise in their equity divisions. They have direct access to the trading floor of a stock exchange. The Volcker rule would allow these nonproprietary trading and equity deals by banks for clients, but not for themselves. If bank holding companies want to continue proprietary trading and private equity operations on their own account, they must give up their banking license. They would lose the special privileges of a bank. "Don't expect the support you would get from being a bank within the club of insured deposits and access to the Federal Reserve and all the loving attention you get as a bank organization," Volcker said.[3]

There was a further catch. Banks that chose to become "nonbanks" would still be subject to regulation and oversight. They would be required to maintain an adequate capital cushion. If a nonbank got into trouble, it would not be saved. A robust resolution trust authority would resolve the moral hazard problem by taking it over and closing it. The resolution process for nonbanks would be "euthanasia rather than life support."[4]

No less than five ex–Treasury Secretaries and several elder statesmen of Wall Street, north of age 70, with solid pedigrees in finance and money making—among them John S. Reed, former chief of Citigroup, and William Donaldson, former head of the SEC—supported the Volcker

(Ingram Pinn / *Financial Times*.)

proposals. But, the bankers asked, did the president go overboard and endorse a set of extreme ideas with a view to placating angry voters in an election year?

As for bankers' compensation, the Volcker proposals did not specify explicit rules. Volcker's views on the issue were clear, however. "I do think that the compensation practices particularly in finance have gotten out of touch and created incentives that are not very helpful. . . . They've gotten obscenely large in terms of the discrepancies between the average worker and the leaders."[5]

The financial turmoil did bring out in the open the issue of Wall Street executive compensation. Did they manage to be rewarded disproportionately for their risk taking? Here and now, how might they be punished for going overboard and the American public be assuaged? Let's explore this issue.

V. Should Government Regulate
Wall Street Executive Compensation?

The administration wanted to send a message to American taxpayers that it was determined to rein in executive compensation of the bailout beneficiaries without subjecting others (who had repaid the bailout money) to similar draconian pay restrictions. These compensation directives were aimed at resolving a short-term political predicament rather than handling the critical issue of a tax system that could be devised for regulating Wall Street executive compensation. Nor did they deal with the long-term issue of bridging the gap between the rich and the poor via an appropriate tax policy.

Thus, the compensation restrictions announced by pay czar Kenneth Feinberg in early November 2009 would apply to 25 top earners at seven companies—Citigroup, Bank of America, AIG, General Motors, Chrysler, and the two automakers' financing units. Their compensation would be cut on average by 50 percent and their perks limited to $25,000. Any executive seeking perks, such as a country club membership, a private plane, or a limousine, in excess of that amount would have to get the necessary permission from the government. And get this—executives of AIG, which was bailed out with $180 billion of taxpayer money, would receive $200,000 each in compensation. In addition, bonuses promised to AIG employees must be cut back or postponed to a future date.

With such cutbacks enforced with a sledgehammer, why would talented executives want to work for these companies? Why would the top 25 executives tighten their belts if they could leave their current employment or go to an offshore company or another private business? Would a junior manager end up receiving more compensation than the boss? But the public was angry and the wayward bosses had to be punished.

As for the too-big-to-fail banks, including laggards such as Citigroup and Bank of America that had finally repaid TARP funding toward the end of 2009, the government was left with making nonbinding suggestions. Their compensation practices should be regulated by independent committees of boards and shareholders. With regard to top executive compensation, Wall Street banks would be left to voluntary restraint and discretion of bank directors despite public fury directed against them. The House Financial Regulatory Reform Bill also settled for the in-house monitoring of bankers' compensation. Indeed, some banks were voluntarily falling in line. In early December 2009, Goldman Sachs announced that it would pay to its 30 executives bonuses in the form of stocks that were locked up for five years. Such a move, if adopted by the banking sector, could generate three positive benefits. Bonus payment in medium-term equity can be linked to recipient performance. It can free up capital in the bank balance sheet. If equity valuation declines as a result, bank investors will take an interest in executive compensation policies. Overall, bankers could accept the approach as inflicting the least misery for their aberrant behavior.

From early on, the U.S. banking industry was poised to confront the regulatory proposals and moderate their restrictive impact. While acknowledging the need for capital-to-asset backing, the bankers wanted to be left alone on the issue of size and method of remuneration, more so because while the measures were being debated by lawmakers, big banks had repaid almost all of the TARP funding they had received from the government by the end of 2009. They had begun raising capital from private investors.

There was, however, a constitutional issue with regard to the enforcement of compensation limits by the pay czar. When Congress approved TARP, it authorized the Treasury Secretary to require that each TARP recipient meet appropriate standards of compensation. In order to carry out this assignment, the Treasury promulgated an emergency rule that waived the standard requirement for a public comment period. It created a special office for setting compensation standards and appointed Feinberg to this position without Senate confirmation. But worried bankers and company bosses asked: Was the process constitutional? Was the pay czar a properly appointed U.S. officer? Weren't his decisions unconstitutional? The House Financial Regulatory Reform Bill provided a reassuring signal on the compensation issue. On December 18, it adopted a compensation policy for banks that would be monitored by board managers and shareholders.

The U.S. regulatory concerns went beyond capital adequacy rules with regard to banks' investment activity, the moral hazard issue of salvaging too-big-to-fail, over-leveraged banks, and bankers' compensation. The debates also faced the issue of the factors leading to the origins of the crisis. Shouldn't the regulatory system prevent the creation of dubious assets with shaky valuations at the source by ensuring that mortgage instruments, which are subsequently securitized in complex derivatives, are sound to begin with? In that case, should insurance companies and mortgage banks be regulated? What about hedge funds outside and inside investment banks and insurance companies, which trade in a variety of assets? Ultimately, why not regulate the activity of stock trading itself, such as over-the-counter derivative transactions?

Administration policy makers and congressional legislators needed to sort out issues relating to derivative traders and hedge fund managers who were acknowledged as permanent actors with debatable roles in the U.S. financial system. Let's see what this involved.

VI. Derivatives and Hedge Funds

Derivative operatives can create perverse incentives for hedging an instrument and create a potential default for a company that holds a significant stock of these assets.

How does one regulate the global $680 trillion over-the-counter derivative market? As I explained in the previous chapter, over-the-counter derivatives consist of swap-based transactions that aim at hedging against changes in interest rates, currency values, commodity prices, and debt obligations of companies (which they may not be able to carry out). Should these transactions be shifted to public venues such as the stock exchanges? Should there be a data warehouse to make the trades more transparent? Should the contracts be standardized? How can contracts that involve a variety of products be standardized?

In mid-May 2009, Treasury Secretary Tim Geithner suggested that over-the-counter deals be separated in standardized and nonstandardized, or customized, categories. The former would be traded on regulated exchanges and be policed for their risk-prone attributes. By contrast, the nonstandardized products would be kept separate from public trading or general regulation. Details of their transactions would be recorded on a "trade repository" only for limited availability to the public.

On October 17, the House Financial Services Committee approved a bill suggesting an overhaul of over-the-counter derivatives. These detailed provisions helped the committee recommend derivative regulation norms for final adoption in the House Financial Regulatory Reform Bill of December 18.

The House Committee Provisional Overhaul of Over-the-Counter Derivative Trading

The bill divided derivatives into standardized and nonstandardized categories and large and small swaps. It also dealt with newly emerging derivative deals that were traded bilaterally. The standardized swaps, big or small, could be traded on a swaps exchange or an electronic exchange. Take a standardized contract that was accepted and executed by a large participant—a bank, for example—along with a number of small participants, against a significant counterparty, along with a number of smaller counterparties that were also party to the contract. The participants and counterparties would be clearly demarcated with regard to their financial obligations. If there were losses, the participants might default on their contractual obligations. The participants would therefore be required to post margins that were large enough to guarantee that the central counterparty would be able to carry out its commitments to all the participating counterparties. If there were losses, the participants would lose their margins. The details of the transactions would be reported to a central registry and their aggregate numbers would be available to the public.

Participants who were not large swap players and who traded in standardized products would be exempted from margin requirements. But if they undertook big and systemically risky ventures, they could be designated as big participants by the SEC and the Commodity Futures Trading Commission.

Next, large nonstandardized contracts, which were traded bilaterally, would have to be reported to a registry that would not be publicly available. They would require large margins.

Finally, small nonstandardized contracts would require smaller margins but would have to be reported to a confidential registry.

Bankers who normally undertook large transactions were opposed en masse to the standardization provision because it would subject them to large margins and would curb innovation and product diversity. Traders, investors, and banks would lose the incentive to undertake profit-making deals. Bankers also desired that the market, rather than regulators, decide margin requirements for newly emerging products. Their details should also be made public.

By contrast, the House Committee's bill recommended that the newly emerging deals that were slightly nonstandard deals and were traded bilaterally should be reported to a registry without being made public. Regulators would prescribe margins for them as they appeared. But according to bankers, it would be appropriate to publicize the details of these newly emerging products and let the market decide their margin requirement and their risk potential.

As a last resort, over-the-counter derivative traders would choose to take their activity to locations with the least restrictions. According to a London banker, "only 25 percent of all OTC trading actually happens in

America. . . . So we don't think what Geithner says is going to change anything for us . . . and even if [Brussels] does the same, activity will shift to Singapore or Switzerland instead."[6] While the banking industry was girding for battle, others insisted that no private derivative should be allowed "to grow in the dark." "For decades, the American financial markets attracted capital because investors believed they were getting the information they needed. That faith has been shaken. . . . All derivatives, exchange traded or private, must be in the sunlight."[7]

The final shape of the derivative legislation awaited congressional decision. Some provisions of the House Committee draft with regard to derivative trading were simplified and softened in the House Financial Regulatory Reform Bill.

The debates over regulating hedge funds were arguably less intense.

Hedge Fund Regulation

To begin with, were hedge funds responsible for the initiation of the crisis? U.S. and European policy makers agreed that hedge funds could not be held responsible for the crisis onset. And yet the U.S. and European approaches for regulating hedge fund activity differed. U.S. hedge fund managers tended to accept proposals for registering hedge funds and collecting information about their trading activities as long as the information remained with a regulator. Such registration would imply that the fund activity could be periodically inspected regarding its borrowing leverage and its investment holdings.

A specific issue related to the rights of investors for withdrawing their cash from a hedge fund. Should hedge funds be allowed to bar frantic investors from withdrawing their cash from the fund? In the second half of 2008, hedge fund managers clamped down on such withdrawals because they would have involved a rapid sale of hard-to-sell assets at prices so low that the process could have harmed the fortunes of the remaining investors. Should a regulator decide the optimum timing of such release of funds and resolve the conflict between the business interests of a hedge fund manager and the monetary calculation of an anxious client?

As discussed in the next section, of all the issues relating to the overhaul of the U.S. financial sector, the Obama administration was most concerned about regulating mortgage and credit card activities with the explicit goal of protecting the American consumer. These were guided by three considerations.

VII. Protecting the American Consumer

First, the American consumer must be protected from the overarching reach of bankers and insurers, credit card issuers, and mortgage brokers. Second, the borrowing and lending must be regulated not only for the welfare of the consumers, but also for the health of the financial institutions. If consumers are protected, then the financial institutions become safe and sound. Finally, the new regime should not stifle innovation and limit consumer choice.

Above all, an agency has to be responsible for monitoring both the health of individual institutions and the systemic risks of the system as a whole. In fact, Congress and the Federal Reserve had adopted regulatory measures with these goals, but the measures constituted as-of-the-moment steps rather than a comprehensive design.

Interim Measures for Consumer Protection

In early 2009, the Federal Reserve issued new regulations on mortgage and credit card policies. Congress had also passed a law with specific features that required banks and credit card companies to give 45 days' notice before they could change interest rates. It also prohibited them from raising rates on existing balances unless a cardholder was delinquent by 60 days on minimum payments.

These were still stop-gap measures, but they got the presidential seal of approval on May 22 when President Obama signed the Credit Card Act of 2009. The new rules relating to personal checking accounts and credit cards were designed to protect Americans by limiting interest rate increases especially on current balances (unless the cardholder was at least 60 days behind in payment) and by requiring card issuers to disclose more information to cardholders. The issuers would have to provide more information in the monthly billing statements relating to the terms and conditions the cardholder must fulfill. The new rules would become effective in February 2010. Not surprisingly, card issuers raced to slip new practices into customer contracts. They closed old accounts, introduced variable interest rates, and slapped on annual fees.

Banks that provided checking accounts came up with novel ideas as well. Perhaps customers should be allowed to choose from options. Perhaps they should receive interest on checking accounts or be allowed to freely use another bank's automated teller machine or be exempted from the minimum balance requirement in their checking accounts. By contrast, a bank might become more restrictive by abolishing free checking completely, raising fees on safe deposit boxes, and charging customers for instructing a bank to stop payment on a check. Community banks tended to be more indulgent toward their checking account customers than the big banks, which imposed fees and restrictive practices.

The final onslaught on the "unfair and deceptive" practices of the $1 trillion credit card industry happened on December 18 when three federal regulatory agencies, the Federal Reserve Board of Governors, the Office of Thrift Supervision, and the National Credit Union Administration, approved the regulatory measures of the earlier enactments. They limited interest rate hikes on past balances by cardholders and required transparent disclosure of cardholding terms; they sought to eliminate several "gotcha" practices of card issuers that cost consumers millions of dollars in fees and interest charges.

The new rules were set to become effective on July 1, 2010. Several card issuers had voluntarily begun falling in line. Their monthly card statements disclosed key terms explicitly. They provided notices of 45 days rather than 15 days in order to alter borrowing and settlement provisions of their cards. While angry customers filed a record number of suggestions with the Federal Reserve and sought relief from mountains of credit card debt, the banking industry reacted by arguing that the measures would hinder a quick response by the issuers to rein in extravagant borrowers and might require some to raise interest charges. They also worried about the availability of credit to American consumers.

The Consumer Financial Protection Agency proposed by the Obama administration would be charged with enforcing credit card and checking account regulations. Its mandate would extend beyond these rules to include regulating the interaction between the suppliers of credit for home ownership and autos and the borrowers.

The Consumer Financial Protection Agency

The administration sent Congress a 150-page document on June 30, 2009, with proposals for setting up a consumer financial protection agency with a threefold focus on regulating mortgages by prohibiting risky loans, monitoring the activities of financial institutions with respect to consumer finance, and protecting credit card customers. The overall purpose was to protect consumers. It would ensure comprehensive authority over banks, credit card companies, credit-granting businesses, and independent, nonbank mortgage companies. The agency would set standards for mortgages. It would restrict mortgages that included hidden fees or contained exorbitant fines for delinquent borrowers. It would allow consumers to opt out of riskier loans. Next, the mortgage documents should be clear and easily comprehensible. At the same time, a state could pass laws that might be stricter. Finally, a data-based agency would track the accumulated mortgage information with a view to forestalling the advent of a subprime mortgage crisis. The agency would also enforce the provision of the law passed by Congress that prohibited banks from arbitrarily raising interest rates. These proposals were opposed not only by big banks such as JPMorgan Chase and Wells Fargo, but also by regional and local banks, all of whom could influence lawmakers via their intense lobbying. Independent mortgage brokers opposed them as well. Among the supporters were Democrats in Congress and consumer groups.

Debates Relating to the Agency in the House Financial Services Committee

The House Financial Services Committee, chaired by Representative Frank, started debating the proposed agency on October 14. Frank had already made a few changes in the proposal since its White House submission in June. He had removed the provision in the bill that would have restricted mortgage brokers to offering customers only a simple 30-year fixed mortgage, the plain vanilla. Brokers could offer exotic products. He had also gotten rid of the reasonableness standard, which would have compelled bankers to ensure that their potential customers clearly understood the mortgage they were undertaking and, more importantly, that they could afford the mortgage. The banks were now absolved of that responsibility.

The agency would be financed by nonbank financial institutions. But didn't these institutions contribute to the housing bubble?

Not surprisingly, the provisions of the agency bill were further diluted in response to pressures from the banking lobby consisting of community bankers sprawled across congressional districts in the country. On October 10, the president himself urged Congress to pass the legislation. He also announced his intention of giving a major role to state regulators and prosecutors for policing financial companies. But bank lobbyists would prefer a federal policing agency with lower standards in order to successfully preempt more rigorous standards by state regulators.

Along with the rapid unfolding of proposals for regulating the financial institutions and the instruments (such as derivatives) through which they operated and the proposed launching of a Consumer Financial Protection Agency, the question of assigning the regulatory functions to specific governmental agencies gathered momentum as well.

The next section deals with questions about the new structure. In particular, will the Consumer Financial Protection Agency require new institutional infrastructure? Will a single agency be in charge of its functions overall? Who should regulate credit derivatives and other complex devices?

VIII. The New Institutional Infrastructure

The pre-crisis regulatory powers with regard to consumer responsibilities, including mortgages, were vested in the Federal Reserve, which supervised bank holding companies; the Federal Deposit Insurance Corporation, which safeguarded households' deposits with commercial banks; and the Comptroller of the Currency, which regulated national banks.

The Consumer Financial Protection Agency was designed to have broader powers (covering mortgage and credit card provisions) than currently held by these supervisory agencies, including the Federal Reserve. Should the new agency be put under the exclusive jurisdiction of the Federal Reserve? The Federal Reserve could rein in the excessive leveraging of financial institutions that went overboard with extravagant mortgages and credit card issues to customers. It could also prevent them from employing exotic instruments, such as credit default swaps, for acquiring securitized assets that proved worthless. But then what would happen to the SEC, which could regulate derivative trading? Or should that job be given to the Commodity Futures Trading Commission, which was created in 1974 in order to regulate trading of commodities—oil, grain, and metals, for example—in futures markets? This oversight agency monitored the options on futures markets so that price distortions and market manipulation could be prevented. Or should the Securities and Exchange Commission and the Commodity Futures Trading Commission be merged?

As the Washington turf battles emerged over the role of the new agency, the SEC felt most at risk from the regulatory overhaul. It had failed to effectively monitor Wall Street investment banks during the boom years beginning in 2001. It had also let Bernard Madoff get away with his nefarious Ponzi scheme. Among its regulatory activities, the SEC monitored mutual funds and investment advisors. In late May 2009, the head of the SEC, Chairwoman Mary Schapiro, shot the first arrow across the bow: "I would question pretty profoundly any model that would try to move investor protection function out of the Securities and Exchange Commission."[8]

The Washington turf wars among these agencies raised issues with regard to the regulatory role of the Federal Reserve.

The Regulatory Role of the Federal Reserve

Should the Federal Reserve be an overall, systemic regulator or should the current agencies with adequate streamlining be put in charge? The president said that the "Fed has the most technical expertise and the best track record in terms of doing that." Senior congressional leaders thought otherwise. Senator Dodd, chairman of the Senate Banking Committee, said, "I get a little uneasy about a single regulator. . . . I think there's value in having overlapping jurisdictions who offer a counterweight from time to time—where you don't place all your eggs in one basket." Representative Frank, chairman of the House Financial Services Committee, also poured cold water on the idea of a single systemic regulator.[9]

Commercial and investment banks, which were traditionally monitored by the Federal Reserve, would accept the Fed's role as a systemic regulator. They did have objections, however, arising from two directions. First, they objected to higher capital adequacy and prudential requirements (discussed above), which reduced their arbitrage opportunities and cut their profitability. They would fight for watering down these provisions. Second, they worried about the Federal Reserve as a systemic regulator extending the sweep of its authority over any financial institution that it deemed too big to fail. Would it require that GE Capital, the financial arm of General Electric, submit to stringent requirements that would slash its profitability? Would its monitoring cover the insurer MetLife and the retailer Walmart?

The House Financial Regulatory Reform Bill aimed at resolving the turf battles by assigning the regulatory roles to the existing agencies rather than concentrating them in the Federal Reserve. The SEC and the Commodity Futures Trading Commission would monitor nonstandard derivatives. The former would regulate hedge funds. The new resolution agency for dissolving over-leveraged banks would consist of four regulators. Perhaps the Treasury would chair the dissolution process in line with the preference of Federal Reserve Chairman Bernanke.

Objections to the emergence of the Federal Reserve as a systemic regulator arose from another direction as well. If it was given wider power, could it lose its independence in formulating monetary policy, which is its main function? In his book, Alan Greenspan says that the idea of the Federal Reserve as a systemwide regulator was "mission impossible."[10] Professor John B. Taylor, Stanford University, agreed with that position. He argued that "if the Fed goes further off its course and doesn't focus on what it did in the 1980s and 1990s, it will have less control over inflation. It will lose its independence. It will have to become more political."[11]

The final shot in consolidating systemic regulatory powers in a single agency was fired by Lawrence E. Summers in an interview published in *BusinessWeek*.[12] He referred favorably to international practice, where a holistic regulator has overall responsibility for the systemic risk posed by institutions. "Our system, where someone's got the trunk and somebody else has the leg of the elephant, hasn't worked so well." In other words, the financial system as a whole cannot be regulated by assigning regulatory tasks, such as capital requirements for banks, safe mortgage provisions, and over-the-counter derivative streamlining, to different agencies. The old approach based on the fallacy of composition must give way to the acceptance of a systemic regulator.

Bernanke's position on the impending institutional overhaul appeared flexible. Rather than have the Federal Reserve take on the role of a super-regulator of risks in the financial system (arising from, say, hedge fund and derivative trading), the Federal Reserve would accept the role of being a player among several in a new council to be chaired by the Treasury. With regard to a consumer protector of mortgages and credit cards, the

Federal Reserve would have to cede the role to the new Consumer Financial Protection Agency. What about its role of bailing out financial institutions in "unusual and exigent circumstances"? Let Congress give that power to the Treasury. "No one is more sick of bailouts than I am," Bernanke said.[13]

On December 18, the House of Representatives approved a financial overhaul bill, the Wall Street Reform and Consumer Protection Act, by a vote of 223 to 202.

On May 20, almost 20 months after the Lehman Brothers collapse, the Senate passed, by a 59-39 vote, a far-reaching financial regulatory bill that had been crafted by Senator Dodd and approved in March by the Senate Banking Committee, which Dodd chaired. The Senate bill would be combined with the House version and sent to the president for final approval. The next section takes a look at these bills.

IX. The House and Senate Bills

Both bills had provisions relating to (i) the establishment of procedures, including a council of federal regulators for monitoring financial markets; (ii) the compensation of Wall Street executives; (iii) derivative and hedge fund regulation; (iv) oversight functions of a new agency to be called the Consumer Financial Protection Agency; and (v) redefining the role of the Federal Reserve.

The House bill also included financial relief for unemployed homeowners, enabling them to avoid foreclosure.

Financial Market Regulation

In the House bill, a council of federal regulators would monitor financial markets, impose strict capital adequacy standards on too-big-to-fail banks, and use a special $150 billion fund for dissolving "large and highly complex," risk-prone financial companies. The provision was calculated to lead to an orderly dissolution of over-leveraged financial units, with the $150 billion to be collected from large companies rather than from taxpayers. But some lawmakers wanted to know why such a unit couldn't be dissolved via the normal bankruptcy proceedings. Wasn't the public tired of company bailouts? In any case, the systematic dissolution of an over-leveraged financial unit would avoid a Volcker-type death sentence.

The Senate proposal, like the House bill, recommended the creation of a Financial Stability Oversight Council of regulators for monitoring and resolving financial risk. The Treasury Secretary would chair the council, which would identify too-big-to-fail banks, monitor their activities, and identify bubble formation. These large banks would also be compelled to keep an adequate capital cushion and be forced to shed some assets. The provision to handle the moral hazard problem for rescuing and liquidating a large financial institution was softened by requiring large financial firms to support a fund of $50 billion, in contrast to the House bill's much larger $150 billion fund. By contrast, banks with more than $50 billion in assets would be required to develop their own liquidation plan in a "living will."

The liquidation of a large institution facing an impending failure and posing a systemic risk to the financial system as approved by the Treasury, the Federal Reserve, and the Federal Deposit Insurance Corporation would be swift. Shareholders could be wiped out, executives fired, and creditors paid from levies to be recouped from industry. The Senate provision was intended to bar the repetition of a Lehman Brothers–style bankruptcy and implicit bailout guarantees for over-leveraged units.

Finally, the Senate proposal went further than the House bill by introducing a modified Volcker rule: Regulators could limit bank proprietary trading and hedge fund and private equity ownership without banning these activities altogether.

Financial Executive Compensation

The House bill specified that shareholders could vote on compensation and severance packages. Independent directors must participate in compensation provisions. Regulators could ban "inappropriate and imprudently risky" compensation practices in banks and financial institutions.

The Senate proposal was similar. It allowed shareholders to have a nonbinding vote on compensation decision making and required independent outside monitoring. Companies must rescind executive compensation based on inaccurate financial statements.

The regulation of derivatives and hedge funds was similar.

Derivatives and Hedge Funds

In the House bill, nonstandardized derivatives would have to be traded via clearinghouses that would be monitored by the SEC and the Commodity Futures Trading Commission. Hedge funds and private equity companies with more than $150 million in assets would be required to register with the SEC and disclose their financial activity.

In the Senate bill, both agencies would regulate derivative trading and monitor the trades by requiring that they occur on regulated platforms and go through a central clearinghouse. The most transformational provision in the Senate bill was the adoption of the proposal by Senator Blanche Lincoln (D-AR), chairman of the Senate Agriculture Committee. It required banks to spin off their derivative trading desks. This extreme measure was opposed by the administration, the Federal Reserve, the Federal Deposit Insurance Corporation, and the banking industry. But the Senate bill adopted a milder version of the Volcker rule, which would prevent banks from undertaking trades for their own accounts and from owning and operating hedge funds and private equity funds. The bill also called for a study of the Volcker rule and recommended a complicated process for implementing it.

Hedge funds greater than $100 million would be required to register with the SEC and provide information about their trades and portfolios. The threshold in the House bill was higher, at $150 million. The commission would discretely exercise its authority by scrutinizing hedge funds' client bases, trading partners, and investments.

The Senate bill would create an office in the Securities and Exchange Commission for rating credit agencies. The bill allowed bond investors to sue rating agencies, thus exposing them to greater legal liability for inaccurate ratings. Debt issuers, including banks, would end up with less influence over which rating agency would grade their issues.

Both bills imposed restrictions with regard to mortgage-backed securities that ultimately turned out to be worthless during the current financial crisis. Companies that issued mortgage-based securities would be required to assume some of the risk by keeping 5 percent of them in their portfolios. The issuers must provide information about the collateral assets that backed these securities.

The Consumer Financial Protection Agency

In the House bill, the Consumer Financial Protection Agency would protect consumers by setting and enforcing rules relating to credit cards, mortgages, and loans. The House bill would give the agency broader enforcement powers and keep it as a stand-alone federal agency independent of the Federal Reserve. Finally, the bill would exclude insurance companies, auto dealers, and accountants from the agency's surveillance. It should be noted that Republicans and a few Democrats would have preferred a council made up of existing regulators rather than setting up a new bureaucracy.

With regard to the new agency, the Senate bill would consolidate responsibilities from seven agencies into a Bureau of Consumer Financial Protection and house it in the Federal Reserve. The bureau would prescribe and enforce regulations with respect to credit cards, mortgages, and other products.

The Senate bill also made specific suggestions with regard to the governance features of the Federal Reserve.

Redefining Federal Reserve Role

Both bills gave the Federal Reserve the responsibility for identifying and mitigating risks to the financial system. But the Senate bill required the Fed to designate a vice chairman for bank supervision. The president, rather than the Federal Reserve Board, would appoint the president of the New York Federal Reserve, who directly supervises major Wall Street firms and serves as vice chair of the Fed's monetary policy committee. No bank officers would be allowed to serve on the boards of the Fed's 12 districts or participate in voting for the Fed presidents.

The Senate bill also proposed an overhaul of the Fed's supervisory role. It would keep oversight of the largest bank holding companies with assets greater than $50 billion. National banks with less than $50 billion in assets would be monitored by the Office of the Comptroller of the Currency. State banks and holding companies would be regulated by either the Federal Reserve or the Federal Deposit Insurance Corporation. The Federal Reserve would be left with supervising the financial activities of 35 of the country's largest banks.

Finally, the House bill redirected $4 billion from TARP for providing financial assistance to unemployed home owners for avoiding foreclosures.

The Dodd-Frank Wall Street Reform and Consumer Protection Act based on these House and Senate bills emerged in the early hours of June 25, 2010, after an all-night 20-hour session of deals, edicts, and adjustments between Senate and House conferees. The vote in the conference committee was along party lines. Democrats in the conference committee voted in favor, Republicans against. House conferees voted in favor by a vote of 20 to 11, and Senate conferees by a vote of 7 to 5. It was passed by the full bodies of the House and the Senate in the first week of July and signed by President Obama on July 21.

The next section takes a look at the Dodd-Frank Act. What does it accomplish? How does it plan an overhaul of the financial regulatory system? How did banking lobbies react to its provisions?

X. The Dodd-Frank Wall Street Reform and Consumer Protection Act

The Dodd-Frank Act mandated the creation of a Resolution Authority that will handle the moral hazard issue by forestalling taxpayer-financed bailouts of too-big-to-fail banks.

The Resolution Authority

The design and functions of the Resolution Authority for seizing and liquidating financial firms followed the guidelines of the Senate bill. The Financial Stability Oversight Council, led by the Treasury, will decide which companies pose a systemic risk and which could be shut down without a bankruptcy. The Resolution Authority will help prevent Lehman Brothers–type bankruptcies and taxpayer-financed bailout of over-leveraged banks.

How much capital will banks be required to hold so that they are better prepared to absorb losses when financial conditions deteriorate?

"Someday, son, this will all be part of a billion-dollar bailout." (From *The Wall Street Journal*, permission Cartoon Features Syndicate.)

Bank Capital Requirements

Banks will not be required to face any reserve requirement rules soon. The G-20 participants at the June 25–26, 2010, Toronto Summit decided to adopt the necessary rules by the end of 2012. They cautioned that the new norms would be phased in over time at rates that maintain global recovery without market disruption. The issue would be discussed at the next G-20 summit in Seoul in November 2010. EU and Asian members of the G-20 group were opposed to the idea of raising their banking sector reserve requirements, and the United States, the United Kingdom, and Switzerland, which pushed hardest on adequate reserves, conceded by allowing a long transition period to everyone in order to minimize the economic impact of the new rules on the ongoing recovery.

How does the Dodd-Frank Act deal with the regulation of derivative trading and hedge funds?

Derivative and Hedge Fund Regulation

Over-the-counter derivatives will be increasingly made public. The requirement implies that derivative swaps will have to be standardized; they will be traded on an open exchange. Their prices and volumes will have to be reported publicly; they will have to be approved by clearinghouses. Contracts that do not fit these criteria may face higher capital charges. The clearinghouses will guarantee that if one party to the derivative contract defaults, the investor holding the other side of the trade will be paid. Clearinghouses will require parties in a derivative contract to put up the necessary collateral to protect against a default. The Commodity Futures Trading Commission will oversee derivative trading for commodities like soybeans, oil, and metals. The Securities and Exchange Commission will cover transactions involving securities, currencies, and interest rate variations. The two agencies not only will monitor derivative transactions for fraud and abuse, but also will prescribe limits on the size of the contract a single firm can control.

Most rules will apply to new contracts, not to existing ones.

Who will clear the derivatives? Brokers on a futures exchange, known as futures commission merchants (FCMs), will clear them by acting as intermediaries between two contracting parties. FCMs will be regulated by the Commodity Futures Trading Commission. The FCMs will process derivative orders and extend credit to customers who are willing to trade. The FCMs must keep adequate capital that is separate from the margins they hold for their clients whom they are clearing. The FCMs can access the discount window of the Federal Reserve for their cash needs. According to information from the Commodity Futures Trading Commission, the top five FCMs are divisions of the major banks that dominate the derivative market. Among these are Goldman Sachs, UBS, Credit Suisse, JPMorgan Chase, and Citigroup. Can these clearinghouses really be independent brokerages? Will they become so large as to be systemically important?

The new rules for regulating the $3 trillion U.S. derivative industry will not be in place until late 2011. The Commodity Futures Trading Commission and the SEC will jointly write the rules. The staff of the former has already split into 30 teams to frame the rules, which are due in 2011. The commission will invite time-bound comments, with strict deadlines, from the public. The commission will be early on some rules, late on others, but the rules will appear by September 2011.

Did the Dodd-Frank Act incorporate the Volcker rule and the Blanche Lincoln proposal in the Senate bill for spinning off derivative trading from banks?

With regard to proprietary trading with banks' funds, the act imposed a limit of 3 percent on banks' capital that could be invested in risky hedge funds, private equity, and real estate funds. But banks can continue earning substantial fees by managing the funds. At Goldman Sachs, a 3 percent limit would cut its $15.4 billion in total investment in such funds to a minuscule $2.1 billion. The bank will have at least four years to cut back its holdings below 3 percent and retire its high-rolling traders. On the other hand, JPMorgan Chase can keep its Highbridge Capital Management hedge fund, valued at $21 billion, because it has cash provided by clients rather than funds raised by the bank itself, but it has begun dismantling its proprietary trading operation. So has Goldman Sachs.

Will banks continue using client activity as a cover for risky bets? Is it possible to distinguish between a trading activity that a bank undertakes for itself, using its own money, and alternatively, for a client, using the client's money? More to the point, will banks stop making overly risky bets on behalf of their clients with their clients' money? According to one report, JPMorgan Chase and Goldman Sachs each lost more than $100 million on transactions they handled for their customers in the period from April to July 2010.[14] In any case, banks have found a solution. They will let their traders make the trading wagers as long as the traders work with the clients.

The controversial Blanche Lincoln plan requiring deposit-taking banks to spin off derivative business from their ledgers was diluted. Banks will not be required to spin off their interest rate, currency, and credit swap derivatives (which are cleared by FTCs) into a separate package. Derivatives involving trading in commodities, agriculture, energy, and equities will be spun off even if these products are cleared.

But how does the act protect consumers?

Consumer Financial Protection Bureau

The new agency, dubbed the Consumer Financial Protection Bureau, will safeguard consumer interests with regard to credit cards, checking accounts, mortgages, and student loans from private sources. Auto dealers, who successfully lobbied, are exempt from the bureau oversight. The agency will get an initial budget, set by the act at about $500 million, for carrying out its purpose of "regulating the offering and provision of consumer financial products and services." It will be located in the Federal Reserve and will be financed by the Federal Reserve, not by congressional appropriations. It will, however, act independently of the Federal Reserve on policy and enforcement issues.

Its evolving course will depend on its first director, who will interpret the Dodd-Frank Act's regulatory mandate, write the rules governing credit cards and mortgages, and seek to enforce them. The director will be nominated by the president, approved by the Senate to serve a three-year term, and operate a budget of $500 million free from congressional scrutiny. The bureau will start functioning in 2011.

How will the emerging regulations affect mortgage and credit card availability for consumers? How will they influence consumer decision making about their checking accounts with banks?

Banks that extend mortgages face an overhaul of rules relating to their services. Mortgage lenders will be prohibited from charging prepayment penalties to borrowers if they pay their loans early. Nor can lenders pay brokers and loan officers extra, which might enable them to steer borrowers to higher interest charges or risky features. Loan officers and mortgage brokers will be prohibited from receiving bonuses for steering borrowers toward deceptively attractive mortgage loans. The lender must also determine a borrower's ability to repay a proposed mortgage by checking his income and assets. Brokers will be required to put their clients' interests first. But not right away. Such a fiduciary standard, which appeared in the House bill, was diluted in Dodd-Frank. The SEC will conduct a six-month study of the brokerage industry for locating regulatory gaps in its current practices.

Most of the regulatory overhaul in the act, however, focuses on the country's mega banks. Small banks with assets of less than $10 billion would be excluded from the bureau's oversight with regard to their activities relating to mortgages, credit cards, and bank deposits. These banks would instead be monitored, with regard to these activities, by state and other federal regulators. The community banks around the country will be free to choose their regulators. This exclusionary privilege comes across as a vote-getting political concession at the grassroots level in favor of small banks, some of whom were responsible for extending trillions of dollars of mortgages that turned out to be subprime. This regulatory exclusivity in favor of small banks could lead to future problems. Community bankers and their supporters claim that the changes will help them compete with big banks.

In any case, will the bureau's impact with regard to mortgages, credit cards, and consumer checking account facilities be altogether benign? Some of the abusive practices will disappear, but stricter controls on mortgage loans, credit cards, and checking accounts will put these beyond the reach of low-income households. The bureau, thinly designed as part of the Federal Reserve, could become a highly intrusive bureaucracy and an aggressive operation with regard to banking sector activities. Banks, in turn, could react by raising the costs of their services, including credit cards and checking accounts.

Finally, how can the functioning of the American corporate sector be made appropriately risk averse by increasing the responsibility of shareholders on issues such as CEO earnings? In particular, how can corporate board members be made more responsive to shareholder concerns?

Shareholder Role in Corporate Management

Shareholders own the company, whereas managers, including the top executives, are hired employees. In a party line 3-2 vote at the Securities and Exchange Commission on August 25, 2010, the SEC voted in favor of the proxy access rule. Companies will be required to include names of all board nominees, even those disapproved by the company, on the standard corporate ballots distributed before the annual shareholder meeting. In order to qualify for nominating a corporate board member, an investor or group of investors must hold 3 percent of the stock and must have held it for three years. Currently, shareholders wage a campaign at their own cost for gaining shareholder support for ousting a board member. They must foot the bill for mailing separate ballots.[15]

It is not clear if shareholders of large companies will participate actively in electing board members. Nor is it certain that board members will play a decisive role in selecting the most qualified CEO for a company.

The CEO compensation and its breakdown in cash and bonus versus company stock will continue to remain flexible. People with narrow agendas may seek seats on boards. Smaller companies will be at an advantage for such proxy access attacks. If a hedge fund shareholder wants to oust a board member in Verizon Communications Inc., he would need $2.4 billion to mount such an attack. For a smaller company, say, the size of Leap Wireless International Inc., the amount an investor would require at 3 percent of the company would be around $28 million.[16]

What does the Dodd-Frank Act accomplish? It is not perfect, but it vastly improves on the status quo. It provides a framework for winding down the largest financial institutions if they fail. It regulates derivatives. It assigns clear and strong responsibility to specific agencies for preventing both systemic risk and consumer abuse. It also instructs regulators to carry out wide-ranging studies and report back to Congress. There will be an almighty tussle as the regulators, mainly the SEC and the Commodity Futures Trading Commission, formulate precise rules and flesh out the act's 2,000-plus pages. The massive directory, which instructs federal regulators to address subjects ranging from derivative trading to mortgage limits to credit card rules, is notably short on specifics. It also perpetuates uncertainty given the amount of work still to be done. It gives regulators significant powers to determine its impact while providing partisans with enough chance to influence its outcome. Will bank lobbyists influence the rules behind the scene? Will consumer groups and trade union activists sway the regulatory outcome in their favor? The decision by the Federal Reserve, the Securities and Exchange Commission, and the Commodity Futures Trading Commission to invite comments from the public on the rule making will test their objectivity to the extreme.

The Dodd-Frank Act seeks a major overhaul of the U.S. financial regulatory arrangements that had been in place for almost 80 years. How effective will it be in preventing a crisis or, if one occurs, moderating its impact? In its preliminary version, ahead of the precise rules that it will generate at the hands of the regulators in 2011, it prompts four comments.

Assessment of the Dodd-Frank Act's Regulatory Provisions

First, the requirements of capital adequacy by banks and hedge funds and of transparent screening of derivatives by clearing agencies will tend to contain excessive risk taking by these institutions. At the same time, the empowerment of regulators to dissolve troubled financial units with cash funding by their cohorts rather than by the taxpayers will constitute progress in dealing with the moral hazard issue. But ultimately, the most exacting rules for disciplining the risk-taking and reward-seeking proclivities of Wall Street titans will turn out to be useless if they are not implemented. They can remain a wake-up call, rather than the start of vigilant execution.

Second, the act provides a role for the Federal Reserve as a financial regulator and a bailout enforcer. While participating in regulatory decision making with other federal agencies, the Federal Reserve will remain in charge of formulating monetary policy. The act steers clear of the adoption by the House, subsequently scuttled, of the provision of congressional auditing of Federal Reserve monetary policy decisions. The auditing provision was counterproductive.

At the same time, the proposal that the Fed oversee only the largest institutions, headquartered mainly in New York City and Washington, D.C., will restrict its supervision to the largest banks. Didn't Congress establish the Federal Reserve in 1913 with 12 banks in a federal structure so that it would counter New York and Washington with a well-informed regional perspective? Federal Reserve Chairman Bernanke was clearly opposed to the provision in the Senate bill: "It makes us essentially the 'too-big-to-fail regulator.' . . . We want to have a connection to Main Street as well as to Wall Street."[17] President of the Kansas City Federal Reserve Thomas Hoenig was similarly concerned, saying that "the Federal Reserve would no longer be the central bank of the United States, but only the central bank of Wall Street."[18]

Third, Dodd-Frank deals with the compensation of Wall Street bankers by relegating it to the watchdog potential of shareholders and board members. Perhaps the lawmakers assumed that the ballooning compensation of Wall Street grandees should be taxed separately via a change in tax rates. In any case, do board directors understand the complex financial instruments that banks employ? As credit default swaps mounted in bank balance sheets, few of them asked: "What would happen if home prices fell?" Besides, how many of them are truly independent?

Finally, the proposed outline of the Consumer Financial Protection Bureau for protecting American borrowers from the evidently nefarious practices of credit card issuers needs to be discretely applied. The consumer-driven American economy operates on credit cards. But the economy needs to grow out of the recession via resurgent consumer demand. From that

(Shannon Stapleton / REUTERS.)

perspective, the bureau will need to act as a prudent bureaucracy in the short run.

Overall, the lawmakers—buffeted by the political uncertainties of the forthcoming congressional elections in the middle of a weak, high-unemployment economy, by pressures of the intense lobbying of the financial sector, and by the continuing wrangling among the federal regulatory agencies—chose to avoid extreme provisions. The Volcker rule of divesting bank holding companies of their proprietary and equity promoting units was diluted. The amendment of spinning off over-the-counter derivative units from their parent bodies for separate rule enforcement was also watered down. In the final version, the lawmakers chose to turn down the extreme version of the Volcker rule, which would have entirely removed proprietary trading on banks' own accounts from their operations. Instead, they adopted a tough mandate for derivative control.

In my view, if the reserve requirements for financial institutions are vigilantly applied and if derivative trading is made transparent, risk taking by financial institutions would be moderated, and the mandate of the

Resolution Authority for breaking up too-big-to-fail financial units would be minimized. Ultimately, the legislation avoided breaking them up to start with. The law gave regulators the authority to monitor financial institutions and the instruments they employed for their activity. It empowered the Resolution Authority to dissolve them in an orderly fashion. In the old days, this mechanism was absent. So Lehman Brothers had to resort to bankruptcy, and AIG was bailed out by the Treasury and the Federal Reserve. The Resolution Authority now has the discretion and flexibility to dissolve any financial institution in distress.

How did EU policymakers react to the flurry of proposals cascading in dizzying succession in Washington? Let's find out.

XI. EU Regulatory Proposals

The European Commission, the executive arm of the European Union, is in charge of recommending regulatory proposals for the European Union's 27 member countries. It formulates the rules, puts them up for open commentary by participating members, and monitors their implementation. The rules relate to bank capital adequacy and the compensation of bank executives as well as regulation of hedge funds and derivatives—in fact, covering all the issues discussed above that must be resolved for stabilizing the financial markets.

A dominant feature that has influenced rule making by the European Commission for preempting excessively risky behavior by EU financial institutions relates to the financial structure of the 27 economies. For example, banks play a much greater role in providing capital to the private sector in the European Union than they do in the United States, where capital markets dominate. Banks provide almost half the financing needs of the private sector in the smaller eurozone, whereas they provide less than 20 percent in the United States.[19] EU banks should be healthy because they have a critical financial role in the economy. For the same reason, they also have an excessive lobbying voice in influencing the regulatory overhaul.

It would seem that, given the importance of banks in their economies, EU governments have, singly or jointly, resisted or accepted regulatory rules for reorienting their banking sector (and other groups such as hedge funds) from five perspectives. These relate to the final shape of the provisional Basel

Committee Rules III; the appropriate regulation of derivative trading and short selling; the limits on the bonus compensations of bank executives who tend to take extreme risks in evident anticipation of higher rewards; the EU rules with regard to the hedge fund and insurance business of foreign units operating in Europe; and finally, the harmonization of all rules across the economies of the 27 EU members.

The critical regulatory issue from the members' perspective has been the ultimate shape of the provisional Basel Committee Rules III (discussed earlier in the chapter), which will apply to banks of all 27 members participating in the Basel process. The need for adequate capital in the form of common equity to cover the banking sector's risky assets is readily acknowledged as an item on the EU regulatory agenda. But the process of cleaning up EU banks as the very first step in banking sector restoration lagged behind the United States. Most EU banks struggled to get back to normalcy, whereas the big players, among them Barclays, HSBC, and Deutsche Bank, had bounced back to active operation much in the style of the U.S. banking titans across the Atlantic. In general, while observing individual country capital adequacy requirements, EU governments gave a nod of approval to the Basel Committee signals announced on September 13, 2010, for consideration of the G-20 November summit in Seoul. EU banks, however, worried about how restrictive the Basel norms would turn out to be.

As I have discussed above, these provisional rules were devised to ensure that banks kept away from taking out-of-bounds financial risk. They related to adequate capital backing by banks against their assets, their global leverage ratio, which must also take account of counterparty risk in their derivative trading, and finally, their liquid holdings, which would help them survive a financial crisis without taxpayer bailout. These three requirements of capital reserves, leverage ratio, and liquidity provision were not only diluted in the mid-September announcement, but also postponed for enforcement at a future date.

Next, in mid-September, the European Commission announced proposals aimed at transforming EU over-the-counter derivative trading by standardizing it, making it more transparent, and aligning it with the provisions of the Dodd-Frank Act. It also unveiled rules that would force short sellers into disclosing details of their short positions to regulators.

Although EU governments have resisted tough rules with respect to banking sector reserve requirements and derivative trading, they readily accepted EU-wide strict rules on bonus payments to bankers. By contrast, the issue of corporate compensation in the United States has been left to shareholders via their choice of board of directors. From the EU perspective, bankers will take less risk if their bonus compensations are regulated by law.

Apart from structural differences in financial activity and the legislative preference for regulatory control of bankers' bonuses, EU decision making has also been influenced by their regulators' desire to enable their financial businesses, among them hedge funds and insurance companies, to compete effectively with their global counterparts. The European Commission would tend to prefer discriminatory rules for restricting operations by foreign units in these activities.

Finally, EU regulatory decision making has been slow in contrast to the decisive speed with which it proceeded in the United States. The process in the U.S. Congress with regard to sorting out the final details of regulatory reform was contentious because of political differences across party lines and pressures from banking and business lobbies. It has moved by fits and starts in the European Union because the rule framers must craft agreement among 27 governments, of which 16 form the Economic and Monetary Union. For example, larger divisions emerged between U.K. and continental European negotiators over the crucial issue of the revision of capital requirements by global banks being negotiated by the group of 27 governments in Basel during the summer. The U.S. and U.K. positions on the issue converged in favor of tougher capital requirements, whereas the continental European view favored vigilant supervision of banks over larger capital reserves.

How did the final rules of Basel III capital requirements, which were announced in late August and finally adopted on September 21, differ from the provisional Basel III proposals I discussed above?

Basel III Requirements

The modified blueprint relating to the three rules responded to the arguments of policy makers and bankers that excessive rule tightening could constrain bank lending amid a fragile recovery, particularly to small and medium-sized businesses. Thus, reserve requirements by banks will include tax credits that they expect in the future, mortgage servicing deals from which banks earn fees, and equity stakes by minority partners in overseas subsidiaries. Thus, if Barclays has minority shareholding by an

(Ingram Pinn / *Financial Times.*)

Indian bank, the Indian bank's equity stake will be counted in Barclays tier 1 capital. The three items in aggregate should remain at 16 percent of total tier 1 capital. The overall tier 1 capital to risky assets is set at 8 percent. Next, the leverage ratio must include banks' exposure to derivatives. Under the new proposal, banks will be allowed to gauge their net exposure by adjusting for derivative contracts in opposite directions. The minimum (tier 1 capital/asset) leverage ratio is set at 3 percent. This rule will be implemented in 2018. Finally, the liquidity requirements by banks in order for them to successfully survive a crisis for 30 days without taxpayer bailout were also softened by the need to redefine specific crisis features as they affected the banking sector. For example, Chinese regulators will manage the impact on Chinese banks of the current property boom in Chinese cities with less difficulty than the financial nightmare of the housing boom that U.S. policymakers had to resolve with regard to large U.S. banks.

The final proposals announced in September raised capital requirements to levels higher than currently in practice. Banks will have to raise their reserve common equity (common shares and retained earnings) to 7 percent of their assets, up from 4 percent in the United States currently. The Basel Committee also suggested that banks should set aside an additional 2.5 percent in reserve backing in good times as a precaution against the emergence of excessive risk taking. The new rules would be applied at a much later date than U.S. regulators had hoped for. That said, the new regime will be tougher than anything in force before the crisis. Bankers, however, greeted the revised package with relief. It could have been worse. Besides, it promised a level global playing field and a transition period of up to eight years.

In mid-September, the European Commission announced detailed proposals for regulating derivative trading and short selling.

European Commission Proposals for Regulating Derivative Trading and Short Selling

The regulatory debates with regard to over-the-counter derivatives raised active dialogue between the European Commission and the U.K. Financial Services Authority.

The European Commission proposed strict rules requiring that these derivatives be standardized and cleared by Central Counter Party (CCP) clearing so as to reduce counterparty risk. This requirement resembled the Dodd-Frank Act, which proposed that derivative trading undertaken by banks and hedge funds be cleared and openly traded. By contrast, the U.K. Financial Services Authority was against forcing nonstandard derivatives into standardized markets. They should remain free in order to be able to hedge against specific risks. As for protecting counterparty risk, CCP clearing, in the U.K. Financial Services Authority's view, should not be mandated for all standardized derivatives. Rather than central clearance, they should be required to keep high capital margins.

It was not surprising that the U.K. financial authority wanted a more flexible monitoring approach and greater freedom for nonstandardized derivatives in London. Why? London, after all, is the mecca for bankers, brokers, and financial risk takers.[20]

According to the proposals released by the European Commission in mid-September 2010, over-the-counter derivatives will have to be processed through clearinghouses and reported to "trade repositories" or data banks and the information will have to be available to regulators. Nonfinancial, over-the-counter derivative trades will be exempted from the clearing obligation. They will, however, be required to keep large capital backing. The nonfinancial lobbies argue that when they float oil, energy, and grain derivatives, they undertake these activities for hedging routine business risks. Why make them more expensive by forcing them to post higher cash margins that clearinghouses may impose on them? If the European Commission were to finally accept dual standards of exemption for financial and nonfinancial derivatives, it would end up ignoring the systemic risks that both types of derivatives pose for financial stability.

The European Commission also unveiled proposals relating to short selling. In short-selling activity, an investor who expects a security price to drop borrows it, sells it at the current higher price, and buys it at a future lower price with a view to repaying it to the original supplier. He makes a profit by selling the borrowed security at the current higher price and buying it later at a lower price for returning it to the initial provider. The proposed rule will require a security trader to disclose his short position to regulators if it exceeds 0.2 percent of a company's issued share capital. If the short position exceeds 0.5 percent, it will have to be disclosed to all traders who are engaged in trading it. Finally, when traders deal in short selling of sovereign debts and credit default swaps, they must release the transaction information to regulators so that buyers of these items can insure themselves against default risks.

European governments and the European Parliament will discuss the proposals on derivatives and short selling before they are finally accepted. The proposals on short selling are expected to be in place by July 1, 2012, and the derivative proposals by the end of 2012.

The European Parliament prescribed new tough bonus rules for member banks.

New Bonus Rules for EU Banks

The issue of bankers' compensation had received a knockout punch with the announcement by Alistair Darling, Britain's Chancellor of the Exchequer, on December 9, 2008, of a one-off, 50 percent tax on any bonus in excess of €25,000 (about $40,000) that U.K. banks paid to their staff. The single-shot levy was not expected to damage the competitiveness of U.K. banks. Nor would it constitute a charge on their retained profits, which could be added to bank reserves. Bank profits had evidently swelled as a result of direct and indirect government bailouts. By contrast, U.S. compensation caps at that time were restricted to bankers who continued receiving tax-financed TARP funding. Britain's banking lobby rose in an uproar for fear that London might cease to be the banking capital of the world. By contrast, France's President Nicolas Sarkozy welcomed the tax as an appropriate departure from excessive Anglo-Saxon liberal capitalism and promised to adopt it in France. Germany's Chancellor Angela Merkel rejected the idea.

A unified approach on the issue did appear on July 7, 2010, when the European Parliament approved strict rules, by a vote of 625 to 28, on bankers' bonuses designed to cap these annual payouts. The parliamentarians had been busy devising the rules since April 2009.

From the bankers' perspective, the rules are full of unsavory ratios. They will limit up-front cash to 30 percent of a banker's total bonus and to 20 percent in the case of very large bonuses. In any case, bankers would need to be patient because between 40 and 60 percent of the bonuses would be postponed for three years and might even be clawed back if the banks underperformed. "Clawbacks" will allow banks to take back part or all of the bonus from an employee who damages the bank's business by taking a bad risk. The rules will apply to managers of commercial and investment banks. Rules on payouts to hedge fund managers will be legislated by the parliament later in the year. National governments will decide if the rules also should apply to traders who undertake big risks.

The draconian rules assume that bankers took huge risks and brought the global economy into financial turmoil because they operated with guaranteed bonuses that were paid in cash. In the lawmakers' view, excessive risk taking occurred from faulty incentives. If the practice were abolished, bankers would cease to misbehave. In any case, senior executives of banks had already adopted bonus deferral practices. At Goldman Sachs, an investment bank with a high-flying bonus culture, managers from the top down had taken their bonuses in stocks. In the United States, the practice may prove short lived. By contrast, the European legislators desired that the enforcement of the rule would rein in bonus-based risk taking by bankers. In late July, the U.K. Financial Services Authority went overboard by extending the bonus payment rules to cover managers of hedge funds, investment banks, and building groups. It also ruled that 50 percent of the bonus package be paid in shares rather than the lower 20 percent prescribed by the European Parliament.

EU debates on hedge fund and insurance regulation centered on the issue of how EU hedge fund and insurance businesses might be protected from the overarching reach of American counterparts in Europe.

EU Hedge Fund and Insurance Regulation Proposals

Toward the end of December 2009, two proposals circulated among European regulators for hedge fund regulation. The regulatory outlines by the European Parliament and by Swedish diplomats differed with respect to a number of issues. Should there be size thresholds? How much latitude for risk taking should fund managers have? Shouldn't there be size limits for offshore funds managed by EU managers? Can non-EU funds raise cash from EU investors? Should managers' pay be linked to risk taking? If so, how? Should managers be forced to disclose remuneration and carried interest that they receive? Must EU fund managers use an EU credit institution or investment fund as a depository unit? Can such a depository be located in the United States? Can a simple, practical solution emerge from the dense fog of proposals and counterproposals?

It would seem that EU policy makers will ultimately favor stringent hedge fund regulations in the belief that global hedge funds pose a systemic risk and must be strictly regulated. By contrast, the thrust of the U.S. hedge fund regulation was both explicit and flexible. Hedge funds should be registered. They must report their activities to a government registry. Restrictions with regard to their size or management compensation or cross-country investment activity were held at bay.

The EU policy stance with regard to capital and other requirements for global insurance companies with European operation also raised concern. Insurance companies based outside the European Union would be exempt from a specific EU requirement if their home country had a comparable regulatory environment. But what if these standards were not formulated and implemented by a single agency overseeing insurance conglomerates? Current U.S. regulatory regime would not pass muster because the insurance industry is regulated state by state. Would European regulators require that U.S. insurers operating in Europe keep extra capital on their books?

These questions raise concern about the extent of discrimination that foreign participants in EU hedge fund activity, insurance businesses, and banking in general may face vis-à-vis local players. In particular, will the EU regulatory regime put U.S. financial firms at a competitive disadvantage? These firms were indeed a source of dubious mortgage securities. They ran the risk of losing EU investors, among them pension funds and insurance companies. According to one regulatory proposal, U.S. hedge funds may need to register with EU regulators if they want to market their financial products to European investors.

Ultimately the regulatory environment needs to be uniform across national boundaries, not only with regard to the extent of control, but also with regard to its exercise in a nondiscriminatory fashion. Unless there is across-the-board international conformity with regard to the rules of banking sector capital requirements and compensation practices, financial markets will become fragmented and cease to be competitive. Without such conformity, hedge funds and insurance businesses will lose their scale economies. The proposed regulations as they relate to foreign participants should be indiscriminatory. Financial groups on both sides of the Atlantic would prefer common standards. A prudent, nondiscriminatory legislative agenda would arouse less overreaction and fragmentation of cross-border activities from banks, insurance companies, and hedge funds, as well as from securities and derivative trading.

While the EU regulatory proposals on hedge fund and insurance activities are being formulated, EU governments approved an intra-EU financial supervision package on September 3, 2010.

EU Adoption of an Intra-EU Financial Supervision Package

The rules will overhaul the monitoring of banks and markets in the region. Under the arrangement, three watchdogs for the banking, insurance, and securities markets will design common technical rules and standards for companies and markets rather than supervise them directly. However, national governments rather than the watchdogs will enforce such supervision. Nor will the watchdogs impose rules on member states relating to budgetary matters. The pact will also create a European Systemic Risk Board with authority to warn about threats to financial stability. The president of the European Central Bank will chair this new agency for the first five years.

In conclusion, the U.S. and EU regulatory processes tend to be different. EU rule making is slow because it must overcome differences among 27 member governments. Even the smaller Economic and Monetary Union with 16 members lacks that feature. The European Union is not a single country marked by political and economic cohesiveness. As a result, the delays and disagreements are apparent in the formulation of the provisions with regard to the banking system overhaul, including executive compensation, over-the-counter derivatives, and the regulation of hedge funds.

It had to be speedy in the United States because the crisis originated in the United States. That said, the EU regulators lack the urgency and the down-to-earth problem-solving approach of U.S. rule makers, who also differ on issues but act in the vigorous American quid pro quo tradition. Again, the U.S. inhibition of how far the legislative authority should interfere in an issue such as bonus payments to bankers differs from the European approach, which is legally more intrusive. Occasionally, socialist Europe regards American financial arrangements as freewheeling and destructive. It sees U.S. regulatory proposals as monitoring devices at best, rather than as regulatory mechanisms. As a result, EU rules will turn out to be more stringent in their coverage of the activities of hedge funds, insurance companies, stock traders, and brokers.

Despite the differences, the process of the U.S.-EU regulatory overhaul will move forward. In my view, a crisis can be expected to occur less frequently and when one does occur, its impact on an economy's decline will be less severe—if the regulatory provisions relating to capital requirements by banks and transparent operations of derivatives are consistently and vigilantly implemented. No law can prevent a bubble created by reckless lenders and crafty traders who will be around. But these two features of the regulatory provisions will need to watch them systematically before they bring the global economy to the brink.

7

The Dollar's Future as
a Reserve Currency

The easy monetary policy that the Federal Reserve undertook by steadily lowering the federal funds rate starting in January 2001 and continuing until mid-2004 contributed to the unsustainable U.S. housing bubble and the financial crisis toward the end of 2007. The Fed's easy monetary policy was also supported by saving inflows from China: The People's Bank of China, the central bank, increasingly invested the country's dollar earnings (from export surpluses) in U.S. Treasury bonds, which amounted to $938 billion in October 2009. China's burgeoning export surpluses, in turn, resulted from a significantly undervalued Chinese currency. If the Chinese authorities allowed the renminbi to appreciate with respect to the dollar, China would export less to the United States and deprive fewer Americans of jobs. As the unemployment rate began moving up in 2009, U.S. lawmakers, led by Senator Charles Schumer (D-NY), the third-most senior Democratic senator, deliberated protectionist levies on Chinese imports.

Chinese leaders have consistently reacted to the global demands for renminbi appreciation with extreme caution. They want their decision making to be independent of outside pressures. They are also determined to steer their renminbi management for advancing China's economic interests. Therefore, their decision to delink the currency (from the declining dollar established in July 2008) and make it flexible would be taken in measured steps, keeping in view China's interests. The spectacular growth of the Chinese economy, averaging to date 10 percent annually over three decades, has been promoted by exports, which in turn have been driven by an undervalued renminbi. This performance cannot be allowed to deteriorate. China's pronouncement on the issue on June 19, 2010, almost on the eve of the G-20 Summit on June 22, promised a flexible currency regime while echoing this policy concern.

The Chinese policy makers also worry about the worth of the dollar-denominated Treasury bonds in the vaults of the People's Bank of China. In their view, the massive U.S. *budget* deficit destabilizes the worth of the Treasury bonds with the Chinese central bank, which helps finance this deficit. In order for foreigners (including foreign central banks) to continue holding these dollar assets and finance the U.S. budget deficit, these asset valuations must remain stable. Furthermore, U.S. consumers, in China's view, must also learn to cut back their excessive spending, which spills into the U.S. *trade* deficit. The dollar could cease to be a reserve currency in which foreigners hold dollar-denominated IOUs for financing U.S. trade deficit if this deficit also becomes excessive.

Similar concern relating to the displacement of the dollar as a reserve currency was voiced by the leaders of Brazil, Russia, India, and China in the summer of 2009 when they proposed that the dollar be supplemented by alternative currencies.

The financial crisis, therefore, initiated debates and demands that revolved around three issues. U.S. policy makers have continued pressuring Chinese authorities for renminbi appreciation. Next, doubts about the continuing role of the dollar as a reserve currency have surfaced in discussions at G-20 summits and mini meetings of the leaders of Brazil, Russia, India, and China (BRIC). Finally, the long-term need for China–United States bilateral balancing, with China saving less and the United States saving more, has raised questions as well. Can renminbi appreciation accomplish such bilateral balancing by slashing Chinese exports in the U.S. market? Should U.S. policy makers also undertake measures to trim the massive federal budget deficit and stabilize the value of the Treasury bonds that are held by foreign banks? Should U.S. consumers also start spending less, especially on imports, and help reduce the size of the U.S. trade deficit? How much balancing is necessary for keeping the dollar stable and preserving its role as a reserve currency?

The issue of renminbi revaluation is complicated and requires a turnaround from a policy framework that has pushed the Chinese economy into a sustained annual growth of nearly 10 percent for more than three decades.

Let's examine this framework: How has it worked?

I. China's High-Growth Model: Its Implications for Renminbi Revaluation

First, the impressive export growth, especially from 2000, has resulted from rising productivity in labor-intensive manufactured goods. China's membership in the World Trade Organization in 2002 also raised the attractiveness of China's domestic investment climate for export-oriented production. "Consequently the process of relocation to China (from Japan, Taiwan, and Korea especially) of final assembly activities of information and communication technology products accelerated."[1]

Second, the domestic investment boom in heavy industrial products (aluminum, machine tools, cement, etc.) has brought about a dramatic fall in import growth. "The overall picture is that there has been both an acceleration of the rate of growth of exports and a decline in the rate of growth of imports."[2]

Third, China's impressive growth rate has occurred under generally low inflation resulting from an effective monetary policy. This in turn has implied that the renminbi released in the foreign exchange market in exchange for the dollars earned from exports must be adequately sterilized. But the demand for money has also kept up in a growing economy, and the sterilization imperative associated with a deliberate exchange rate policy has been manageable.

Fourth, the intervention in the foreign exchange market has also been aimed at preventing an excessive appreciation of the renminbi against the dollar. Such an appreciation would create significant unemployment in export industries and in urban areas. The exchange rate must be maintained at an undervalued renminbi with regard to the dollar. A floating rate was ruled out, and a sharp change in the fixed-but-adjustable low rate would be too destabilizing.

Finally, the import-substituting heavy industry focus and export-promoting manufactured goods activities have been concentrated in large, state-owned enterprises. "Enterprise savings have been exceptionally high . . . and have steadily increased owing to low wages and absence of payments of taxes or dividends to the government."[3] Household savings are high too because of low social welfare arrangements and lack of pensions. "Relative to GDP, aggregate savings are estimated to have been about 50% of GDP in 2006."[4]

What would be the implications of this two-decade-long policy framework for a possible renminbi revaluation?

Implications of the Policy Framework for Renminbi Revaluation

A stronger renminbi would imply that the export-driven monopoly industries operating under state supervision would need to switch production to domestic consumption. Similar import-substituting heavy industries in the state sector would need to compete with cheaper imports. These massive structural shifts would be resisted by entrenched state operatives and monopoly producers who have operated in tandem under planners' policy guidelines. The Chinese commerce ministry, which is in charge of exports and imports, is opposed to renminbi appreciation, which would tend to damage the export and domestic import-substituting sectors. Notwithstanding, a modest renminbi appreciation may be favored by the National Development and Reform Commission, China's state planning agency, although the agency is opposed to a fully floating exchange rate. The People's Bank of China is more flexible on the issue than the ministry of commerce and the planning agency because a moderate intervention in the foreign exchange market with a view to managing the exchange rate gives it an additional policy instrument for controlling inflation. Despite slightly varying shades of policy choices from the commerce ministry to the central bank, a fast-paced switch from state-directed investment to diversified business enterprises operating under market incentives with widespread employment possibilities and diversified household earnings is considered totally unrealistic. As a realistic, intermediate policy option, the authorities may consider opting for a slow-paced upward movement of the renminbi in order to manage the mounting external pressure for such a move.

In mid-2005, the policy makers had delinked the currency from the dollar and allowed it to appreciate for three years by 21 percent until July 2008. Then the dollar peg was reinstated in July 2008, and the renminbi was allowed to move with the declining dollar in order to maintain the export markets (figure 7.1).

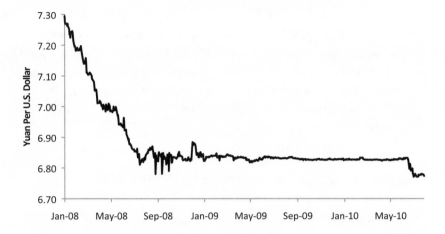

Figure 7.1.
Chinese Yuan in Exchange for One U.S. Dollar. (Federal Reserve.)

Note: The Chinese currency is referred to as the renminbi, but the exchange rate is expressed in terms of yuan exchanged for $1.

A competitive renminbi is an essential tool in the central bank's policy kit, and a dramatic policy switch of renminbi appreciation is unlikely. A slow-paced, modest appreciation of the renminbi in 2010 would be a safe bet. But the imbalances in favor of China in early 2010 were massive from the perspective of the rest of the world, which the next section explores. Other countries clamored that the renminbi was too cheap: The Chinese trade surplus was close to $150 billion, and the foreign exchange reserves of the People's Bank of China approached $2.4 trillion.

II. Renminbi Appreciation: The Chinese View Versus Outside Pressures

In December 2009, China's Premier Wen Jiabao reacted with the following words to the international chorus that the renminbi was exploitatively undervalued: "We will not yield to any pressure of any form forcing us to appreciate."[5] It would seem that the renminbi's unofficial peg to the declining dollar, which had been in place since July 2008, would continue despite continuing protests from outsiders about China's exchange rate policy.

Soon thereafter, Zhou Xiaochuan, chairman of the People's Bank of China, signaled a cautious policy management. He suggested that the dollar peg, which linked the renminbi to the devaluing dollar, was a special measure. It was designed to keep Chinese exports moving in foreign markets for weathering the recessionary impact of the financial crisis.

Pressures for renminbi appreciation were also building among Asian and European suppliers.

Escalating Pressures from Outside

Asian suppliers competed with Chinese exporters in world markets. The link of the renminbi to the declining dollar since July 2008 had left it undervalued, giving Chinese exporters a massive competitive advantage in relation to Asian suppliers as they fought their way out of the gathering financial crisis. At the same time, the renminbi's official peg against the declining dollar had lifted the euro against the Chinese currency by 15 percent in the 12 months ending November 2009. It had created an unfair advantage for Chinese exporters vis-à-vis eurozone suppliers.

However, following the November 2009 mini summit in Nanjing between European and Chinese leaders, Premier Wen Jiabao announced that the exchange rate of the renminbi would be kept at a "reasonable, balanced level." An immediate revaluation, in his view, could undermine the ongoing economic recovery in China. An 8 percent trade-weighted real depreciation of the renminbi since October 2008 had kept the current account surplus at 6 percent of the GDP in 2009 (down from a high of 10 percent in 2007). Of course, the stimulus package of 15 percent of the GDP, energetically navigated via bank lending for infrastructure buildup and household spending on consumer durables, would play a role as well.

But questions remained. When would the renminbi appreciation begin? How sharp would it be? How long would it last? More to the point, would it mark a departure from China's long-standing export-led growth strategy supported by an undervalued exchange rate? In the eurozone economies as well as in the United States, both afflicted with a recession and high unemployment, protectionist calls emerged in 2009 with demands for more barriers by domestic producers who lost their markets to cheap Chinese imports. Are these demands, which go against free movement of goods, justified?

The Rising Protectionist Tide

In a classic paper, the late Paul Samuelson argued that the rules of free trade did not apply in the current situation: "With employment less than full . . . all the debunked mercantilistic arguments [that is, claims that nations who subsidize their exports effectively steal jobs from other countries] turn out to be valid."[6] He then went on to argue that persistently misaligned exchange rates create "genuine problems for free trade apologetics."[7] The best answer to these problems is getting exchange rates back to where they ought to be. Given the misalignment, a renminbi appreciation emerged as an indispensable measure for rebalancing United States–China disequilibrium by curtailing Chinese exports and investment and lifting consumption by Chinese households.

If the Chinese authorities would not undertake a currency revaluation, the U.S. Congress would consider imposing tariffs on Chinese imports. U.S. Senators proposed legislation in early April 2010 that would brand China a currency manipulator and allow emergency trade tariffs against Chinese imports. Senator Schumer threatened the heavy ordnance of currency legislation in the following words: "After five years of stonewalling, punctuated by occasional, but halting action by the Chinese, we have lost faith in bilateral negotiations."[8] At the same time, following a time-bound resolution of the U.S. statutory calendar relating to anti-dumping duties, the Senate set 30 to 90 percent duties on Chinese-made steel pipes worth more than $1 billion.

By contrast, Treasury Secretary Tim Geithner postponed a report that might have labeled China a currency manipulator and promised instead to press the American case of renminbi manipulation at the June 2010 G-20 summit in Canada. In return, China's President Hu Jintao reacted diplomatically to the Treasury's nuanced handling of the issue during his visit to the United States in connection with the nuclear nonproliferation summit in Washington, D.C., on April 12 and 13. Finally, it happened. On June 19, just three days before the G-20 summit, the People's Bank of China announced that it would remove the renminbi peg to the dollar and make it more flexible so that its exchange rate reflected demand and supply "with reference to a basket of currencies." Let's take a look at what this meant.

III. Announcement of a Flexible Renminbi

With its impeccably well-timed move of adopting a managed float against a basket of currencies, the Chinese central bank had scored several points. It had successfully removed the hot-button issue of its exchange rate policy from the agenda of the June summit. It had defused the simmering protectionist pressures against Chinese imports in the U.S. Congress. It made a virtue out of the need to raise the renminbi's value against other currencies because the economy showed signs of an inflationary buildup. A stronger renminbi would tame inflationary pressures.

Renminbi Appreciation for Dealing with Inflation Buildup

As early as mid-November 2009, shortly before President Obama's visit to China, the People's Bank of China had signaled a soft touch in its quarterly monetary policy report. It had declared that the exchange rate policy would take into account "international capital flows and changes in major currencies." It meant that the bank would buy fewer dollars from dollar export earners and release fewer renminbi in the foreign exchange market in order for it to appreciate against the dollar.

At the same time, a stronger renminbi would stem the inflationary buildup and the housing bubble that the recovering Chinese economy confronted toward the end of 2009. Several policy initiatives were launched in November to deal with the inflationary pressures. Commercial banks had to hold 50 basis point–higher reserves. More to the point, the People's Bank of China began mopping up excess renminbi (which it released as it acquired dollars) by issuing central bank bills. The end-of-the-year pickup in sterilization signaled renminbi appreciation as an inflation-fighting device.

Indeed, by early 2010, the consumer price index had moved up and a bubble was developing in property values. Although the central bank had adopted measures forcing banks to cut back lending to borrowers (discussed in chapter 4), it needed to raise the renminbi in relation to other currencies. That would cut back exports, cheapen imports, make more goods available within China, and lower inflationary expectations. In other words, a moderate appreciation of the renminbi would be in China's interest. The latest June 2010 adoption by the central bank of a flexible exchange rate could help it contain the inflationary buildup. A week after the official announcement of the policy, the renminbi had crawled up by 0.5

percent against the dollar and, in the judgment of currency traders, was expected to move up in the futures market by 2 percent by the end of the year. It could be raised higher if inflationary pressures in the economy needed a stronger renminbi as an anti-inflationary policy instrument. But how long would it last?

The Policy Reversal in Favor of a Lower Renminbi

On August 12, 2010, almost two months after the People's Bank of China had loosened the renminbi peg against the dollar, it lowered the currency sharply, wiping out the gains from a flexible exchange rate arrangement. The move coincided with the authorities' intention of lifting exports as the Chinese economy showed signs of a slowing recovery. Industrial output had dropped in July, and retail sales were declining. The central bank chose to promote exports in order to counter the sluggish domestic demand. At the same time, foreign companies faced exclusion from the Chinese government procurement market valued at $500 billion. Renminbi depreciation would raise exports, and preferential treatment of domestic companies to the exclusion of foreign suppliers in government procurement would lift economic recovery. As before, the issue of imposing tariffs on Chinese imports in the United States resurfaced in early August when the latest U.S.-Chinese trade deficit, $26.2 billion in June, showed the biggest rise since October 2008. The House Ways and Means Committee was ready to hold a hearing on the renminbi issue in September after Congress returned from the September recess.

Indeed, the contentious issue came back to life on September 23, 2010, in New York when President Obama asked Premier Wen Jiabao to revalue the Chinese currency. As the November elections to the House and Senate approached, the president put the issue of American jobs and competitiveness at the top of his meeting with the Chinese premier, who barely budged beyond his familiar talking points about gradual reform of the Chinese currency. This standard response revived the usual political theater in Congress and in the Treasury Department. Representative Sander Levin (D-MI), chairman of the House Ways and Means Committee, was ready to present a bill that would declare that China was manipulating its currency, that such manipulation constituted an illegal export subsidy in favor of Chinese goods, and that the United States could not only impose emergency tariffs on Chinese goods it considered subsidized, but also make a case before the World Trade Organization. In his response before the Senate Banking Committee, Treasury Secretary Geithner expressed his reservation about naming China a currency manipulator. This prompted a sharp rebuke from Senator Schumer: "I'm increasingly coming to the conclusion that the only person in this room who believes that China is not manipulating the currency is you."[9] Perhaps the U.S. lawmakers' threat of imposing emergency tariffs on Chinese goods would prompt Chinese authorities to raise the renminbi by a small percentage ahead of the forthcoming G-20 November Summit in Seoul. The Chinese policy makers were ahead of U.S. lawmakers in practicing the art of diplomacy and challenging them over an issue they regarded as vital to China's interests.

While the U.S. Congress once again deliberated over the uncooperative renminbi management by Chinese authorities, the announcements by the BRIC group for supplementing the dollar as a reserve currency with additional instruments had died down. These suggestions, examined in the next section, had swirled around in early 2009.

IV. Why the Demand for an Additional Reserve Currency?

The first salvo in favor of a supplemental reserve currency was fired by Xiaochuan, chairman of China's central bank, in March 2009 on the bank's website. He had said that the reserve currency should be "disconnected from economic conditions and sovereign interests of any single country."[10] Following that announcement, the campaign for a supplemental reserve currency gathered momentum. Russia's President Dmitri Medvedev argued for a diversified currency regime on his Kremlin website as the April 2, 2009, London summit approached. The call was repeated at the mini BRIC summit when leaders of Brazil and India joined the chorus. In December 2009, the four BRIC members held about $3.3 trillion as foreign exchange reserves, including $2.4 trillion by China, $406 billion by Russia, $259 billion by India, and $232 billion by Brazil. They had been worried about the dollar's continuing decline since March against a trade-weighted basket of the major global currencies (figure 7.2).

The size and mix of alternative currencies by a central bank will depend on the trade participation of the country of currency origin. Quite often, a currency's value is announced against a basket of currencies rather than only the dollar. The Russian central bank announces the ruble's value in terms of the dollar and the euro, with weights of 0.55 for the dollar and

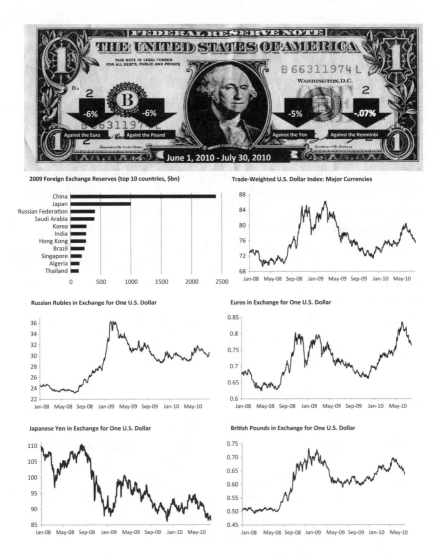

Figure 7.2.
The U.S. Dollar in Exchange for Major Currencies: 2008–2010. (Federal Reserve, International Monetary Fund.)

Note: The trade-weighted average of the foreign exchange value of the U.S. dollar is calculated against the subset of a broad index of currencies that circulate widely outside their country of issue. The heaviest-weighted currencies in order are the euro, the Canadian dollar, the renminbi, and the yen.

0.45 for the euro. Of course, Russia's trade with the United States is minuscule, but the prices of its major exports, energy and commodities, are specified in terms of the dollar. As for the euro, Germany is Russia's largest trading partner.

By March 2009, China was not only the largest holder of foreign exchange reserves, but also the largest holder, at $1 trillion, of U.S. Treasury bonds. As the largest foreign creditor of U.S. public debt, Chinese authorities worried about the dollar's value, although the U.S. economy had been exhibiting a GDP recovery toward the end of 2009. However, U.S. growth in the coming months could come with higher inflationary expectations because of the imploding budget deficit and the exorbitant money supply associated with the Federal Reserve's easy monetary policy. If the inflation onset turned out to be higher and quicker, the Fed might be compelled to lift the interest rate. As a result, Treasury bondholders, including the Chinese, would earn higher yields. But the Chinese authorities worried about the declining value of these dollar assets in their central bank portfolio and were ready to diversify their holdings. (As I set forth in chapter 3, however, U.S. recovery had become somewhat uncertain in July 2010, and the danger of an inflationary onset at that point had receded.)

Central banks around the world hold a basket of currencies, among them the dollar, the euro, the yen, and gold. The dollar occupies a dominant share because it has a sustained history of foreigners wanting to invest in the U.S. economy in general, beyond acquiring U.S. Treasury bonds. It continues to be the world's largest economy, and it chooses to consume more than it produces. Over the years, U.S. current account deficits have been financed by investment flows with foreigners, governments, and institutions holding dollar-denominated IOUs. This was facilitated by an ample supply of dollars in recent years. As examined in the next section, the dollar emerged as the global reserve currency.

V. The Dollar's Emergence and Prospects as a Reserve Currency

As early as 1960, Nobel laureate Robert Triffin had suggested that in order for the United States to continue being the supplier of a reserve currency, it had to incur persistent current account deficits.[11] In the course of analyzing the role of the dollar as a reserve currency, Triffin traced not only the replacement of gold by the dollar in that role, but also the constraints that the emergence of the dollar imposed on U.S. policy making. Thus,

> [g]old has long ceased to provide more than a fraction of the minimum requirements for the preservation of adequate reserve and liquidity levels. Most—although not all—countries, however, have shown themselves willing to accumulate a substantial portion of their monetary reserves in the form of foreign exchange—primarily sterling and dollar balances—alongside of gold itself. The trouble with this solution—known as the "gold exchange standard"—is that it is bound . . . to impart an increasing vulnerability to the world monetary superstructure built upon these so-called key currencies. Indeed, the additions to international liquidity made possible by the system are entirely dependent upon the willingness of the key currency countries to allow their own net reserve position to deteriorate, by letting their short-term liabilities to foreigners grow persistently and indefinitely at a faster pace than their own gold assets.[12]

The dollar replaced the sterling and emerged as the reserve currency because countries around the world were willing to hold and use dollar-denominated assets for financing their expanding trade. From early on, the dollar has continued to be freely traded in foreign exchange markets, enabling the dollar-denominated IOU holders to freely move out of their holdings should they so choose. The emergence of the dollar as the reserve currency replacing gold became final when President Richard Nixon abolished the dollar's convertibility into gold in 1971.

The availability of dollars to outsiders as a reserve currency, however, has depended on the ability and willingness of the Federal Reserve to issue dollars. On the one hand, if it chooses to adopt a strict monetary policy and release less currency in order to ease inflationary buildup at home, it may fail to meet the demand for dollars in an expanding global economy. On the other hand, if it pumps excess liquidity into the economy as it has done from the end of 2008 till now, it forces outsiders—among them, China—to hold low-yielding dollar assets. This seesaw of the dollar assets in possession of foreigners, the up-and-down fluctuation as a result of U.S. policy requirements, called the Triffin dilemma, has currently begun the phase of a dollar glut and low-yielding dollar assets.

Shouldn't, therefore, the global economy have an alternative reserve currency? Can the Chinese renminbi take on that role?

Can the Renminbi Become a Reserve Currency?

Will the Chinese policy makers need to follow the American model, that is, undertake a somersault and convert China's massive current account surplus into a deficit? Will China have to be a net dis-saver and entice foreigners to finance this saving gap by accepting renminbi-denominated IOUs? Not necessarily. A stable and growing Chinese economy with significant foreign trade participation can be expected to float renminbi-denominated bonds and attract foreign buyers. However, the renminbi will need to be fully convertible in order for foreign holders of the bonds to convert them into other currencies. But a fully convertible renminbi may appreciate against the dollar, which is what the U.S. Treasury, the International Monetary Fund (IMF), and several countries around the world want. Such an appreciation will undermine Chinese policy makers' export-led, high-growth, and abundant-employment strategy.

By contrast, the renminbi can occupy the less-than-domineering status of an important currency for bilateral trade transactions. For example, China and Brazil occasionally use their currencies for mutual trading, with China paying for its imports from Brazil in renminbi and Brazil financing its Chinese purchases with the Brazilian real.

Can the dominance of the dollar as an unreliable reserve currency be dislodged by an alternative arrangement proposed by Brazil, Russia, India, and China? They have actively supported the plan to increase the financing role of the IMF Special Drawing Rights (SDRs) by members.

Current Role of IMF SDRs

Three features currently mark SDRs, which were created in 1969 to replenish the gold and dollar reserves with the IMF of member countries, which in turn were determined according to a country's GDP.

First, the value of the SDR varies with the exchange rates of the dollar, the euro, the yen, and the British pound sterling, whose relative weights in the SDR are determined according to the currency's importance in the global trading and financial system. These weights are reviewed every five years. The U.S. dollar value of the SDR is posted daily on the IMF website. On August 25, 2010, one dollar exchanged for 0.663416 SDR.

Second, SDRs are allocated to IMF members in proportion to their quotas. An SDR holding does not represent an automatic claim on the

IMF, but a member can acquire a hard currency in exchange for its SDR via a voluntary exchange with another member or via IMF intermediation, which can persuade a member to acquire SDRs from another member country that needs hard currency. The acquisition of hard currency could enable the member country to run a budget or current account deficit or pay its hard currency debt or import from a hard currency source.

Finally, new SDRs can be issued by the IMF when the consenting members represent 85 percent of the total IMF quota. The United States, with a quota of 16.75 percent, can therefore veto an increase in SDRs with the IMF. The G-20 agreed in London on April 3, 2009, to increase the size of IMF SDR holdings tenfold, by $250 billion, of which $100 billion would go directly to emerging markets and developing countries. In June 2009, Congress approved the additional SDR creation with a U.S. contribution of $10 billion.

However, the SDRs becoming an international reserve currency with the IMF in charge is neither likely nor desirable. An international reserve currency has to be accepted by market participants rather than imposed by an agency of international economist-bureaucrats. But the demand of the Chinese authorities that the Chinese renminbi be included in the composition of the SDR carries more weight. At the same time, the dollar must remain strong in order for it to serve as a stable reserve currency.

The recent movement of the dollar, examined next, does not provide a reassuring signal.

VI. The Volatile Dollar

From mid-2008 till June 1, 2010, the value of the dollar against a trade-weighted index of the major global currencies indicates three phases. The dollar's value against the euro, the yen, and the pound shows a similar threefold trajectory (figure 7.2). Despite the complex motivation that induces currency traders to move in and out of the dollar, it is possible to make a reasonable guess about the greenback's movement against other currencies. In the first phase, the dollar rose from July 2008 until March 2009. The global recovery prospects during this period were uncertain and the dollar served as a safe haven for risk-averse currency holders. In the second phase, it fell, from March 2009 until early 2010. During this phase, which represented a massive carry trade from the dollar into other major currencies, speculators profited from borrowing dollars at near 0 percent interest and converting them into higher, interest-bearing, nondollar assets. In the final phase, it rose in the first half of 2010 as the prospects for U.S. economic recovery kept ahead of those in the eurozone, Britain, and Japan. However, in the two months ending July 31, 2010, the dollar had dropped against the euro by 6 percent, against the yen by 5 percent, and against the pound by 6 percent (figure 7.2).

The dollar's volatility has not converted U.S. policy makers, especially the Federal Reserve, into believers of the Triffin dilemma. In any case, the value of the dollar does not feature in the Fed's policy mandate, which must employ monetary policy for ensuring low inflation and unemployment. Neither the Federal Reserve nor the Treasury regards the slide of the dollar as a cause for worry. Its decline would moderate as the U.S. economy continued improving, and the Federal Reserve would eventually signal an exit strategy targeted at soaking up the excess liquidity.

That view, however, does not meet the approval of global leaders. During their September 2009 summit, the G-20 leaders desired that the United States bring its fiscal deficit under control, save more, and export more as the dollar declined. In the days leading up to his mid-November visit to Beijing, President Obama got an earful from East Asian leaders who pegged their currencies to the dollar and faced an asset bubble in their economies as speculators borrowed the greenback at low U.S. interest rates and invested them in higher-yield Asian assets. Indeed, Liu Mingkang, China's chief banking regulator, took a swipe at the Federal Reserve, saying that a declining dollar and a 0 percent interest rate threatened a global asset bubble. "Put your house in order. The dollar is your currency, but it is becoming our problem," the chorus chanted in unison.

This call was reminiscent of Triffin's warning about the consequences for U.S. policy making of the replacement of gold by the accumulation of short-term dollar liabilities:

> Such a movement obviously could not continue indefinitely without ultimately undermining foreigners' confidence in the dollar as a safe medium for reserve accumulation. The time will certainly come, sooner or later, when further accumulation of short-term foreign liabilities will either have to be slowed down or substantially matched by corresponding increases in our already bloated gold assets. If this were not done on our own initiative, foreign central banks would do it for us by stopping their own accumulation of dollar assets and re-

quiring gold payment instead [until the unilateral U.S. cancellation of the convertibility in 1971] for their overall surplus with the United States.[13]

Does the dollar's movement vis-à-vis other major currencies and against gold during the financial crisis that began in December 2007 exhibit such a drastic and continuing decline as to require a switch by holders of dollar assets into gold?

Are Dollar Assets a Liability?

As I have argued above, the dollar's volatility against major currencies in the past two years was marked also by occasional upswings when the U.S. economy was seen by the market as performing better relative to other economies. For example, as it posted signs of recovery in the first half of 2010 ahead of the eurozone, Britain, and Japan, the dollar had rebounded against the three currencies. In early 2010, the massive budget deficits and public debts of several eurozone peripheral economies, from Ireland in the north to Greece, Portugal, and Spain in the south, threatened the stability of the zone and the future of its single currency until the ailing economies got remedial support from the European Central Bank and the eurozone governments as they implemented austerity measures. Outside the eurozone, cautious investors weighed in against the British pound sterling as the British Exchequer sought to fix budgetary woes in mid-2010. In the Far East, Japan's new leaders struggled to pull the economy out of persistent deflation. In the early months of 2010, the dollar was once more in demand. However, the dollar weakened against the euro in July as the eurozone recovery signs improved and the U.S. growth prospects became uncertain.

The dollar's recent slide does not signal its impending collapse. However, as discussed in the next section, its steady, predictable value against the major currencies clearly depends on a decisive lowering of the federal budget deficit. In the long run, the trade deficit also needs to be lowered via suitable incentives designed to encourage Americans to consume less and save more.

VII. Long-Run Issues Relating to the Dollar
as a Reserve Currency

The scenario of the dollar continuing as a reserve currency will depend on tough policy choices, no less demanding than those facing the Beijing bosses. Slashing the U.S. budget deficit from the 2009 high level of 10 percent of GDP would constitute a continuing policy challenge in the near future for the policy makers. So would a steady maintenance of Americans' recent 6 percent saving rate from their disposable income. The declining personal saving rate of the past decade marked a departure from the significant long-standing saving behavior of American households (figure 7.3). It can be restored with appropriate incentives. In the end, only a stable U.S. current account deficit of around 3 percent of GDP managed via a low budget deficit and high personal saving rate can safeguard the dollar's role as a reserve currency.

Five decades ago, Triffin talked about rebalancing the world economy in the context of the dollar problem as the dollar came under pressure because of troubling U.S. trade deficits in the 1960s. "The real danger which we face is not that of a dollar collapse. It is the fact that such a collapse can

Figure 7.3.
U.S. Personal Saving as Percent of Disposable Income. (Bureau of Economic Analysis.)

ultimately be avoided only through a substantial slowdown of contributions to world liquidity derived in the last nine years [in the 1960s] from the persistent weakening of our net reserve position [via large trade deficits]."[14] Triffin, however, did not recommend an elimination of the overall U.S. balance of payments deficits, which would, by definition, put an end to the constant deterioration of U.S. monetary reserves. Such an elimination, in his view, "would have deprived the rest of the world of the major source—by far two-thirds to three-fourths—from which the international liquidity requirements of an expanding world economy were met in recent years, in the face of a totally inadequate supply of monetary gold."[15]

Triffin's message for the long-term stability and strength of the dollar was clear. The U.S. economy must maintain a sustainable current account position as a deficit economy via appropriate cutbacks in government and consumer spending. More decisively, the advantage that the dollar's status as a reserve currency confers to the economy should ultimately prevail in U.S. policy making. Not only are costs for U.S. borrowers lower, but they also repay their debts with the greenbacks. With the dollar standard in place, the United States exerts a dominant sway in the global economy. A gyrating dollar can carry adverse consequences, not only for the U.S. economy, but also for the global financial and trading system. In my view, the current policy debates in the high-unemployment U.S. economy tend to overemphasize the role of the mismatched U.S.-Chinese trade imbalance and push the rebalancing imperative via renminbi appreciation on China's policy makers. Ultimately, a strong dollar and its continuing role as a reserve currency call for determined and sustained policy initiatives in the United States. The responsibility for maintaining the dollar's status as a reserve currency must remain with the decision makers in Washington rather than in Beijing.

8

The Great Depression and the Current Financial Crisis

From the hindsight of almost seven decades, the Great Depression of the 1930s comes across as an incomprehensible combination of a lightning financial meltdown, a massive impact on the real economy, a staggering unemployment rate, and a damaging policy flip-flop in 1937 that set back the course of the fragile recovery.

The devastating episode raises three issues of relevance for the current financial crisis. First, which factors operating in the real economy and the financial sector during the 1920s contributed to the emergence of the Great Depression of the 1930s? Second, what institutional and policy measures were undertaken in the 1930s under Franklin Delano Roosevelt's two presidencies, from 1933 to 1940, for dealing with the chaos in the financial sector and in the real economy that faced massive unemployment and GDP decline? And third, how do the policy measures and the institutional changes implemented during the Great Depression compare with similar undertakings during the current financial crisis?

These issues, as they relate to the Great Depression, have been dealt with exhaustively by historians and economists from varying perspectives. These analysts also have sought to address controversial subjects, such as whether the stock market crash of 1929 led to the Great Depression and whether FDR's New Deal policies contributed to its persistence. Instead of reviving these debates, this chapter focuses on the salient features of the Roaring Twenties that developed into the traumatic events of the 1930s. It narrates the measures that were implemented under FDR for reducing the Depression's severe impact on the economy, and finally, it compares them with the policies of the Obama administration for dealing with the current financial crisis and with the regulatory overhaul proposed by Congress for preempting similar turmoil in the future.

In the first section, we take a look at the portents of what was to come. What were the underlying symptoms of the Great Depression? Why did they arise?

I. The Symptoms and Their Origin

The symptoms by all accounts were devastating.

On Black Tuesday, October 29, 1929, the stock market crashed, declining by 23 percent in a single day. Banks, which held these stocks as assets, suffered serious losses to the point of avoiding their depositors' claims. By 1931, 2,294 banks had collapsed, their number reaching 5,000 by March 1933. These failures wiped out the savings of millions of people.

The financial turmoil hit the real economy as demand declined, factories closed, people lost jobs, and farms were foreclosed. The Hawley-Smoot Tariff Act of 1930, which imposed the highest tariffs on imports in American history in order to promote sales of American goods, prompted a chain reaction of retaliatory tariffs from other countries, which worsened the situation further.

The policies of the Hoover administration (1929–1932) remained noninterventionist. In its view, a countercyclical fiscal policy involving a budget deficit and a high public debt would damage the government's credibility. Monetary easing would damage the value of the dollar and further weaken the economy.

The U.S. economy hit bottom in 1932. From 1929 levels, manufacturing was down by almost half, farm prices were down by 44 percent, and the stock market was down by 80 percent. Twenty-five percent of the workforce was unemployed.

How did these symptoms arise?

Origin of the Crisis

During the Roaring Twenties, the American economy was marked by rapid productivity growth, which in turn was led by unprecedented technological advances. These advances appeared not only in mass electrification and in assembly line production, but also across the board in a variety of new and better consumer goods, from refrigerators, washing machines, and vacuum cleaners to radios, furniture, and clothing. The automobile changed the way Americans went to work, shopped, and traveled. Increasingly, gas stations, repair shops, motels, and shopping malls appeared across the country. Extraordinary inventions proliferated in the entertainment industry. Philo Farnsworth came up with the dissector tube, which paved the way to the invention of the television. The first sound movie, *The Jazz Singer,* appeared in 1922. The first movie with sound and color followed in 1926. The first television drama, *The Queen's Messenger,* came out in 1926. Americans earned more and spent more on a variety of goods and services. As sales rose, manufacturers plowed back their profit, set up new facilities, and hired more workers. Prices declined as more goods and services became available. The wholesale prices of commodities such as cotton went down as well, affecting the economic well-being of Southern farmers. The American economy functioned vigorously by reacting appropriately to price and wage signals.

The Roaring Twenties was not a period of smooth growth in per-capita GNP, employment, and the inflation rate. Economic growth took off in 1923 after a brief recession in 1921 and a slight recovery in 1922. Figure 8.1 shows that real per-capita GNP rose from $641 in 1921 to $847 in 1929 at an average annual rate of 3.7 percent. Figure 8.2 shows that the unemployment rate fell from 12 percent of the workforce in 1921 to 3 percent in 1929. At the same time, with rising productivity led by widespread use of electricity and assembly line production in manufacturing, the inflation rate, measured via movements in consumer prices, rose from –11 percent in 1921 to 0 percent in 1929 (figure 8.3).

From 1921 to 1929 the inflation rate averaged –1.6 percent. Clearly, the Federal Reserve monetary policy must have played a role in the deflationary scenario during this period.

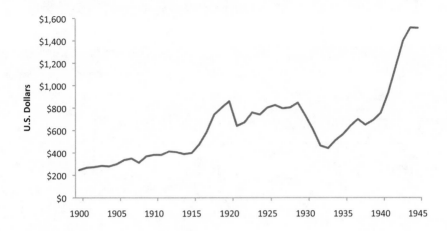

Figure 8.1.
Real Gross National Product per Capita in Dollars: 1900–1945. (U.S. Census.)

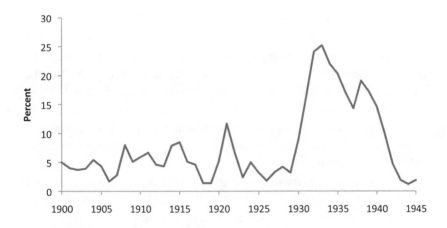

Figure 8.2.
Unemployment Rate as Percent of Labor Force: 1900–1945. (U.S. Census.)

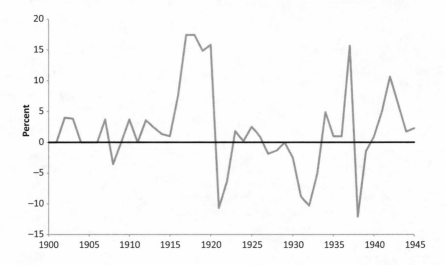

Figure 8.3.
Yearly Percentage Change in Consumer Price Index: 1900–1945. (U.S. Census.)

Monetary Policy During the 1920s

The policy-making expertise of the Federal Reserve was challenged to the hilt in the 1920s by a set of exceptional circumstances. Across the Atlantic, the war-ravaged European economies suffered from destruction of their productive capacities and high inflation rates. High wartime inflation resulting from excessive cash emission reached its pinnacle in war-torn Germany. Several European governments were also burdened by massive debts incurred during the war.

The Fed's inflationary worries arose from the fact that European countries, which had borrowed from U.S. creditors, including banks, began repaying their debts either in dollars or in gold. Under the prevailing gold standard, the Federal Reserve was expected to increase money supply as the gold inflow made its way via an American creditor's commercial bank account to the district Federal Reserve to the New York Federal Reserve. Until the United States went off the gold standard in 1933, this, in principle, was the automatic money creation process. As banking sector reserves rose (in exchange for the Fed's purchases of gold from the banks), the Federal Reserve worried about the increase in money supply these reserves could create.

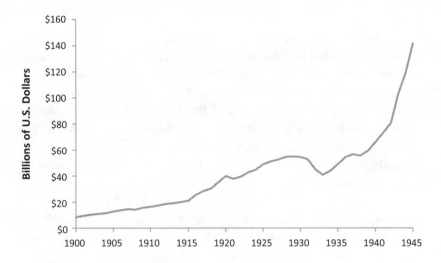

Figure 8.4.
Money Supply M2 in Billions of Dollars: 1900–1945. (*A Monetary History of the United States, 1867–1960*, by Milton Friedman and Anna Schwartz.)

Note: M2 includes currency in circulation plus demand and time deposits.

Since its establishment in 1913, the Federal Reserve had three policy instruments for containing surges in money supply. It could raise the discount rate it charged commercial banks when they borrowed from it. It could raise the reserve requirements that banks must keep for covering their deposit liabilities. And finally, it could sell securities in the market and soak up the excess money supply. For most of the 1920s starting in 1922, the Federal Reserve sold securities in order to soak up the excess reserves of banks and the rising money supply. It was not playing by the strict rules of the gold standard. The Fed's mission of the time was stated by Benjamin Strong, president of the New York Federal Reserve and the most influential member of the Federal Reserve's Board of Governors: "It was my belief . . . that our whole policy in the future, as in the past, would be directed toward the stability of prices so far as it was possible for us to influence prices."[1]

According to Milton Friedman and Anna Schwartz, "[g]old movements were not permitted to affect the total of high-powered money [bank reserves and currency]. They were . . . sterilized, inflows being offset by open market sales, outflows by open market purchases."[2] As figure 8.4 shows, M2, the measure of money supply consisting of currency in circulation, plus demand and time deposits, increased at 3.7 percent a year overall from 1921 to 1929. During that time, however, M2 increased and decreased in spurts as the Federal Reserve fine-tuned monetary policy. M2 increased in 1922, 1924, 1925, and 1927 and declined in 1923, 1926, late 1928, and early 1929. Indeed, the monetary policy management during the period evoked an encomium from no less a person than John Maynard Keynes: "The successful management of the dollar by the Federal Reserve Board from 1923 to 1928 was a triumph . . . for the view that currency management is feasible."[3] In hindsight, the Fed's excessively restrictive monetary policy kept the economy in intermittent deflation from 1921 to 1929.

From 1921 to 1929, there was an improving progression in terms of per-capita GNP (figure 8.1) and employment (figure 8.2) while inflation averaged –1.6 percent (figure 8.3). There were, however, two outlier observations, in 1921 and 1930, amid this improving performance.

Two Exceptions to the Roaring Twenties in 1921 and 1930

As the post-war U.S. economy took off in 1919 leading into 1920, the Federal Reserve, fearing an inflationary buildup, applied an excessive monetary brake and brought down M2 growth rate between 1920 and 1921 by –5.39 percent. Per-capita real GNP declined from $860 in 1920 to $641 in 1921; the unemployment rate moved up sharply from 5.2 percent in 1920 to 11.7 percent in 1921; and the consumer price inflation rate crashed from 15.8 percent in 1920 to –10.6 percent in 1921. However, the economy bounced back from the sharp recession of 1921 with quick adjustments in prices and wages across different sectors. The adjustments would have been difficult if the 1921 recession had resulted from a financial crisis. In reality, it was brought about by the Federal Reserve's tightening monetary policy in 1919 and 1920.

The second outlier, in 1930, had sharp recessionary features as well. Real income per capita was down. The unemployment rate had soared to 30 percent of the workforce. The consumer price inflation rate had dropped from zero in 1929 to –10 percent in 1932. In August 1929, the Federal Reserve raised the discount rate from 5 to 6 percent. The economy, in its judgment, was overheating with an abnormal rise in the stock market.

The growth of the stock market in the 1920s (figure 8.5) would seem a normal feature of the growing economy of the period. But why did it crash in October 1929?

Figure 8.5.
Dow Jones Industrial Index: 1900–1945. (Bloomberg.)

Note: The Dow Jones Industrial Index during this period was composed of between 12 and 30 major U.S. industrial companies.

Why Did the Stock Market Crash in October 1929?

Was the crash anticipated? Was it a crash?

WAS THE STOCK MARKET CRASH OF OCTOBER 29, 1929, PREDICTED?

The real economy from 1921 to 1929 showed steady real GNP growth. The Federal Reserve Bulletin reported improvement in the production index from 87 in 1920 to 125 in 1929. The annual rate of change of total factor productivity from 1919 to 1929 was more than 5 percent. The price/earnings ratios of companies and the dividends they paid out indicated a healthy performance.[4]

Shortly before the crash, economist Irving Fisher had made a pronouncement that has earned him a permanent place in history books: "Stock prices have reached what looks like a permanently high plateau."[5] By contrast, economic historian Charles Kindleberger, following an exhaustive, ex post facto analysis, provided details of the underlying speculative orgy. "Early in 1928, the nature of the boom changed. The mass escape into make-believe, so much a part of the true speculative orgy, started in earnest."[6]

Prior to October 29, the stock market was unstable. From 1925 to 1929, the Dow Jones Industrial Average (figure 8.5) kept rising, reaching record highs every year. From 1925 to the third quarter of 1929, common stocks increased in value by 120 percent in four years, a compound annual growth of 21.8 percent. This was an exceptionally high rate of appreciation.

On Black Tuesday, more than 16 million shares were traded, a record that was not broken until 1968 (when many more shares existed). From that perspective, it was a crash. And the speculative orgy that it represented resulted from stock trading by investment firms and individuals with borrowed cash in a regulation-free environment.

WHY DID THE STOCK MARKET CRASH ON OCTOBER 29, 1929?

At the turn of the 20th century, stock market speculation was restricted to professionals, but the 1920s saw millions of 'ordinary Americans' investing in the New York Stock Exchange. By August 1929, brokers had lent small investors more than two-thirds of the face value of the stocks they were buying on margin—more than $8.5 [billion] was out on loan.[7]

A significant institutional development from the early 1900s in U.S. banking consisted of the development of investment trust companies that engaged both in the issuing and underwriting (i.e., distributing) of securities as well as receiving their customers' deposits. States granted most commercial banks powers to engage in investment activities that were practiced by investment trusts. Banks also formed securities affiliates that carried out investment activities. From 1927 to 1929, commercial banks and their affiliates became increasingly involved in the securities business.

Around that time, only 16 percent of Americans held securities, in contrast to more than 60 percent currently. However, they borrowed in order to acquire them. People sold their Liberty bonds and used the cash to buy shares. When the cash did not cover the full value of the stock purchase, they borrowed. Brokers lent smaller investors, cooks and chauffeurs among them, 90 percent of the value of the shares they bought. In other words, the margin requirement was 10 percent. During the 1920s, these margin ratios were controlled by the brokers. On selected stock, they demanded a margin requirement as high as 25 percent. As the market became unstable after 1925, brokers raised the requirements from the average of 50 percent to around 75 percent toward the end of October 1929. In the process, while the brokerage firms safeguarded their own interest by demanding abnormally higher cash payments from their customers, the customers, who acquiesced in the deal, borrowed and faced financial ruin. When the market crashed, they not only lost their investment in the shares, but also faced a heavy debt burden.

Individual Americans were small players, however. Among the big investors in the stock market were investment trusts (similar to modern bank holding companies) that bought massive stocks of the expanding public utility companies. They also bought the shares on margin with funds loaned by nonbank creditors. However, the public utility companies in New York City, in New York State, and in Massachusetts faced increasing regulation from the Federal Trade Commission with regard to the pricing of electricity they sold to the public. As a result, prices of their stocks weakened. Sell-off of utility stocks from October 16 to October 23, 1929, weakened their prices, finally leading to panic selling. In addition to the troubled utility sector, real estate values were declining from their peak in 1925. On October 25, 1929, President Herbert Hoover referred to the "excellent state of business," but then added a caveat, saying that building and construction had been adversely "affected by the high interest rates induced by stock speculation."[8]

After the collapse on October 29, the market continued to spiral down at an unprecedented rate for a month. Periods of selling and price declines were followed by buying and price recovery. After Black Tuesday, the Dow Jones Industrial Average recovered partially in late 1929 and early 1930, then crashed again in 1932. On July 8, 1932, the Dow hit its lowest level of the twentieth century and did not gain its pre-1929 levels until November 1954.[9] The stock market lost 90 percent of its value from 1929 to 1932. By that criterion, it was overvalued.

The crash was followed by the economy's slide into the Great Depression and FDR's inauguration as president on March 4, 1933. Let's look at the years of the Great Depression and how FDR's policies affected the outcome.

II. The Great Depression: Symptoms, Policies, and Institutional Buildup

Throughout the period of 1929 to 1933, banks that held stocks as assets closed in large numbers. As a result of the severe contraction of the banking system, M2 declined sharply in 1929, 1932, and 1933. By 1933, M2 was 25 percent less than its 1929 level. By February 1933, the gold holdings of the Federal Reserve banks had increased to $3.36 billion, from $2.86 billion in 1929. However, although gold and other reserves had increased by $700 million, M2 had increased by only $680 million.[10] The contraction in the real economy turned out to be severe because of these waves of bank failures.[11]

In 1932, real GNP had declined by 23 percent from its 1931 level (figure 8.6). The unemployment rate was at 24 percent. Consumer price inflation was –10 percent. Amid this devastating scenario of the Great Depression, Franklin Delano Roosevelt conducted the presidential election on behalf "of the forgotten man at the bottom of the pyramid." He won by a landslide. His campaign pledged better economic prospects—to the workers via the rights to unionize and to claim fixed working hours and to the farmers via agricultural price supports. He promised to regulate the securities and mortgage markets via a stronger Federal Reserve. He implemented the New Deal, which he had promised to the American people during his campaign, and created an extensive institutional infrastructure. The four most important were the Federal Deposit Insurance Corporation, the Glass-Steagall Act, the Securities and Exchange Commission, and the Social Security Act providing benefits to retirees.

Institutional Buildup Under the New Deal

On taking office on March 4, 1933, FDR called a special session of Congress and declared a four-day bank holiday with congressional approval. Insolvent banks were closed and viable ones were reorganized and reopened. By mid-April, 12,800 banks, 4,000 fewer than before, were operating.

"Only with the New Deal's rehabilitation of the financial system in 1933–35 did the economy begin its slow emergence from the Great Depression."[12] The establishment of the Federal Deposit Insurance Corporation (FDIC) and the Securities and Exchange Commission (SEC) laid the foundation for rehabilitating the financial system.

The Banking Act of 1933 created the FDIC, which insured individual deposits with commercial banks in the amount of $5,000 each. Friedman and Schwartz described the setting up of the FDIC as "the structural change most conducive to monetary stability since . . . the Civil War."[13]

The Glass-Steagall Act of 1933 was designed to strike at the root of the securities trading of commercial banks, which, in the view of the act's promoters, played a role in the stock market crash of 1929. The act separated commercial banking from investment banking by defining the investment activities that member banks of the Federal Reserve System (including state-chartered banks) could undertake. They could act as agents for their customers in securities transactions, but were prohibited from using their depositors' accounts to buy securities for the banks' own accounts. The law also banned these banks from underwriting/distributing securities to the public.

Glass-Steagall banned national and state member banks from affiliating with any institution engaged principally in the issuance or underwriting/distribution of securities. By the same token, corporations that were engaged in issuing and distributing securities were barred from receiving public deposits. Congress later repealed these provisions in 1999 via the Gramm-Leach-Bliley Act.

The SEC was created as a federal agency on June 6, 1934, for enforcing federal securities laws, regulating the securities industry, and monitoring the nation's stock and options exchanges. Prior to its creation, the so-called Blue Sky Laws, which were formulated and enforced at the state level, regulated the offering and sale of securities. These laws were ineffective. As early as 1915, the Investment Bankers Association argued that companies could ignore these laws by offering securities across state lines through mail. Congress passed the Securities Act of 1933 for regulating interstate sales of the original issues of securities at the federal level. The law required companies to register securities trading with the SEC before they sold them across state lines. The public must have information about the financial condition of the issuing company and the risk the company securities carried. A subsequent 1934 act regulated the sale of secondary trading between individuals and companies. The 1934 act also required brokers to get a license, publish their prospectus, and fully disclose their financial activities.

Currently, the five SEC commissioners are appointed by the president with the advice and consent of the Senate. No more than three can be from a single political party. The SEC's broad mandate of safeguarding the financial system from fraud by enforcing federal securities laws was easier to implement in the 1930s when stocks were traded on open exchanges without fast electronic trading and flash orders; derivative trading was minimal, and credit default swaps were absent.

In 1935, Congress enacted the single most important federal program of the four institutional infrastructures, the Social Security Act of 1935 to keep seniors out of poverty. The act established an initial 1 percent payroll tax on both employers and employees to fund a guaranteed minimum income for seniors. A national minimum wage of 25 cents an hour was established in 1938.

In the early years of FDR's first presidency (1933–1936), Congress enacted several laws that were designed to promote the GDP and employment recovery in a stabilizing financial and regulatory environment.

The Tennessee Valley Authority Act of May 18, 1933, created a federally owned corporation that provided flood control, electricity generation, and agricultural relief in the Depression-impacted Tennessee Valley covering seven states. It turned out to be the largest regional planning agency of the federal government. The Agricultural Adjustment Act of May 12, 1933, allowed farmers to cut back or destroy crop production and get rid of livestock so that they could raise farm product prices. The National Industrial Recovery Act of June 16, 1933, established the National Recovery Administration with the aim of reviving growth, encouraging collective bargaining, and setting maximum work hours and minimum wages. The Chamber of Commerce proclaimed it an important step in progress toward business rehabilitation. The National Association of Manufacturers and Henry Ford opposed it.

In all, 17 landmark laws were enacted with a view to setting standards for dealing with the problems of a shattered economy so severe that machine guns protected government buildings out of fear that they might be attacked.

The stabilization of the banking system and the stock market had a positive impact on the real economy. In the four years from 1933 to 1936, "[a]nnual real GNP growth averaged over 9%, unemployment fell from 25% to 14%."[14] During FDR's two presidencies, from 1933 to 1940, the real GNP grew at average annual rates of 9 percent except during 1938. During the growth years, unemployment dropped from a high of 25 percent of the workforce in 1933 to 14 percent in 1937. It climbed to 19 percent in 1938 before dropping to 15 percent in 1940. The inflation rate measured in consumer prices improved from –10 percent in 1932 to 5 percent in 1934. It dropped to –12 percent in 1938 before rising to 0 percent in 1940. The stock market improved steadily except for a sharp decline of 34 percent in 1937.

Clearly, these numbers provide a record of widespread recovery during FDR's first term. Beyond the pickup in agriculture and manufacturing, the improving employment prospects, and the rehabilitation of the banking system and the stock market, men and women at the bottom of the pyramid felt more hopeful. Their bank deposits were safe. Their home mortgages were secure. The elderly had social security. The institutional apparatus that was set up under the New Deal for ensuring these benefits, from the Civil Works Administration for creating a massive public works program to the Rural Electrification Authority and the Tennessee Valley Authority for bringing power to the rural South, became powerful agents for betterment and renewal.

This momentum came to a halt in 1937 in the first year of FDR's second presidential term. What went wrong?

A Counterproductive Policy Switch in 1937 with Negative Impact in 1938 and 1939

A switch to contraction-prone fiscal and monetary policies halted the recovery and raised unemployment to 19 percent in 1937. By 1936, 4 million veterans had received $1.5 billion in benefits. These payments were discontinued from the federal budget. However, federal budget spending, measured in 1937 dollars, declined by less than 0.7 percent of the GDP between 1936 and 1937.[15] The budget deficit was reduced via higher taxes. Social security taxes were raised. A bigger impact on deficit reduction came from sliding tax rates on undistributed corporate profits. The sliding tax rose to 27 percent if a company retained 70 percent of its net income. The tax raised the cost of investment in companies that financed it from retained profits. The tax rate on dividends also went up, from 10.14 percent in 1929 to 15.98 percent in 1932 and then doubling in 1936. These increases in capital income tax can account for much of the 29 percent decline in fixed business investment that occurred in 1937 and 1938.[16] In a word, the budget deficit was cut back in the middle of a fragile recovery with tax measures that discouraged investment.

At the same time, the Federal Reserve worried about excess reserves in banks that might fuel inflation if "speculative excess" resurfaced once again. The Banking Act of 1935 had reconstituted the Federal Reserve policy apparatus by establishing the Federal Open Market Committee (FOMC) and had raised reserve requirements against the deposit liabilities of commercial banks. Congress had raised the price of gold to $35 an ounce in 1934. The political situation in Europe was unstable. As a result of these inducements, U.S. banks received gold from buyers that made its way to the district Federal Reserve banks. By 1936, gold with commercial banks and with the Federal Reserve banks was in excess of the required amounts against their liabilities.

The Fed was worried that the excess reserves might lead to increased money supply and fuel inflation if "speculative orgy" resurfaced once again. The Federal Reserve Board raised the reserve requirement of commercial banks in three steps: by 50 percent in August 1936, 25 percent in March 1937, and the final 25 percent in May 1937. In other words, the reserve requirement for commercial banks was doubled from, say, 7 percent of deposit liabilities to 14 percent. As a result, banks extended fewer loans to clients, and the recovery was stifled. The decision under FDR in 1933 to suspend the gold standard enabled the Fed to employ these monetary measures. As a result, the exit in 1936 and 1937 from the expansionary monetary policy of 1933–1936 came prematurely.

At the University of Chicago on November 8, 2002, in a speech honoring Milton Friedman on his 90th birthday, Federal Reserve Chairman Ben Bernanke said: "I would like to say to Milton and [his wife] Anna: Regarding the Great Depression, you're right, we did it. We're very sorry. But thanks to you, we won't do it again."[17]

This leads us right to a comparison of the two crises.

III. The Great Depression and the Current Financial Crisis: Contrasts

The origins of the two crises suggest a significant contrast.

Differences in Crises Origins

The stock market crash in October 1929 toward the end of the Roaring Twenties initiated bank and business failures, crumbling household finances, and massive unemployment, which stretched into the Great Depression of the 1930s. The current financial crisis originated with a housing boom that was fed by the Federal Reserve's liberal monetary policy starting in 2001. The lax regulatory setup resulted in excessive mortgage buildup by Americans. These mortgages, which turned out to be subprime, appeared in the balance sheets of Wall Street banks, which acquired them as investors via credit default swaps. In short, by the end of 2007, Americans held massive debts and banks around the country and on Wall Street carried

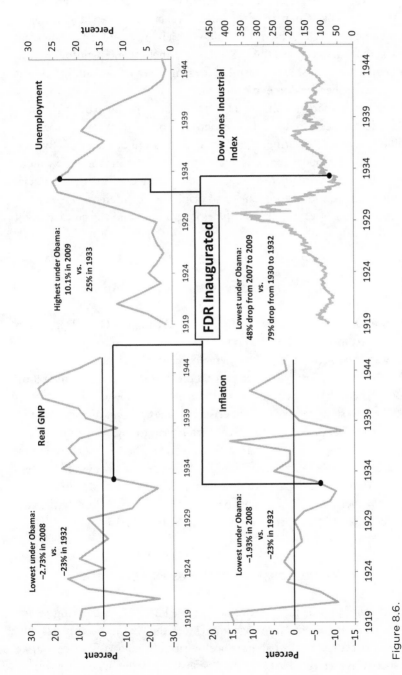

Figure 8.6.
The Great Depression and the Current Crisis: A Comparison. (Bloomberg; U.S. Census.)

near worthless mortgages that were taken over by Fannie Mae and Freddie Mac. The shaky finances of the financial sector threatened its collapse, whereas the heavily indebted consumers, which provided up to 66 percent of consumption outlays in the U.S. GDP, withheld their spending. Investment cutbacks by businesses resulted in rising unemployment, which was 9.6 percent of the workforce in mid-2010.

The stock market collapse of 1929 devastated the banking sector, household finances, and the U.S. economy from 1930 through 1932. The decline continued, resulting in the Great Depression of the 1930s. By contrast, the housing boom that was financed in an environment of easy monetary policy and lax regulatory environment initiated the current financial crisis toward the end of 2007. The crisis origins were different.

The impact of each crisis on the real economy and the stock market differed as well.

Crises Impacts on the Real Economy

As figure 8.6 shows, the growth of real GNP during the Great Depression had plunged to –23 percent in 1932. Its largest decline during the current crisis was –2.73 percent in 2008. Unemployment in 1933, at 25 percent, was higher than the highest rate of 10.1 percent under the Obama administration in 2009. The inflation rate during the former was as low as –12 percent in 1938. The lowest during the current crisis was –1.93 percent in 2009. Finally, the stock market plunge of 90 percent from 1929 to 1932 was more severe than the decline of 48 percent from 2007 to 2009. The American economy was severely crippled in terms of all the indicators during the Great Depression. By contrast, the impact of the current crisis appears moderate.

The responses and their sequencing by policy makers during the two episodes reflected their priorities in dealing with the crisis.

Policy Responses: Similarities and Contrasts

On becoming president in early March 1933, FDR placed banking sector reform as the first item on his agenda. Under the Obama administration, the Fed's stress test of the balance sheet health of the 19 Wall Street banks was speedy as well. Under FDR, the Reconstruction Finance Corporation bought $1 billion worth of preferred shares, which were one-third of banking sector assets. The Troubled Asset Relief Program funding provided to major Wall Street banks ran into $250 billion out of a total of $700 billion.

FDR's program of bailing out American home owners was incomparably manageable in contrast to the Treasury's continuing support of Fannie Mae and Freddie Mac, which hold vast amounts of subprime mortgages. In 1933, the Home Owners' Loan Corporation was established to help home owners refinance their homes and avoid foreclosures. The purpose was to enable lenders and investors to take losses so that mortgage holders could afford their mortgages. Ultimately, 200,000 owners defaulted, but 80 percent were saved. These are minuscule numbers in contrast to the subprime mortgages running into $5.5 trillion originally held by Fannie and Freddie out of an estimated total $10 trillion.

The stimulus provided by the New Deal public works program, which began in 1933, brought down unemployment from 25 percent in 1933 to 14 percent in 1936. The stimulus of $862 billion, approved by Congress in early 2009, has raised intense controversies about its impact on output and employment growth. In my view, the recessionary decline of GDP and employment would have been higher in the absence of the stimulus spending, which will continue into 2011.

Clearly, the *absolute* scale of the impact of the current crisis in terms of employment and output loss has been incomparably higher than at the height of the Great Depression. It would also seem that the economic benefit from the stimulus, dollar for dollar, flowed more speedily in the 1930s than currently. The public works program undertaken under the New Deal of building bridges, roads, and schools was perhaps less demanding in terms of construction know-how, engineering technology, organization, and public-private coordination. The program was geared to creating rapid employment, and it succeeded in its mission. A significant number of these structures are currently certified as outdated or crumbling in terms of current technology, and their upgrading demands superior training and advanced skills from unemployed job seekers.

The Great Depression and the current crisis provide contrasts and lessons with respect to monetary and fiscal policy making as well.

Monetary and Fiscal Policies: Contrasts and Lessons

Fiscal and monetary policy implementation during most of the 1920s and 1930s tended to be conservative and at times counterproductive. A significantly low growth rate of money supply during the 1920s kept the economy in deflation. In the midst of a fragile recovery in 1936–1937, the Federal Reserve raised reserve requirements of commercial banks in 1937. At the same time, the budget deficit cutback via higher taxes on dividends and retained profits of businesses turned out to be counter-productive. FDR's fiscal conservatism prevailed. He was not an ardent follower of Keynesian pump priming. By contrast, monetary and fiscal policies during the current crisis have continued to be expansionary. The substantial budget deficits running at 10 percent of GDP in 2009 and at the same projected level in 2010 have aroused debates about the need to cut them back with a view to containing the public debt–to–GDP ratio. The Federal Reserve has continued to maintain the federal funds rate at close to 0 percent and has released more cash into the economy via pur-chases of long-term Treasury bonds. U.S. banks, however, have been cau-tious in extending loans to businesses, which in turn await a pickup in retail buying by consumers.

The hasty tightening of monetary and fiscal policies in 1937 in the midst of a fragile recovery with high unemployment provides a major les-son to policy makers for managing the current recession with slow GDP recovery prospects and an unemployment rate of 9.6 percent of the work-force. They must avoid the temptation of opting in favor of a premature fiscal and monetary policy tightening. The timing of the exit from the cur-rent expansion to monetary tightening in the next phase is critical.

The Great Depression created a number of government agencies that stabilized the banking system and the stock market. The regulatory over-haul and the necessary institutions proposed by the Dodd-Frank Act are no less impressive.

The New Institutions: Then and Now

The New Deal resulted in the creation of the Federal Deposit Insurance Corporation, the Securities and Exchange Commission, and the social se-curity program. These have continued to function, although with mixed operational records. The financial resources of the FDIC have been overly stressed in bailing out small and medium-sized banks that carry subprime mortgages. The SEC failed to track down the trading of highly leveraged securities, which in turn were positively rated by credit rating agencies like Standard & Poor's. With cash outflows in excess of inflows, the social security program will continue to contribute to the federal budget deficit. This New Deal arrangement for promoting the welfare of retirees is more manageable than Medicaid and Medicare, but it is currently in poor shape.

Under the Dodd-Frank Act, the over-leveraging by big banks will be monitored by a Resolution Authority. Consumer interests with regard to mortgages and credit card activities will be regulated by the new Consumer Financial Protection Bureau. These two agencies' performance in preventing a new crisis by winding down big failing financial units in time and protecting consumer interests will depend on whether the legislative provisions of Dodd-Frank can be converted into specific regulatory rules and whether the rules in turn will be implemented effectively. Will the new rules promote consumer benefits via credit card transactions, checking account deposits, and home ownership via mortgages? This is a debatable issue (discussed in chapter 9).

Each crisis originated in America and each became global.

American Crises Turning Global

Cross-border connections are far more interactive in trade, finance, and technology today than in the 1930s. The scale of globalization is vast and complicated. China's historic emergence as a major creditor of U.S. Treasury debt and an aggressive policy enforcer of its exchange rate policy (analyzed in chapter 7) has immeasurably complicated policy making around the globe. In the 1930s, by contrast, American-European interaction was decisive. It was particularly close as a result of gold inflows and outflows, which in turn complicated U.S. monetary policy choices. In the current crisis, the European Union was badly hit from crisis impact on European exports and the European banking sector. In addition, fiscal mismanagement by some members of the Economic and Monetary Union (discussed in chapter 4) weakened the euro to the point of its survival. But current European problems appear more manageable than during the 1930s when severe political instability continuing after the weak post-war recovery dragged Europe and the United States into World War II.

But World War II turned out to be the recovery trigger that pulled the United States out of the Great Depression. When the war began in 1939, U.S. unemployment was 17.2 percent. It was a low 2 percent in 1945. Much of the employment, however, was temporary. It consisted of 10 to 12 million soldiers who were sent overseas and an additional 10 to 15 million workers who produced military items, from bullets to tanks, at home. Nevertheless, within the two-year period of 1939 to 1941, manufacturing output had gone up by 50 percent. The GNP had almost doubled from 1940 to 1945.

At the end of the war, the U.S. economy faced a massive, peacetime conversion of its production capacity. It nevertheless took off in an unprecedented boom, aided in part by a liberal corporate tax policy. With a Democratic majority in both chambers, Congress slashed the top effective marginal corporate tax rate from 90 percent to 38 percent. FDR's "excess profit" tax was repealed. The top marginal income tax rate, which was 94 percent on all income over $200,000, was cut to 86.4 percent. The lowest rate was cut from 23 percent to 19 percent. It exempted 12 million Americans from tax rolls entirely.[18]

The United States is currently engaged in two wars (however, with continuing disengagement in the Iraq operation). Their contribution to the growth of the economy's production and employment possibilities has been minuscule at best. At the same time, the cost of the dual military engagement has continued to represent a significant burden on the federal budget. More to the point, unlike in the post–World War II phase, current decision making in Congress and the administration with regard to federal tax and spending policies has been charged with irresolvable interparty political intransigence. Will the outcome of the November elections and a reconstituted Congress promote a workable compromise on the issue?

How different is the political environment today from that under FDR going into the post-war recovery?

The Political Environment: Then and Now

The political climate under FDR was no less contentious than it is under Barack Obama. The ideological battles in the 1930s, as they related to presidential decision making, were no less clamorous. The Left believed that FDR was not going far enough in its direction. On the Right, opponents of the New Deal, among them Republican congressmen and the U.S. Chamber of Commerce, argued that new taxes and the institutional overhaul would inevitably retard growth and harm America. That is a familiar Republican position now also. Under FDR, however, his opponents believed that the New Deal was un-American. He was converting the United States into "Amerika." In their view, he was no different from Stalin and Mussolini. The worst epithets Obama has been given are that he talks like a professor and acts like a socialist. His concern for the common man is genuine, but, his opponents ask, is it heart-warming? FDR, by contrast, fought for the common man with an intimate personal bond as it were, with joyous energy, and political savvy occasionally bordering on wiliness. People believed him when he said that the ravaged nation had a rendezvous with destiny. He gave Americans a sense of what they could expect from their government. He was a fiscal conservative who nevertheless believed that "modern society, acting through its government, owes the definite obligation to prevent the starvation or the dire want of any of its fellow men and women who try to maintain themselves but cannot."[19] Obama argues relentlessly for the welfare of the common man, but his speeches, unlike FDR's radio talks, fail to bring him into the listeners' living rooms. In maneuvering the decision making at every turn and implementing it, at times incorrectly as in 1937, FDR redefined the relationship of the American people with their government. Will Barack Obama rise to the challenge? Too early to tell.

9

The Future of American Capitalism

The financial turmoil that threatened a meltdown of U.S. financial institutions toward the end of 2008 raised questions about the enduring power of American capitalism. Nobel laureate Joseph Stiglitz suggested that its destructive impact could resemble the fall of the Berlin Wall in 1989, which ended the Soviet Union in 1991. That was a misplaced analogy. Moscow's domination of East-Central Europe had to end. The authoritarian political system that prevailed in the Soviet Union for seven decades needed to disappear as well. By contrast, post-crisis American capitalism called for its renewal.

By all accounts, American capitalism comes across as a special brand of a private enterprise system distinguished not only by remarkable entrepreneurial drive, innovative ingenuity, and risk taking, but also by a complex financial and technological underpinning. Viewed from this perspective, American corporate arrangements have evolved at a frantic pace from the original conception of a market system articulated by Adam Smith as far back as 1776. More than a century and a half later, John Maynard Keynes warned about the inherent instability of the arrangements in which the separation of corporate managers and owners interacted with the destabilizing influence of stock markets in investment decision mak-

"Wasn't that Paul Krugman?"

(© David Sipress / The New Yorker Collection / www.cartoonbank.com)

ing. The economywide consequences of excessive risk taking in his design will ultimately appear in a declining economy with decreased investment and consumption spending. As a result, government stimulus spending will become indispensable.

Both Smith and Keynes, as I argue in this chapter, suggested that a "prudent" financial order was indispensable for the stability and growth of a market system. Following their analyses, I seek to answer a specific question, namely, will the new regulatory rules stabilize the U.S. financial sector in order for the economy to grow and the corporate model to endure? What concessions were made by U.S. legislators with that aim in view? Do the evolving responses by U.S. banks to the new rules on derivative and proprietary trading and credit card issuance provide positive signals to the effect that they are ready to face the challenges of the regulatory overhaul? The ongoing signals are affirmative and resilient. They suggest that worries about the demise of the corporate arrangements that characterize American capitalism are premature.

As the financial storm gathered momentum, policy makers in the administration and in Congress confronted the issues, mounted a stimulus for softening its recessionary impact, and adopted a slew of new regulations. Two aspects of relevance for the future of the American arrangements emerged at the center of the process.

How did Adam Smith define a market system that forms the basis of American capitalism? Did a reckless departure by U.S. financial institutions from the strictures he laid down with regard to financial practices plunge the economy into a deep recession? Let's examine this.

I. Adam Smith's Market System

Adam Smith's oft-quoted example of the butcher, the baker, and the brewer conveyed the essential driving force that forms the basis of market transactions, namely, that individuals motivated by self-interest undertake profitable exchanges in a marketplace.[1] Indeed, commenting on the propensity to truck, barter, and exchange one thing for another, Smith wrote: "Whether this propensity be one of those original principles in human nature, of which no further account can be given; or whether, as seems more probable, it be the necessary consequence of the faculties of reason and speech, it belongs not to our present subject to enquire. It is common to all men, and to be found in no other race of animals."[2] The propensity to undertake profitable market transactions will continue to be the underlying feature of American capitalism.

Indeed, Smith extended the concept of profitable exchanges based on the division of labor to the international arena as well. "If a foreign country can supply us with a commodity cheaper than we ourselves can make it, better buy it of them with some part of the produce of our own industry, employed in a way in which we have some advantage. The general industry of the country . . . will not thereby be diminished . . . but only left to find the way in which it can be employed with the greatest advantage."[3]

Could Adam Smith's baker take out a loan for setting up a bakery? He could, but under such stringent conditions that a modern-day baker, or a banker for that matter, would regard Smith's operational requirements for the purpose draconian.

The Banking System Under Adam Smith

Smith notes: "What a bank can with propriety advance to a merchant . . . is not either the whole capital with which he trades, or even any considerable part of that capital; but that part of it only, which he would otherwise be obliged to keep by him unemployed, and in ready money for answering occasional demands."[4] In other words, the baker would continue to pay the flour mill for his purchase of flour and his workers for their services from the cash he received by selling the bread. He could resort to a bank loan if the bakery had to be closed during an emergency or if a buyer or two failed to pay him on time.

This revolving door policy that required the borrower to cover his bank loans via receipts from his sales operations imposed constraints on banks as well. Thus, "if . . . the sum of the repayments from certain customers is, upon most occasions, fully equal to that of the advances, it [the bank] may safely continue to deal with such customers. Though the stream which is in this case continually running out from its coffers may be very large, that which is continually running into them must be at least equally large."

And himself a thrift-prone Scotsman, he continues:

The banking companies of Scotland, accordingly, were for a long time very careful to require frequent and regular repayments from all their customers, and did not care to deal with any person, whatever might be his fortune or credit, who did not make, what they called, frequent and regular operations with them. By this attention, besides saving almost entirely the extraordinary expense of replenishing their coffers, they gained two other very considerable advantages. First, by this attention they were enabled to make some tolerable judgments concerning the thriving or declining circumstances of their debtors, without being obliged to look out for any other evidence besides what their own books afforded them. . . . Secondly, by this attention they secured themselves from the possibility of issuing more paper money than what the circulation of the country could easily absorb and employ.[5]

Smith's rules for banking sector loan activities seemed to exclude fractional reserve requirements. Bank advances had to be matched by bank receipts over a period of time. The practice would rule out indiscriminate credit and cash flows in the economy. He worried about excessive currency circulation resulting from overtrading. "The over-trading of some bold projectors in both parts of the United Kingdom was the original cause of this excessive circulation of paper money."[6] The most conservative modern-day banker would regard the norm overly restrictive. The rule would be observed under Adam Smith's regime because bankers' loans were to extend to customers about whom banks had "tolerable judgments concerning [their] thriving or declining circumstances" based on their books and only for moderate periods of time.

> A bank cannot, consistently with its own interest, advance to a trader the whole or even the greater part of the circulating capital with which he trades; because, though that capital is continually returning to him in the shape of money . . . yet the whole of the returns is too distant from the whole of the outgoings, and the sum of his repayments could not equal the sum of its advances within such moderate periods of time as suit the convenience of a bank. Still less could a bank afford to advance him any considerable part of his fixed capital; of the capital which the undertaker of an iron forge, for example, employs in erecting the forge.[7]

In other words, banks might choose to advance a fraction of the capital required for a foundry, but the dominant share would have to come from the personal savings of the foundry owner(s). The rudimentary institutional underpinning implied that some capital was raised by the butcher, the baker, and the candlestick maker from people who moved money around, and Smith was aware of them, but it is not clear if he described these arrangements as capitalism involving the use of capital. The transactions were based on mutual trust and were personalized.

Did the notion of private property belong to the model?

Property Ownership, Private Interest, and Public Awareness Under Adam Smith

The baker, who took out a short-term loan for operating his bakery and repaid it promptly, owned his bakery. He sought to run his bakery in pursuit of profit, but Smith emphasized the role of traditional values in disciplining the role of the profit motive when individuals pursued self-interest as members of a social group. "Prudence of all virtues is most helpful to the individual, whereas humanity, justice, generosity, and public spirit are the qualities most useful to others."[8] The market system, in other words, can be viewed as involving a moral pursuit. Of course, he did not believe that the confluence of private virtue and public awareness would produce self-regulatory markets. Profit seeking, in his view, could produce "prodigals and projectors" who were animated by excessive risk taking. The invisible hand of the market could get out of control and create dangerous consequences for society.

Adam Smith and the Invisible Hand of the Market

Can the invisible hand generate correct prices and create stable markets? Clearly banks existed, people borrowed, and governments provided a rudimentary underpinning of rules for economic actors. Individuals motivated by "self-interest" undertook "market transactions," with a view to making "profit" in the microeconomic arrangements of *The Wealth of Nations*. However, the macroeconomic conflict between private gain and public interest in his framework was resolved via traditional values rather than via imposition of a regulatory mechanism involving, for example, adequate capital requirements by banks, which are the dominant concern currently of the Basel Committee (as discussed in chapter 6). Needless to say, the overarching role of the stock market and of over-the-counter derivative transactions via fast electronic trading in generating macroeconomic turbulence was not relevant in his framework. Bilateral business deals of his days, driven by mutual trust, were to take place via personal contacts or, failing that, via painstaking postal negotiations.

Almost two centuries later, Keynes focused on the macroeconomic consequences of risk-prone microeconomic investment decisions that drove an economy into a downward spiral. The next section explores Keynes's perspective.

II. Macroeconomic Consequences of Microeconomic Decision Making in Keynes

In Keynes's view, long-run expectations of investors during the upswing of a business cycle were marked by exuberant risk taking. His *General Theory of Employment, Interest, and Money* drew its lessons from the stock market crash of 1929 and the "animal spirits" that drove people into undertaking precarious decisions. He came out strongly in favor of a policy agenda of government pump priming designed to fill the gap in private spending during an economic downturn.

Keynes attributed the risk-prone nature of business decision making of his time to the interaction of three factors. First, in contrast to the old days, ownership of a business unit, he argued, was increasingly separated from its management. Second, the emergence of the stock market, in his view, tended to add to the instability of investment activity. And finally, he emphasized the role of animal spirits in creating the upswing of a business cycle. Despite the uncertainty and even ignorance of estimating yields from long-term projects, investors choose to act "as a result of animal spirits, . . . a spontaneous urge to act."[9]

How did the separation of ownership and management influence investment activity?

Owner Versus Manager According to Keynes

In former times, when enterprises were mainly owned by those who undertook them or by their friends and associates, investment depended on a sufficient supply of individuals of sanguine temperament and constructive impulses who embarked on business as a way of life, not really relying on a precise calculation of prospective profit. The affair was partly a lottery, though with the ultimate result largely governed by whether the abilities and character of the managers were above or below the average. Some would fail and some would succeed. But even after the event no one would know whether the average results in terms of the sums invested had exceeded, equaled or fallen short of the prevailing rate of interest; though, if we exclude the exploitation of natural resources and monopolies, it is probable that the actual average results of investments, even during periods of progress and prosperity, have disappointed the hopes which prompted them. Business men play a mixed game of skill and chance, the average results of which to the players are not known by those who take a hand. If human nature felt no temptation to take a chance, no satisfaction (profit apart) in constructing a factory, a railway, a mine, or a farm, there might not be much investment merely as a result of cold calculation.[10]

Thus, businessmen, according to Keynes, increasingly took a chance at investing. They were not necessarily driven by "cold calculation" of profit making. As a result, the average stream of returns discounted over time fell below the current rate of interest. This happened less frequently in the old days because the decision was taken by men of "sanguine temperament" and "constructive impulses" jointly with their friends of similar inclinations. By contrast, managers, divested from old-fashioned ownership commitments, produced results that were below average.

Does this argument appear outdated? Modern corporations and financial institutions have become so large that they require separation of ownership and management. Indeed, during the current financial crisis, the shareholders of Lehman Brothers discovered that they were far removed from the decision-making maneuvers of its management team. Because of such flaws, Treasury regulators sought to tie managers' compensation to their long-term performance in the large banks that had received funding from the Treasury in 2009. Among the latest regulatory rules suggested by the Dodd-Frank Act, boards of directors are urged to vet managerial decisions. Shareholders, who will elect members of company boards via proxy votes, are asked to monitor the fortunes of the companies they own. The separation of management from ownership in large financial institutions, which Keynes worried about, is here to stay except in mom-and-pop stores in the trade and service sectors.

How did the stock market fare in Keynesian analysis of investment decision making? He managed the stock portfolio of King's College and spoke with firsthand familiarity.

Keynes and the Stock Market

According to Keynes, the stock market allowed a continuing revaluation of investments and added to the instability of investment decision making. Thus,

> Decisions to invest in private business of the old-fashioned type were, however, decisions largely irrevocable, not only for the community as a whole, but also for the individual. With the separation between ownership and management which prevails to-day and with the development of organised investment markets, a new factor of great importance has entered in, which sometimes facilitates investment but sometimes adds greatly to the instability of the system. In the absence of security markets, there is no object in frequently attempting to revalue an investment to which we are committed. But the Stock Exchange revalues many investments every day and the revaluations give a frequent opportunity to the individual (though not to the community as a whole) to revise his commitments. It is as though a farmer, having tapped his barometer after breakfast, could decide to remove his capital from the farming business between 10 and 11 in the morning and reconsider whether he should return to it later in the week. But the daily revaluations of the Stock Exchange, though they are primarily made to facilitate transfers of old investments between one individual and another, inevitably exert a decisive influence on the rate of current investment. For there is no sense in building up a new enterprise at a cost greater than that at which a similar existing enterprise can be purchased; whilst there is an inducement to spend on a new project what may seem an extravagant sum, if it can be floated off on the Stock Exchange at an immediate profit. Thus certain classes of investment are governed by the average expectation of those who deal on the Stock Exchange as revealed in the price of shares, rather than by the genuine expectations of the professional entrepreneur. How then are these highly significant daily, even hourly, revaluations of existing investments carried out in practice?[11]

Keynes wondered if the stock market helped investment activity by providing correct profitability signals with respect to alternative choices. If there were no stock market, an investment decision would be irrevocable. It would sink or swim on its own merit. The stock market, he argued, influenced current investment decisions. Why build a new factory at a higher cost when a similar one could be acquired via a stock transaction? In this instance, it provided a helpful clue. By contrast, a risk taker might undertake a new business venture at enormous costs because the stock market flashed high immediate profitability for it. In the end, it might turn out to be misdirected.

In raising questions about the role of stock trading in investment activity, Keynes seemed to suggest that the stock market signals should be interpreted carefully. Were he to watch the current advances of stock trading via fast electronic platforms, flash orders, and derivative operations, he would have come out in favor of their regulation. "It is generally agreed that casinos should, in the public interest, be inaccessible and expensive. Perhaps the same is true of Stock Exchanges."[12]

The third and final element in his framework related to the uncertainty of long-term investment decisions in which animal spirits rather than careful estimates of yields prevailed.

Keynes and Animal Spirits

The outstanding fact is the extreme precariousness of the basis of knowledge on which our estimates of prospective yield have to be made. Our knowledge of the factors which will govern the yield of an investment some years hence is usually very slight and often negligible. If we speak frankly, we have to admit that our basis of knowledge for estimating the yield ten years hence of a railway, a copper mine, a textile factory, the goodwill of a patent medicine, an Atlantic liner, a building in the City of London amounts to little and sometimes to nothing; or even five years hence. In fact, those who seriously attempt to make any such estimate are often so much in the minority that their behaviour does not govern the market.[13]

In other words, long-term investment decisions are based on scant knowledge of the underlying yields, indeed on knowledge that amounts to little and sometimes to nothing. But in Keynes's example, the hard-to-evaluate assets were concrete items ranging from a railroad to a building in the city of London. He did not have in mind the animal spirits of a London-based group of 100 financial dervishes who sliced and diced billions of dollars' worth of mortgage-based securities of American Insurance Group (AIG) and sold them to global investors. They not only contributed to the financial turmoil, but also endangered the jobs and livelihood of 120,000 AIG employees.

Transmitted to the American financial sector, Keynesian animal spirits provided a refreshing insight with regard to its volatility. During the upswing that started in early 2007, bank and hedge fund managers acquired mortgage-based securities with scant knowledge about the likely future yields of these assets. But the sagging animal spirits of the financial operators hit bottom at the end of 2007 and remained there in 2008. As I have noted earlier, the stock market experienced one of its sharpest weekly declines in October 2007; the yields on three-month Treasury bills hit the negative range in September 2008 with investors seeking them out as safe havens; huge losses on securitized assets ate up massive amounts of major bank capital in June and November 2007.

As the erosion of Keynesian animal spirits spilled over from the U.S. financial sector into the real economy, his recipe for reviving the U.S. economy from the devastating downturn in income and employment that began in December 2007 acquired policy relevance. Doubts about the efficacy of the stimulus package (discussed in chapter 3) have continued, although all but $100 billion of the $862 billion had been disbursed by September 1, 2010. The budget deficit also has prompted widespread concern about the government's ability to bring it under control over time. Keynes would have no doubt that the U.S. economy's downturn in 2009 with continuing high unemployment in 2010 required a government-led deficit.

Keynes and Budget Deficits

Keynes provided a formidable analytical framework in favor of government pump priming in his inimitable writing, which was occasionally cumbersome, but always precise and illuminating. He was above all driven by robust pragmatism. It was pointless to resort to long-winded arguments for resolving a conflict between political expediency and a policy decision when resolute action was called for. "If the barometer is high and the clouds are black, don't waste time on a debate on whether to take an umbrella," he had said.[14] Again, a budget deficit, in his view, might be necessary right away and for a short duration. In one of his most famous quotes, he had said: "The long run is a misleading guide to current affairs. In the long run we are all dead. Economists set themselves too easy a task . . . if they can only tell us that when the storm is past the ocean is flat again."[15] Capitalist markets are inherently unstable. They need occasional and timely intervention via deficit spending for dealing with economic downturns, which are marked by output and employment decline. With this caveat in mind, he assessed the system favorably. "For my part, I think that capitalism wisely managed can probably be made more efficient for attaining economic ends than any alternative system yet in sight, but that in itself, it is in many ways extremely objectionable."[16]

Can the endemic instability of capitalist markets be moderated by government regulations? In particular, will the regulatory rules that will follow the Dodd-Frank Wall Street Reform and Consumer Protection Act signed by President Obama on July 21 accomplish that task? Will the rules effectively handle the recurrence of future financial crises and preserve American capitalism? The next section investigates answers to these questions.

III. The Likely Impact of the New Regulatory Rules

While the new rules are being formulated by the regulatory agencies— among them the Federal Reserve, the Securities and Exchange Commission, and the Commodity Futures Trading Commission—the signals provided by the Dodd-Frank Act, as I discussed in chapter 6, are directed at preempting the occurrence of a future financial crisis.

A Resolution Authority will monitor the activities of large U.S. financial institutions and arrange for their systematic dissolution if they appear on the brink of a collapse. In order to minimize their out-of-bounds risk taking, they will be allowed to undertake proprietary trading of only 3 percent on their own accounts. As growth picks up decisively among the crisis-hit global economies, including that of the United States, global banks will be required to keep substantial reserves, which will prevent them from over-leveraging. Derivative trading will be regulated. Financial derivatives relating to currencies, interest rates, and securities will remain with banks, but derivatives relating to commodities will be spun out of banking sector coverage. Derivatives must be cleared by special agencies and traded openly on exchanges. Hedge funds will need to keep adequate reserves and register with a regulator; rating agencies will have to be careful in proclaiming a security or bond issuer as deserving a AAA rating. The new Consumer Financial Protection Bureau is in charge of mortgage and credit card rules, which will require the issuing banks to be more prudent in their transactions with clients.

The regulatory process, which began in early 2009, ended after almost 16 months with President Obama signing the Dodd-Frank Act on July 21. The initiatives in Congress on reforming the financial regulatory system were dominated by the administration, its economic advisors, and the Democratic leadership in Congress. Unlike the health reform bill, which was drafted and navigated in Congress by the Republican leadership, Republicans hardly offered concrete, debatable proposals on financial reform. The Republican minority was short on substantive responses and long on obstructive tactics.

The Democratic control of the process raises three questions: Did the framers of the rules steer the process in the direction of restructuring the American corporate model based on risk and reward? Next, did they tighten the rules for regulating the financial sector and some of its practices while safeguarding the corporate arrangements? And finally, what concessions did they make along the way with that aim in view?

Impact of the Proposed Rules on the American Corporate Model

In the American corporate arrangements, managers take risks and promote growth of their businesses by outcompeting rivals. They generate profits and shareholder dividends. Successful managers receive large paychecks, abundant perks, including stock options, and name recognition. At the same time, the stock market and the shareholders, the corporate investors and the rating agencies ceaselessly track the quarterly earnings of the major corporations. Higher quarterly earnings imply bigger profits and larger dividends to shareholders.

In the wake of the financial turmoil, this model of shareholder values has come under attack from three directions. First, the emphasis on quarterly earnings takes attention away from the long-term goals of a corporate enterprise. Next, the goal of shareholder value ignores the interests of workers and, beyond that, of creditors and suppliers. And finally, advocates of corporate social responsibility argue that businesses should broaden their goals beyond profit making and shareholder value and worry about the impact of their operations on the environment, for example. General Electric had no business polluting the Hudson River with toxic waste, which it subsequently cleared up.

To what extent will the corporate search for profit be modified by government regulators, trade union activists, social responsibility advocates, and even stalwarts of American business such as Jack Welch, who recently warned about the model's focus on quarterly earnings as "the dumbest idea in the world"? It is doubtful that the multipronged pressures to chip away at the high-risk, high-reward corporate model will degenerate into a full-scale, European-style socialist adventure.

That said, the crisis revealed that the profit-maximizing managers operated in an environment of cursory oversight by directors and lax monitoring by regulators. It brought into the open the issue of the best way of rewarding top U.S. executives. In 2007, the earnings of top American CEOs had reached 275 times the average pay of a worker. At the same time, rewarding CEOs with stock options raises the question of whether they contribute to the upswing of the stock market only at a given point. They can be rewarded with stock options at the time of their retirement on the basis of their long-term contribution to the fortunes of the company. Can the methods of rewarding CEO profit-making savvy be determined by legislative rules? Should top management's pay be capped by congressional lawmakers?

That would be highly intrusive, according to the regulatory signals built into the Dodd-Frank Act. They indicate that company directors rather than legislative rule makers should assess managerial performance and determine its reward. Shareholders with significant equity holding should be actively monitoring the performance not only of the top CEOs, but also of directors who are supposed to be the watchdogs of shareholder interests. Dodd-Frank implies that the best approach is responsible activism within the private sector marked by checks and balances, rather than intrusive legislation. As a result, the act's regulatory proposals are aimed at inducing corporate responsibility through increased participation by shareholders who will elect corporate boards via proxy votes. The Securities and Exchange Commission and the Commodity Futures Trading Commission are busy devising procedures for decisive participation by shareholders in corporate management.

Do the provisions of the Dodd-Frank Act manage an appropriate balance between an autonomous financial system and regulatory guardrails with a view to nurturing the American corporate arrangements?

Balance Between Financial System Autonomy and Regulatory Guardrails

The long history of the financial reform process that began in early 2009 provides an answer to this question. Undoubtedly, the president's pragmatic view was swayed by political considerations, as when he introduced the Volcker rule for assuaging public anger against bankers. Representative Barney Frank (D-MA), who steered the Troubled Asset Relief Program legislation in late 2008, had pacified congressional resentment on the issue by arguing that bankers occasionally got wayward, but the country needed them. Senator Christopher Dodd (D-CT), who crafted the Senate bill, not only sought a balance among the various regulatory agencies, but also forcefully affirmed the vital role of American banks by arguing on May 21, 2010, that "improving regulation made more sense than restraining an industry that was critical to the American economy and that faced fierce competition from foreign banks, which would not be placed under similar restrictions. . . . I'd rather rely more on our ability to do that than to somehow shrink our capacity for this nation to lead in financial services."[17] And finally, Lawrence E. Summers, the administration's chief economic advisor, had this assessment: "[T]he legislation did not simply rely on an improved performance by regulators. It also creates larger margins for errors and tries to give companies incentives to behave."[18] He compared the approach to "increasing highway safety through seat belt laws and guardrails rather than relying on driver education. This is not a system that relies on people being smarter in the future."[19]

The system allows regulators a margin of error. They may occasionally underestimate the banking system's reserve requirements or fail to track down the derivatives that must go through a clearinghouse and be traded openly. But their overall record must be positive. Banks, by contrast, must take fewer risks or invite regulatory screening and pull back. No banks were broken up, and no limits were imposed on their size. No taxes were levied on their transactions, and no bans were imposed on bankers' compensation. Of course, their profits would be scaled back as they kept more reserves and avoided outlandish derivative trading. In the legislators' view, an adequately targeted regulation of the financial system will help the financial actors reshape their activities and shake off the burden of the pervasive malaise from their operations. In time, they will resort to traditional banking services of advancing loans to businesses and promoting economic growth. The basic arrangements of a free enterprise system, marked by private initiative and innovative drive, do not need to be altered.

And finally, what concessions did the lawmakers make for achieving a balance between the regulatory framework and a steady momentum of financial activity in order for U.S. market arrangements to endure and prosper? Let's examine this.

IV. Concessions Along the Regulatory Reform Route

Three major concessions were made by congressional lawmakers during their intense negotiations in drafting the Senate bill that formed the core of the final legislation. These were the postponement of higher capital requirements by banks against their assets; the dilution of the original Volcker rule and of the Blanche Lincoln proposal for spinning off all derivative trading from banks; and finally, locating the Consumer Financial Protection Bureau inside the Federal Reserve instead of keeping it as an independent regulatory agency.

Postponement of the Requirement for Higher Bank Reserves

Banks naturally want the capital requirement provision to be diluted. According to a study prepared by the Institute of International Finance, a lobbying group of large global banks, a higher requirement would knock 3 percentage points off the collective GDP of the United States, the eurozone, and Japan by 2015 and cost almost 10 million jobs.[20] Sheila Bair, chairman of the Federal Deposit Insurance Corporation, played down these scare tactics, saying that banks always argue against high capital requirements. In good times, they will say higher requirements are not necessary because their losses are low. In bad times, they argue that tougher rules will crimp lending.[21] In any case, the impact of capital requirement on bank lending is difficult to measure. In a study correlating capital buffers and loan prices, Douglas J. Elliot, a fellow at the Brookings Institution, found that a 4 percentage-point increase in capital ratios might cause loan prices to rise by 0.2 percentage point, which is "essentially trivial."[22] According to the Basel Committee, a 1 percent increase in the ratio of capital to assets in bank balance sheets would lead to a minuscule 0.04 percent decline in annual GDP growth over four and a half years. That said, the capital requirement norms need to be internationally coordinated. The Basel Committee's final standards relating to banking sector reserve requirements (discussed in chapter 6) are moderate and will be applied in 2018 following a decisive global recovery.

Modifications of the Volcker Rule and the Blanche Lincoln Proposal

Bankers feared the adoption in the final legislation of a punitive Volcker rule, similar in intent to the Glass-Steagall Act, which separated commercial and investment banking. Equally worrisome from their perspective was Senator Blanche Lincoln's (D-AR) proposed amendment, which was designed to spin off derivative and swap trading from the banking business. These were both massively redistributive features that would require banks to cut back their lucrative businesses of hedging their risks via derivative trading and underwriting stocks and bonds for their corporate clients. This in turn would wipe out billions of dollars of annual revenues and send bankers in search of alternative sources of funding. However, the lawmakers must avoid rejecting the two proposals altogether. That would be seen as benefitting the bankers or doing their bidding, and for that, the lawmakers would be punished in the forthcoming November elections. Both provisions were watered down in the final legislation (as discussed in chapter 6).

The equally controversial idea proposed by President Obama of setting up an independent Consumer Financial Protection Agency for safeguarding American consumers' financial interests, such as home mortgages and credit cards, became a divisive issue among Senate Democratic leaders. Its adoption in the final legislation as a bureau within the Federal Reserve required deft handling for its passage.

A Tamer Consumer Financial Protection Bureau?

The idea of a consumer protection agency, which was mooted by President Obama in June 2009 (as I outlined in chapter 6), had staunch supporters among consumer groups and virulent detractors among business and banking lobbies. Occasionally it faded from the scene, but was resurrected by Representative Frank in the House bill in December 2009. It was not unequivocally popular among the president's advisors. His chief economic advisor, Summers, was concerned that the agency might not be insulated from political pressures in view of the fact that the agency proposal was popular with consumers, trade unions, and other activists. Senate Republicans and business groups worried about the creation of an ungovernable bureaucracy, a "nanny state" according to Senator Richard Shelby (R-AL), the ranking Republican on the Senate Banking Committee. Perhaps housing the agency in the Federal Reserve would keep it pliable. The concession to keep the auto dealers and several businesses beyond its reach also paved the way for its final acceptance and passage in the Senate and ultimately in the full Congress.

Even before the modified proposals were incorporated in the final bill, banking and business groups, which had actively lobbied against its evidently extreme provisions, were ready to respond to the bill's impact on their revenues. The next section takes a look at this.

V. Banking Sector Response to the Legislation

The response of major banks to the legislative overhaul relating to derivative transactions and proprietary trading accelerated as the final legislation took shape.

Response to Restrictions on Derivative and Proprietary Trading

The new rules will cut bank profits in the short run by an estimated 11 percent, but over time banks will plug that hole by doing what they do best. They will invent new products that fall in line with the regulations. At JPMorgan Chase, 90 project teams were meeting daily to review the rules and retool their business practices. According to Jamie Dimon, chairman and chief executive of JPMorgan Chase: "If you are a restaurant and you can't charge for the soda, you're going to charge more for the burger. . . . Over time, it will all be repriced into the business."[23]

Banks were already geared to the new rule of having their derivative contracts approved by clearinghouses. In the old days, they arranged the contracts, took the underlying risk, sold the contracts directly to investors, and collected a fee for the transaction for which they undertook a risk. Under the new arrangement, they will simply broker the transaction, and the clearinghouses will bear the risk, collect the profits, and incur the losses. But as brokers of derivative business, banks could still provide customer services, negotiate contract prices, deal with large volumes, and earn mega fees. Banks have already spent vast sums to expand and rewire their computer systems. JPMorgan Investment Bank has retooled its giant derivative business as a brokerage undertaking.

The Dodd-Frank Act is also designed to transform relationships between banks and retail consumers. A federal law, which I discussed in chapter 6, had already limited a card issuer's clout to raise interest charges on cardholders who had missed a payment for more than 60 days. Down the regulatory reform road, the Senate bill was designed to limit the charges that banks imposed on merchants for debit card transactions. The final legislation, embedded in the Dodd-Frank Act, promises all these features and more. Will they work in favor of consumers?

Banking Sector Response to Rules Relating to Consumer Financial Protection

How will banks react to the emerging rules with regard to credit and debit cards? Even before the adoption of the Dodd-Frank Act in late July 2010, banks had begun responding to the earlier, mid-2009 regulatory provisions (discussed in chapter 6) by raising rates for their current cardholders before the limits imposed by these rules became effective in February 2010. A few of them had lifted rates in June and early July 2009 in anticipation of the new rules. They scrutinized their cardholders' credit history to distinguish between those who showed signs of improvement and those who deteriorated. If a holder signaled excessive use of his credit card, he was denied a new card or charged a higher rate. Bank of America started favoring its large depositors at the bank by providing them with a lower credit card charge, higher credit availability, and more lucrative rewards. Cards that currently carried variable rates had a higher rate imposed on the borrower.

In response to the adoption of the Dodd-Frank Act, a few banks planned to switch from punitive measures on cardholders to behavior modification alerts for them. Citigroup will issue a MasterCard with an "inControl" service, which automatically cuts off the card service at the holder's choice when a spending threshold is reached. Citigroup will become a partner in a cardholder's self-restraint rather than an enabler of his profligacy. Merchants will join in via proposals for implanting similar chastity belts on their customers. They will vary their discounts according to whether a customer pays cash, for which the discount is higher than for a purchase via a debit or credit card. The new rule will allow them to turn down a customer's credit card purchase of $10 or less. However, they will not be allowed to vary their discounts across credit cards and opt in favor of MasterCard and against Visa.

Across the industry, banks have begun finding new sources of earnings in order to counter the revenue losses arising from lower fees on debit cards. Bank account holders will lose free checking. Of course, the coverage of insured bank deposits for personal accounts, put in place by the Federal Deposit Insurance Corporation at $250,000 during the crisis, will continue, but account holders must pay for checking account services. Along with Wells Fargo, Regions Financial of Alabama and Fifth Third of Ohio will charge new customers a monthly maintenance fee of $2 to $15 a month, amounting to almost $180 a year on most basic accounts. By contrast, Bank of America started offering a fee-free, bare bones account on July 14, 2010. There was a catch, however. Customers cannot use tellers at their local branches, they can use only Bank of America automated teller machines, and they will receive only online statements of their accounts. Banks will also keep scores of their clients' credit performance, including how much they owe and whether they clear their credit card balances on time. These numerical snapshots derived from customers' credit history will be available to them from their banks or their companies free of charge.

These escalating developments suggest that bankers and merchants will keep ahead of retail consumers in their business dealings. Financial operators will continue exploring profitable opportunities and innovative new avenues and instruments. The new rules in effect will create a zero-sum environment in which Americans are unlikely to benefit at the expense of the providers of credit and debit cards and checking accounts. More to the point, the rules will inhibit widespread offers of mortgages as banks face more rules and potential home owners encounter detailed inquiries into their financial status, mountains of paperwork, and interminable delays. The intention of the Consumer Financial Protection Bureau to create safer *and* larger home ownership for Americans will actually result

in less of it in the years ahead. In a word, Joe the plumber will find it difficult to obtain a mortgage and own a home.

It would seem that although the intention of the regulatory overhaul
has been to promote prudent behavior among financiers, bankers, and
merchants, it will end up inducing a desirable behavior modification among
American consumers as well. They will learn to borrow less recklessly as
their brokers chalk out a bumpy road to home ownership and their banks
invoke new rules and, in the process, keep an upper hand in the decision
making.

From a broader perspective, the relevant question relates to the potential of the regulatory overhaul for preempting a financial crisis. The American corporate model requires a stable financial underpinning for its continuation marked by exceptional resilience and entrepreneurial drive. No
rules can provide a complete guarantee for a crisis-free environment in the
days ahead. However, the rules that will emerge from the Dodd-Frank Act
promise to be an adequate safeguard for anticipating a crisis, softening its
destructive impact on the economy, and preserving American corporate
arrangements.

NOTES

1. Financial Crisis Origin

1. Martin Wolf, "Beijing Should Dip Into China's Corporate Bank," *Financial Times*, October 4, 2006, 15.

2. Keith Bradsher and David Jolly, "Global Stocks Fall; Oil Slips Below $90," *New York Times,* October 6, 2008, www.nytimes.com/2008/10/06/business/worldbusiness/06iht-06markets.16713116.html (accessed December 29, 2010).

3. Edward Luce, "Few Escape Blame Over Subprime Explosion," *Financial Times*, May 6, 2009, 3.

4. Michael M. Phillips, "Would You Pay $103,000 for This Arizona Fixer-Upper?" *Wall Street Journal,* January 3, 2009, A1.

5. Ibid.

6. Luce, "Few Escape Blame," 3.

7. James Politi and Alan Rappeport, "Greenspan Grilled Over Role in Meltdown," *Financial Times,* April 8, 2010, 3.

8. Ibid.

9. Ibid.

10. Frank Rich, "No One Is to Blame for Anything," *New York Times,* April 11, 2010, 8.

11. Catherine Rampell, "Lax Oversight Caused Crisis, Bernanke Says," *New York Times,* January 6, 2010, A1.

12. Sewell Chan, "Greenspan Criticized for Characterization of Colleague," *New York Times*, April 11, 2010, B2.

13. David Wessel, "Economics—Financial Crisis: Inside Dr. Bernanke's E.R.: As Obama Considers Reappointing the Fed Chairman, a Look at How He Took on More Power," *Wall Street Journal*, July 18–19, 2009, W3.

14. Suzanne Kapner, "Geithner Rejects Full Privatization of Fannie and Freddie," *Financial Times*, March 24, 2010, 4.

15. Nick Timiraos, "Reluctant Realtors: Fannie Mae and Freddie Mac," *Wall Street Journal*, September 17, 2010, C1.

16. Joe Nocera, "Lehman Had to Die, It Seems, So Global Finance Could Live," *New York Times*, September 12, 2009, A3.

17. Henry Paulson, *On the Brink: Inside the Race to Stop the Collapse of the Global Financial System* (New York: Headline Business Plus, 2009), 438.

18. Anonymous, "Blaming Bank of America," *Wall Street Journal*, February 6, 2010, A12.

19. Wessel, "Economics—Financial Crisis," W3.

20. James B. Stewart, "Eight Days: The Battle to Save the American Financial System," *The New Yorker*, September 8, 2009, 79.

21. Ibid.

2. Banking Sector Stress Tests

1. Louise Story, "Report on Bailout Says Treasury Misled Public," *New York Times*, October 5, 2009, B2.

2. John Cassidy, "No Credit: Timothy Geithner's Financial Plan Is Working—and Making Him Very Unpopular," *The New Yorker*, March 15, 2010, 29.

3. Michael R. Crittenden, " 'Problem' Banks Up to 775," *Wall Street Journal*, May 21, 2010, C3.

4. Damian Paletta and Michael R. Crittenden, "Bank-Bailout Fund Faces Years in Red as Failures Jolt System," *Wall Street Journal*, September 30, 2009, C3.

5. Eric Dash, "Investors Ease Strain on F.D.I.C.," *New York Times*, May 20, 2010, B1.

6. Ibid.

7. Jack Ewing, "French and Germans Most Exposed in Euro Debt Crisis," *New York Times*, June 14, 2010, B8.

8. Jack Ewing, "Report Lists Dangers for Banks in Europe," *New York Times*, June 1, 2010, B1.

9. Christopher Bjork, Joe Ortiz, and Stephen Fidler, "EU, Spain Move to Soothe Bank Fears," *Wall Street Journal*, June 30, 2010, A10.

10. Patrick Jenkins and David Oakley, "Lenders Braced for Stress Test Results," *Financial Times*, July 9, 2010, 17.

11. Ibid.

12. Ibid.

3. Is the U.S. Economy on the Mend?

1. Michael Sherer, "What Happened to the Stimulus?" *Time,* July 1, 2009, 14.

2. Ibid., 41.

3. Carl Bialik, "To Count New Stimulus Jobs, Help Really Wanted," *Wall Street Journal,* September 16, 2009, A23.

4. Chrystia Freeland, "Lunch with the FT: Larry Summers," *Financial Times,* July 10, 2009, www.ft.com/cms/s/2/6ac06592-6ce0-11de-af56-00144feabdc0.html (accessed December 29, 2010).

5. Jackie Calmes, "Summers Says Stimulus Plan on Track Despite Job Losses," *New York Times,* July 18, 2009, B7.

6. Kevin A. Hassett, "Democrats Ride Into Sunset, Your Wallet in Hand," *Bloomberg Commentary,* January 4, 2010, 1.

7. Ibid.

8. Sewell Chan, "On Hill, Geithner Makes the Case for a Bank Tax," *New York Times,* May 5, 2010, B4.

9. Phil Izzo, "Optimism About the Economy Grows," *Wall Street Journal,* July 16, 2010, 7.

10. Martin Vaughn and John D. McKinnon, "Democrats Dissent on Bush Tax Cuts," *Wall Street Journal,* July 22, 2010, A2.

11. Editorial, "Liberal Tax Revolt," *Wall Street Journal,* July 23, 2010, A10.

12. President Obama at Democratic Congressional Campaign Committee/Democratic Senatorial Campaign Committee General Reception, Roosevelt Hotel, New York, September 22, 2010.

13. Izzo, "Optimism About the Economy Grows."

14. Editorial, "A Taxing Divorce: Ben Bernanke vs. Tim Geithner," *Wall Street Journal,* July 26, 2010, http://online.wsj.com/article/SB10001424052748703700904575391573478916924.html (accessed December 29, 2010).

15. Sudeep Reddy, "Panel Decides It's Too Soon to Pinpoint Recession's End," *Wall Street Journal,* April 13, 2010, A4.

16. Mark Whitehouse, "Evidence Mounts of Strong Recovery," *Wall Street Journal,* April 15, 2010, A3.

17. Izzo, "Optimism About the Economy Grows."

4. Global Recovery Prospects

1. Robert Wade, "Iceland as Icarus," *Challenge* 52 (May–June, 2009): 15.

2. Ibid.

3. Floyd Norris, "Fraying at the Edges," *New York Times,* February 5, 2010, B1.

4. Martin Wolf, "New York and London: Twins in Finance and Folly," *New York Times,* May 9, 2009, B6.

5. Renminbi is the name of the Chinese currency, similar to the pound sterling; however, the main unit of the Chinese currency is the yuan.

5. Hedge Funds and Derivatives, Credit Default Swaps, and Rating Agencies

1. David Smith, "Hedge Fund Industry Climbs Its 'Slope of Enlightenment,'" *Financial Times,* June 3, 2009, 24.

2. Ibid.

3. Steven M. Davidoff, "To Reduce Hedge Fund Risk, Let Everyone In," *Wall Street Journal,* September 17, 2009, 8.

4. Aline van Duyn, "Regulators Warn Over Derivatives Law Loopholes," *Financial Times,* October 8, 2009, 22.

5. David Gillen, "In Rating Agencies Investors Still Trust," *New York Times,* June 5, 2009, 7.

6. David Oakley, "Short Selling Ban Has Minimal Effect," *Financial Times,* December 8, 2008, 27.

7. Tony Barber, Ben Hall, and Gerrit Wiesmann, "German Curbs Raise Tensions in Europe," *Financial Times,* May 20, 2010, 1.

8. Michael Mackenzie and Jeremy Grant, "High-Speed Traders Keep Their Technology Close By," *Financial Times,* September 30, 2009, 35.

9. Fawn Johnson, "SEC Plans Trader ID System," *Wall Street Journal,* April 15, 2010, C3.

10. Randall Smith, "Keeping the Shroud on 'Dark Pools,'" *Wall Street Journal,* December 8, 2009, C4.

11. Tom Braithwaite, "Volker Supports Tax Transactions Between Banks," *Financial Times,* September 25, 2009, 2.

12. Ibid.

13. Edward Wyatt, "Regulators Vow to Find Way to Stop Rapid Dives," *New York Times,* May 11, 2010, B8.

14. Fawn Johnson and Kristina Peterson, "'Flash Crash' Plan: Circuit Breaker for Every Stock," *Wall Street Journal,* May 19, 2010, C1.

6. U.S. and EU Regulatory Proposals

1. Mervyn King, Speech at the Lord Mayor's Banquet for Bankers and Merchants of the City of London, Mansion House, London, June 17, 2009.

2. Sewell Chan, "Reform Bill Adds Layers of Oversight," *New York Times*, March 15, 2010, B1.

3. Chrystia Freeland and Francesco Guerrera, "Goldman Faces Stark Choice on 'Volcker Rule,'" *Financial Times*, February 12, 2010, 1.

4. Ibid.

5. Chrystia Freeland, "Volcker Lays Fresh Legacy as Rule Takes Centre Stage," *Financial Times*, February 12, 2010, 3.

6. Gillian Tett, Aline van Duyn, and Jeremy Grant, "Let the Battle Commence," *Financial Times*, May 20, 2009, 7.

7. Frank Partnoy, "Danger in Wall Street's Shadows," *New York Times*, May 15, 2009, 17.

8. Robert Schmidt and Jesse Westbrook, "U.S. May Strip SEC of Powers in Regulatory Overhaul," www.bloomberg.com/apps/news?pid=newsarchive&sid=a18ctNv3FDcw&refer=home (accessed November 23, 2010).

9. Mary Schapiro and Tom Braithwaite, "Congress Joins Turf War on Regulation," *Financial Times*, May 29, 2009, 3.

10. Alan Greenspan, *The Age of Turbulence* (New York: Penguin Press, 2007), 528.

11. Stephen Labaton, "Behind Scenes, Fed Chief Advocates Bigger Role," *New York Times*, June 23, 2009, B1.

12. Lawrence E. Summers, interview by *BusinessWeek*, July 6, 2009, 9.

13. Edmund L. Andrews, "Bernanke, in Nod to Critics, Suggests Board of Regulators," *New York Times*, October 2, 2009, B3.

14. Nelson D. Schwartz and Eric Dash, "Despite Reform, Banks Have Room for Risky Deals," *New York Times*, August 26, 2010, A1.

15. Jessica Holz and Dennis Berman, "Investors Gain New Clout," *Wall Street Journal*, August 26, 2010, A1.

16. Ibid.

17. Sewell Chan, "Fed Fights to Keep Oversight of Banks That Aren't Big," *New York Times*, March 18, 2010, B1.

18. Thomas Hoenig, "Keep the Fed on Main Street," *New York Times*, April 18, 2010, WK 11.

19. Peter Engberg Jensen, "Basel Rules Must Recognize Performance of Covered Bonds," *Financial Times*, July 28, 2010, 22.

20. Megan Murphy, "City Limits," *Financial Times*, December 14, 2009, 5.

7. The Dollar's Future as a Reserve Currency

1. Max Corden, "China's Exchange Rate Policy, Its Current Account Surplus, and the Global Imbalances," *Economic Journal* 119 (November 2009): F432.

2. Ibid.

3. Ibid., F436.

4. Ibid.

5. Geoff Dyer and Jamil Anderlini, "Hopes Fade of Rapid Removal of Peg to U.S. Dollar," *Financial Times,* March 8, 2010, 1.

6. Paul Krugman, "Chinese New Year," *New York Times,* January 1, 2010, A29.

7. Ibid.

8. Alan Beattie and Jamil Anderlini, "Battle Lines Are Blurred in Dispute Over Renminbi," *Financial Times,* April 6, 2010, 3.

9. Alan Beattie, "Geithner Turns Up Heat Over Renminbi," *Financial Times,* September 17, 2010, 1.

10. Steve LeVine and Dexter Roberts, "China Thinks Beyond the Dollar," *BusinessWeek,* May 28, 2009, www.businessweek.com/magazine/content/09_23/b4134024721528.htm (accessed December 29, 2010).

11. Robert Triffin, *Gold and the Dollar Crisis* (New Haven, CT: Yale University Press, 1961).

12. Ibid., 8–9.

13. Ibid., 63.

14. Ibid., 64.

15. Ibid., 9.

8. The Great Depression and the Current Financial Crisis

1. Richard M. Ebeling, "Monetary Central Planning and the State, Part 3: The Federal Reserve and Price Level Stabilization in the 1920s," *Freedom Daily* 87 (March 1997): 2.

2. Milton Friedman and Anna J. Schwartz, *A Monetary History of the United States, 1867–1960* (Princeton, NJ: National Bureau of Economic Research and Princeton University Press, 1963), 297.

3. John Maynard Keynes, *Treatise on Money* (London: Macmillan, 1953), 258.

4. Harold Bierman Jr., "The 1929 Stock Market Crash," *Economic History Services,* February 5, 2010, http://eh.net/encyclopedia/article/Bierman.crash (accessed December 29, 2010).

5. Edward Teach, "The Bright Side of Bubbles," *CFO Magazine,* May 1, 2007, www.cfo.com/article.cfm/9059304 (accessed December 29, 2010).

6. John Kenneth Galbraith, *The Great Crash 1929* (New York: Houghton Mifflin Harcourt, 2009), 11.

7. Richard Lambert, "Crashes, Bangs, and Wallops," *Financial Times,* July 19, 2008, 22.

8. Special to *The New York Times,* "President Hoover Issues a Statement of Reassurance on Continued Prosperity of Fundamental Business," *New York Times,* October 26, 1929, 1.

9. Anonymous, "U.S. Industrial Stocks Pass 1929 Peak," *New York Times,* November 24, 1954, 12.

10. Friedman and Schwartz, *A Monetary History of the United States,* 608.

11. Ibid.

12. Ben Bernanke, *Essays on the Great Depression* (Princeton, NJ: Princeton University Press, 2000), 41.

13. Friedman and Schwartz, *A Monetary History of the United States,* 434.

14. Christine Romer, *The Economist,* June 20, 2009, 82.

15. Thomas F. Cooley and Lee E. Ohanian, "FDR and the Lessons of the Depression," *New York Times,* August 27, 2010, A17.

16. Ibid.

17. Editorial, "FDR's New Deal Prolonged the Great Depression," *Examiner,* October 30, 2008, 1.

18. Burton Folsom Jr. and Anita Folsom, "Did FDR End the Great Depression?" *Wall Street Journal,* April 12, 2010, A17.

19. Jean Edward Smith, *FDR* (New York: Random House, 2007), 250.

9. The Future of American Capitalism

1. Adam Smith, *The Wealth of Nations* (New York: Random House, 1937), 14.

2. Ibid., 13.

3. Ibid., 291.

4. Ibid., 288.

5. Ibid., 289–291.

6. Ibid., 289.

7. Ibid., 291.

8. Adam Smith, *The Theory of Moral Sentiments* (Edinburgh: Millar, Kincaid, and Bell, 1767), 282.

9. George Akerlof and Robert D. Shiller, *Animal Spirits* (Princeton, NJ: Princeton University Press, 2010), 3.

10. John Maynard Keynes, *The General Theory of Employment, Interest, and Money* (New York: Harcourt, Brace, Jovanovich, 1964), 150.

11. Ibid., 151–152.

12. Ibid., 159.

13. Ibid., 150.

14. Robert Skidelsky, *Keynes: The Return of the Master* (New York: PublicAffairs, 2009), 86.

15. Ibid., 88.

16. John Maynard Keynes, *Essays in Persuasion* (New York: W. W. Norton & Company, 1991), 321.

17. Eric Dash and Nelson D. Schwartz, "As Reform Takes Shape, Some Relief on Wall Street," *New York Times,* May 24, 2010, B1.

18. Ibid.

19. Ibid.

20. David Enrich, "Studies Question Bank Capital Fears," *Wall Street Journal*, August 4, 2010, C1.

21. Ibid.

22. Ibid.

23. Eric Dash and Nelson D. Schwartz, "U.S. Banks Aim to Turn Rules to Their Advantage," *New York Times*, July 18, 2010, 9.

INDEX